ALAN LIVINGSTONE MACLEOD

CAPITALS,

VICTORIA'S HOCKEY

ARISTOCRATS,

PROFESSIONALS, 1911–26

and COUGARS

HERITAGE

Heritage House Publishing Company Ltd.
heritagehouse.ca

Cataloguing information available from
Library and Archives Canada
978-1-77203-373-1 (paperback)
978-1-77203-374-8 (ebook)

Edited by Karla Decker
Cover design by Jacqui Thomas
Interior design by Setareh Ashrafologhalai
Cover photograph: Tommy Dunderdale, courtesy David
MacDonald

The interior of this book was produced on 100% post-consumer
paper, processed chlorine free and printed with vegetable-
based inks.

Heritage House gratefully acknowledges that the land on which
we live and work is within the traditional territories of the
Lkwungen (Esquimalt and Songhees), Malahat, Pacheedaht,
Scia'new, T'Sou-ke, and W̱SÁNEĆ (Pauquachin, Tsartlip,
Tsawout, Tseycum) Peoples.

We acknowledge the financial support of the Government of
Canada through the Canada Book Fund (CBF) and the Canada
Council for the Arts, and the Province of British Columbia
through the British Columbia Arts Council and the Book
Publishing Tax Credit.

25 24 23 22 21   1 2 3 4 5

Printed in Canada

In memory of Frank Fredrickson, 1895–1979

Flier, Royal Flying Corps and
Royal Air Force, First World War

Leader of the first Olympic gold-
medal hockey team, 1920

Leader of the last non-NHL team
to win the Stanley Cup, 1925

Friend to Albert Einstein, 1933

Member of the Hockey Hall of Fame, 1958

CONTENTS

PREFACE

On THE LAST day of March in 1925, a headline in inch-and-a-half type stretched across the front page of the Victoria *Daily Colonist* from one margin to the other: COUGARS WIN STANLEY CUP. Accompanied by a photograph of a dozen seated and standing men, all facing the camera, the first of four subheadings reported that VICTORIA'S OWN ARE WORLD HOCKEY CHAMPIONS. The evening before, the Victoria Cougars had defeated the Montreal Canadiens by a margin of 6-1 to win the Stanley Cup. In the *Daily Colonist*'s view, the Victoria hockey players had thereby upheld the honour of the city in a crucial conflict.

Eleven of the men in the photo wear matching sweatshirts. The twelfth man, standing tall in the middle at the back, is dressed in a suit and tie, looking more formal than the others. He is Lester Patrick, the owner, operator, manager, and coach of the Cougars—and sometime player too. With his younger brother, Frank, he also founded the Pacific Coast Hockey Association (PCHA), the major professional hockey league the brothers had established in collaboration with their father, Joe, in 1911 in order to compete with the National Hockey Association (NHA) for recognition as the best hockey league in the world. The Stanley Cup victory of 1925 was the culmination of the Patricks' vision and, though no one realized it at the time, a milestone event that still resonates nearly a century later.

In part, the subject of this book is the cast of characters Lester Patrick assembled to deliver his dream of making Victoria a hockey mecca. From 1911 through 1925, some forty-nine men took their turn as players with the Victoria hockey professionals. Some played only a single season in Victoria, some just a few games, but several played season after season. A good number of these players flourished in Victoria. Seven of the men did so well they would one day be awarded a place in the pantheon: members of the Hockey Hall of Fame, the very best to have ever played the game.

Who were these men, not just the Hall of Fame players but the entire cast who had taken their part in the drama leading to the 1925 triumph? That is one question addressed in this book.

There are other questions. What was the context in which these hockey players went about their business? What was the milieu—social, cultural, political—in which they played? What did the people of Victoria *care* about in the second and third decades of the twentieth century? Who were their heroes? Their villains? What worried them? What inspired them? Where did they turn for relief from daily toil and trouble? Where did they find entertainment and edification?

Though the Stanley Cup victory was the big story in Victoria at the end of March 1925, there was other news for the people of the city to contemplate. The front page of the March 31 edition of the *Daily Colonist* reported that a collapse in the price of wheat was causing distress among Canadian prairie farmers. Post-war Germany was in political turmoil over how to deal with the wreckage of the war and what to do about the burdensome reparations imposed by the winning side of the conflict. In British Columbia, members of the provincial legislature worried about immigration from China and Japan (referred to by the racist term "yellow peril") and what to do about it. In a more lighthearted vein, the paper reported that the city had been invited to take part in the annual spring tulip festival in the neighbouring city of Bellingham, Washington. Spring had sprung.

Local politicians and the people of the city put together a cele-
bration to honour their hockey heroes. Ordinary people pitched in
to pay the cost of striking medals to bestow on the players. A huge
crowd gathered in the Board of Trade auditorium to laud the men
who had brought such great glory to the city.

In the fifteen years leading up to the 1925 pinnacle, Lester Patrick had called upon a varied cast to help him get there.

One man was an Australian who had come to Canada as a boy
and mastered the skills enabling him to lead Victoria in scoring
for four different seasons. Another was an effective player despite
being profoundly deaf. Fans and teammates called him "Dummy"
or "Silent," and so did the city's newspaper. A Regina lad spent time
as an inmate at Alcatraz, the notorious prison near San Francisco,
the price he paid for failing to comply with demands that he register
for the US wartime draft.

Ten of the Victoria players had served as Canadian soldiers
during the Great War, either as volunteers or conscripts. Two of
these were bona fide war heroes, soldiers awarded medals for gallantry. Perhaps the most consequential of Lester Patrick's hockey
recruits had been an airman in the Royal Flying Corps who went on
to lead the Canadian team to the first Olympic hockey gold medal.
In his six years in Victoria, he led his team in scoring every season.

Foraging through the pages of the *Daily Colonist* in the years 1911
through 1926 delivers a kind of time travel, a journey accompanied
by delight, discovery, dismay, surprise—even amazement. The *Colonist* is the oldest newspaper in British Columbia. It was established
in 1858, eight years before the British colonies of Vancouver Island
and British Columbia were joined and thirteen years before BC
joined the Canadian Confederation.

The newspaper was founded by a man born William Smith at
Windsor, Nova Scotia, who eventually decided that "William Smith"
was a name not worthy of his significance; he changed it to *Amor
de Cosmos*, meaning "Lover of the Universe." In 1872, when de
Cosmos became British Columbia's second premier, his Victoria

daily—originally called the *Daily British Colonist*—was the newspaper of record in the BC capital.

By 1911, the *Colonist* was fifty-three years old. By then there was a second Victoria daily, the *Victoria Daily Times*, but the *Colonist* was the morning paper and the one people turned to first for news of their community and the world at large. It was also the one the city's sports fans relied upon to tell them what had happened in last night's hockey game.

By 1911, the Patrick brothers had established themselves as hockey players of consequence. Born December 31, 1883, Lester Patrick had already made a name for himself in Montreal by the turn of the century. He played amateur hockey in Montreal before travelling to Manitoba to play for the Brandon club of the Manitoba and Northwestern Hockey Association in 1903-04. In 1905, he joined the Montreal Wanderers of the Eastern Canada Amateur Hockey Association (ECAHA) and made significant contributions to that team's Stanley Cup victories in 1905 and 1906.

Two years younger than his brother, Frank Patrick also established his early hockey reputation as an amateur in Montreal. He played two years, from 1905 through 1907, with the McGill University Redmen, and one with the ECAHA's Montreal Victorias in 1907-08.

Lester and Frank were the sons of Joseph Patrick, an entrepreneur who by 1907 had established himself as owner-operator of the Patrick Lumber Company at Nelson, British Columbia. For a couple of years, the brothers supported their father in the lumber business while playing hockey with the Nelson club of the West Kootenay Senior Hockey League. In 1908-09, playing the rover position, Lester scored twenty-two goals in just six games. One of his collaborators on that team was his kid brother Frank, who managed nine goals in the five games he played.

By 1909, both brothers had made the big time as players in the National Hockey Association, the major *professional* league in its time. The NHA comprised seven teams in 1909-10; three in Montreal, one in the nation's capital, and three in Ontario communities no longer deemed suitable locations for major professional hockey: Cobalt, Haileybury, and Renfrew.

The Patrick brothers skated with the Renfrew Creamery Kings and led their team to a very good record in 1909-10: eight victories and one tie in the NHA's twelve-game season—which was good, but not good enough to match the Wanderers, who had turned professional and who finished 11-1 that year. The brothers did well in their professional debut. Lester led the Renfrew club with twenty-three goals, and Frank scored nine. Five members of the Creamery Kings would eventually be inducted in the Hockey Hall of Fame.

Having had a taste of professional hockey in the NHA and experience as hockey movers and shakers in the West Kootenays, the brothers were seized by a dream as 1910 passed into 1911. What a good idea it would be, they thought, to establish a new major professional hockey league in the west, one that would produce a brand of hockey every bit as good—or better—than that played in the NHA, a league that would enable them to apply their boundless ideas for improving the game.

The brothers were fortunate because in Joe Patrick they had a father who believed in them, wanted to support them, and most importantly, had the financial means enabling them to realize their dream. Thus was born the Pacific Coast Hockey Association.

Joe Patrick sold his lumber business in Nelson and, with the proceeds of the sale, financed the construction of something never before built in Canada: hockey arenas that had facilities for making artificial ice. Travelling to study artificial ice plants in the US, Frank made himself an expert on the subject. Lester took a lead role in the construction of the new arenas.

A Victoria architect, Thomas Hooper—once as well known and fully occupied in Victoria as Francis Rattenbury and Samuel Maclure—designed both arenas. Many of his buildings remain standing, still well used in the city. Located at the corner of present-day Epworth Street and Cadboro Bay Road in Oak Bay, the Victoria arena had room to accommodate four thousand spectators. The Vancouver facility at Denman and Georgia in the downtown core was much larger: it could accommodate 10,500, the biggest hockey arena in Canada at the time.

Shot through with ambition, determination, and energy, the Patricks saw to it that construction of the new buildings, begun in August 1911, was completed in time for the first season of the Pacific Coast Hockey Association.

In addition to teams in Vancouver and Victoria, there would be a third franchise established at New Westminster, a club that for the time being would share the Denman rink as its home base.

In some cases, men who would be playing hockey a bit later on picked up tools and helped complete the construction. Both buildings were ready on time. To celebrate the imminent arrival of major pro hockey on the west coast, the Patricks opened the doors to both arenas to allow people to admire their new facilities, go for a skate, and fill themselves with anticipation of the hockey soon to arrive in their cities. Fifteen hundred people participated in the Vancouver opening on December 20, while six hundred shared in the fun on Christmas Day in Victoria.

On the last day of 1911—Lester Patrick's twenty-eighth birthday—the sports section of the *Daily Colonist* featured an item reporting on the first game of the new hockey league two days hence: "All roads will lead to the Victoria Arena on Tuesday night," the piece began, "when the first hockey match of the Pacific coast league for the Paterson Cup will take place between the fast Victoria team, captained by Mr. Lester Patrick, and the New Westminster septette, under the direction of Jimmy Gardner."

Lieutenant-Governor Thomas Wilson Paterson would look after the ceremonial opening faceoff, and the arena was expected to be crowded with spectators "keen to see the introduction of the game that for years has held the enthusiasts on their toes in the east." The city band would attend and the BC Electric Company would put on extra streetcars to accommodate the rush of fans wanting to be in their seats by the 8:30 PM start. A separate arena ad informed fans to take the Willows streetcar to see the "fastest men and the fastest game on earth."

The fastest men and the fastest game on earth.

And so it begins: an account of Victoria's hockey professionals in the years 1911 to 1926 and of the tempestuous times in which they played and lived.

ONE

1911-12

A CAPITAL BEGINNING

IN AN AGE when tastes in the naming of major league hockey teams run to the likes of "Hurricanes," "Sharks," and "Predators," it may mystify the modern observer that "Creamery Kings" could once have been a hockey moniker of first choice. But it was. In 1909-10, Lester Patrick had led the NHA's Renfrew Creamery Kings in scoring, with twenty-three goals in twelve games. Lester's brother Frank was a teammate on that squad, as were future Hall of Famers "Cyclone" Taylor and Fred Whitcroft. Two other Creamery Kings on the 1909-10 roster—goaltender Bert Lindsay and defenceman Bobby Rowe—would be targeted by Patrick when the time came to build his Victoria squad for the inaugural 1911-12 season of the Pacific Coast Hockey Association. Patrick also poached from the 1910-11 Creamery Kings roster, persuading rover Don Smith to migrate 2,660 miles from Renfrew to the southern tip of Vancouver Island. The effect of Patrick's powers of persuasion is that fully half of the first Victoria pro team were former Creamery Kings.

Patrick's Victoria club would eventually become the Cougars, a name consonant with modern hockey sensibility. But in the early years of professional hockey, the Victoria players would come to be known by a name not much more macho than Creamery Kings: Aristocrats.

The Victoria team was not born to the name. The *Daily Colonist*'s game accounts never called its new team the Aristocrats during that first season. It is conventional understanding that the three teams of the new PCHA arrived fully formed as the New Westminster Royals, Vancouver Millionaires, and Victoria Aristocrats. It wasn't so. Not once in 1912 did the *Colonist* refer to the city's new hockey team as the Aristocrats. Occasionally the Vancouver squad was called the "Terminals," never the Millionaires. New Westminster is, of course, "the Royal City," so that team was sometimes called the Royals. In the beginning, the hockey professionals playing in the BC capital were simply the "Victoria team."

The very first professional hockey game in Victoria took place on January 2, 1912, in the spanking-new Epworth Street arena. It was one of only two artificial ice arenas in Canada, the other being the one in Vancouver, where Frank Patrick's septet went about their business in 1911–12.

The headline news in the January 3 issue of the *Daily Colonist* was that Canada's prime minister—now *Sir* Robert Borden—had been knighted. The front page also reported on a mutiny of Chinese troops in Lanchow—today known as Lanzhou—and new developments in the election of the German Reichstag. But none of those things compared to the day's truly exciting news.

Over in the sports section, under the headline HOCKEY MAKES ITS DEBUT HERE, the *Colonist* delivered a breathless account of that momentous first game. "Ice hockey with all the thrills that the west has heard of was introduced in grand style to over 2,500 people at the Victoria arena last night."

BC Lieutenant-Governor Thomas Wilson Paterson dropped the ceremonial first puck after the national anthem—"God Save the King"—had ushered His Excellency onto the rink. The game began late by today's standards, at 8:45 PM.

As was the custom at the time, seven players—the rover being the seventh man—played the entire game for each team, all sixty minutes. Some might observe that men were men back then.

The 1910 Renfrew Creamery Kings of the National Hockey Association were an all-star cast that included four players who would one day be inducted into the Hockey Hall of Fame. Lester Patrick, centre, his brother Frank—behind Lester's left shoulder—and Cyclone Taylor, behind Lester's right shoulder, would all star in the Pacific Coast Hockey Association the Patricks founded in 1911. AUTHOR'S COLLECTION

"The cheers rang in every corner of the structure," the *Colonist* reported, but the Victoria fans went home disappointed: the former Creamery Kings and their mates fell to visiting New Westminster, 8-3. A star of the game and future Hall of Famer, New Westminster's Ernie Johnson scored twice and greatly impressed the *Colonist* scribe: "He stands in a class by himself," the reporter gushed.

Former Creamery Kings did all the scoring for Victoria in that first game: two by Don Smith, one by Bobby Rowe. Encouraged by Lester Patrick, Smith had jumped his contract with Renfrew in November. Though tiny by today's player standards, at five feet, six inches and just 160 pounds, Smith was not unusually small by comparison to most other players of his era. He was twenty-five by the time of his Victoria debut, a seven-year hockey veteran. After the

First World War erupted in 1914, Smith would enlist in the Canadian Expeditionary Force (CEF). He would lose three years of his hockey career for doing his duty to King and Country, but he did not lose his life as dozens of other hockey players did before the Armistice was signed in late 1918. Smith scored the first goal in the team's history and he would score a good many more over the course of the 1911–12 season.

It was another future member of the Hockey Hall of Fame, Tommy Dunderdale, who would lead the team in 1912, with twenty-four goals in the team's sixteen scheduled games, but Smith was no slouch either, with nineteen goals. That first season would turn out to be Smith's only one in Victoria. In a time when players enjoyed far greater freedom of movement than they would in years to come, Smith boarded a train after the season and went to Montreal, where he joined forces with future Hall of Famers Newsy Lalonde and Didier Pitre of the Montreal Canadiens.

Bobby Rowe, the other former Renfrew star who scored in that first game, was twenty-six when he came to Victoria. In today's National Hockey League, the average player is six feet, one inch tall and weighs two hundred pounds. Rowe's measurements were identical to Smith's: five feet, six inches and 160 pounds. By 1911, he had been a player in organized hockey nearly a full decade. In contrast to Smith, Bobby Rowe didn't break a contract in answering Lester Patrick's siren call: after two years in the National Hockey Association, the Renfrew team had disbanded and departed the NHA. Rowe signed with Patrick's club without breaking a promise or giving offence in Ontario.

Rowe liked the west coast well enough to spend fourteen years in Victoria and Seattle. In that first season, 1911–12, he would tie with Lester Patrick for third in team scoring—ten goals in sixteen games. Over the course of his long PCHA career, he would be a league all-star five times.

Another first-year player drew attention in the *Daily Colonist* on January 3, not for what he put in the net but what he spilled on the ice. The newspaper account reported that the game had been rough.

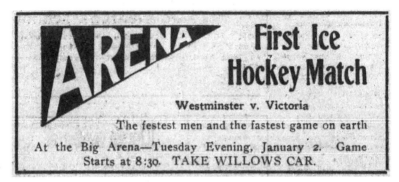

First Ice Hockey Match

Westminster v. Victoria

The festest men and the fastest game on earth

At the Big Arena—Tuesday Evening, January 2. Game Starts at 8:30. TAKE WILLOWS CAR.

The newspaper ad for the first-ever game of the new Pacific Coast Hockey Association, January 2, 1912, at the "Big Arena" at Epworth Street and Foul Bay Road in Oak Bay. Note the spelling mistake: The 'festest' men and the fastest game on earth. *DAILY COLONIST*, DECEMBER 31, 1911

One of the on-ice casualties was Walter Smaill, who was badly cut and bled all over the place. Smaill was taken off but "soon came back and pluckily continued." That was typically the way it was back then.

It was the Montreal Wanderers that Lester Patrick had raided to secure Smaill's services. The Wanderers were a star-studded cast. Of the nine skaters who played for Montreal in 1910–11, seven would eventually be inducted in the Hall of Fame, including Ernie Johnson, the New Westminster star who so impressed the *Colonist* reporter in that first PCHA game, on January 2.

At five feet, ten inches and 180 pounds, Smaill was somewhat bigger than his teammates Smith and Rowe. He was a journeyman— he had not been a front-line star in Montreal and he wasn't one in Victoria either—but he contributed, scoring nine goals in the team's sixteen games. For three more seasons in Victoria, Smaill remained a reliable cover point. (In those early days, the term for a defence-man was "point," the "cover point" being the one having licence to roam a little more widely from his base in front of his own goalten-der.) Two years later, in 1913–14, Smaill was better than ordinary: he made the all-star team.

A goaltender shutout was a rarity in that first 1911–12 PCHA sea-son. The man in the Victoria goal never once managed to bar the opposition from scoring in a game, nor even limit enemy sharp-shooters to a single goal. Bert Lindsay's finest hour was perhaps the game of January 23, when he allowed just two goals in Victoria's 3-2 win over New Westminster. Lindsay's goals-against average was 5.52 in 1911–12, a figure that could not induce comparisons to the greats of the game, but Lindsay had his moments.

The January 23 game gave the *Daily Colonist*'s hockey reporter—the paper gave him no byline—another opportunity to go over the top in verbiage. In a game "said by many to be the greatest game which they have ever witnessed," Victoria prevailed. When Smith evened the score at 2-2 in the third period, "pandemonium broke loose, and for several seconds the huge ice palace was filled with shrieks and yells, and sounds of horns and cowbells." When Smith scored the winner in the sixteenth minute, the *Colonist* reporter was lost for words to describe the fans' rhapsody.

The *Colonist*'s reporter was not the only one in town who felt obliged to go over the top in describing the January 23 game. The *Victoria Daily Times* reporter—just as anonymous as his *Colonist* counterpart—called it "the most wildly exciting game seen in Victoria." An exciting game, and a rough one too.

Bert Lindsay was the goaltending hero of the January 23 game. In his case, it was the NHA's Toronto Tecumsehs—the Creamery Kings' successors in the NHA—who were the victims of Patrick's manipulations. He induced the goaltender to jump his Toronto contract and bring his gear bag to Victoria.

He would never make the Hall of Fame himself, but Bert Lindsay produced a son who did. Ted Lindsay was both a skilled and tenacious player and a union-organizer thorn in the side of Detroit Red Wings management. He played alongside Gordie Howe and would be inducted in the Hall of Fame in 1966.

Son Ted was still thirteen years in Dad's future when Bert Lindsay joined forces with Lester Patrick's men in 1911. That year he was a thirty-year-old veteran in his eighth hockey season. Lindsay Sr. would play four years in Victoria and have a best GAA—goals-against average—of 3.62 in his second Victoria season, 1912–13.

Benalla, Australia, about 130 miles northeast of Melbourne, is not the sort of place one imagines as likely to be the spawning ground of a great hockey player. The Benalla of our time, situated in the floodplain of the Broken River at latitude 36 degrees south, is a small city of fewer than ten thousand whose first name—*Swampy*—conveys a little about its geographic context. Benalla's mean minimum temperature is about fifteen degrees Celsius, its maximum about double that. But appearances belie fact: Benalla is the birthplace of the other member of the 1911–12 Victoria team—the one not named Lester—who is a member of the Hockey Hall of Fame, class of 1974: Tommy Dunderdale.

Dunderdale was the prize catch in Lester Patrick's 1911 effort to assemble a winning Victoria team for the inaugural season of the new Pacific Coast Hockey Association. In the previous hockey season, 1910–11, Tommy had been a leading light with the Quebec Bulldogs of the National Hockey Association. Patrick managed to lure him, as a free agent, to Victoria. As events unfolded, Dunderdale would shine even more brightly in the BC capital than he had done in the Quebec one.

At five feet, eight inches and 160 pounds, Dunderdale was marginally taller but no heavier than his teammates Smith and Rowe. He was nonetheless a colossus of a hockey player. On February 9, 1912, playing before an Epworth Street crowd of 3,100, the Victorias lost narrowly to Frank Patrick's Vancouver seven, 8-7. The loss could not be blamed on Dunderdale: he scored five of his team's seven goals. The Benalla native was very good at scoring goals. Over the course of his thirteen seasons in the PCHA, he would net 198 of them, more than anyone else in league history.

Dunderdale had not remained long in the iceless reaches of the Broken River. At age seven, he migrated with his family to a place whose minimum mean temperature was a good deal cooler than Benalla's—Ottawa. A few years later, he moved to a still colder locale, Winnipeg. At age eighteen, Tommy was scoring at a goal-a-game pace for the Winnipeg Ramblers of the Manitoba Hockey League. Just one year after that, he would be playing not just for joy but for cash too. By 1909–10, Dunderdale was in big-league hockey, with the Montreal Shamrocks of the National Hockey Association. That season, he tied for the team lead in scoring with Don Smith, each of them scoring fourteen goals in a twelve-game schedule.

Dunderdale's journey to the west coast in 1911 was not a short-term arrangement: he would never play another season for a team based in the east. By the time the western league went under in 1926, Dunderdale's hockey résumé reflected long stays in Victoria and Portland, Oregon, as well as whistle stops in Saskatoon and Edmonton.

A standard detail of the *Daily Colonist*'s 1912 scoring summaries was a list of the men who officiated in games. Each game featured two on-ice officials, the referee and "judge of play." There were no linesmen because in these early days of hockey there were no lines. The judge of play was the man who assessed penalties; the referee's task was to call offsides—the forward pass being an innovation whose time had not yet come. Inasmuch as Canadian hockey was still mostly an outdoor game often played in deep sub-zero temperatures, on-ice officials didn't bring a frozen metal whistle to their lips to signal infractions. Instead, they rang a wooden-handled bell.

In 1912, on-ice officials were not selected from a roster of men recruited solely to fill that specialized role but from ranks of the players themselves. In a game between Teams A and B, it would be two players from Team C that would officiate the game. In the February 9 game, both officials were men who would one day be enshrined in the Hockey Hall of Fame: New Westminster players Jimmy Gardner and Harry Hyland.

Of course, events other than hockey commanded attention in the *Daily Colonist*'s pages. On February 17, a few days after Dunderdale's five-goal splurge, the British Columbia legislature considered a resolution sponsored by Conservative premier Richard McBride putting limits on Chinese immigration. BC was a "white man's province," the premier proudly asserted, and he worked assiduously to keep it that way. His resolution passed without opposition.

Tommy Dunderdale was a twenty-four-year-old established star in the
National Hockey Association when, in 1911, Lester Patrick persuaded him
to abandon the Quebec Bulldogs and join the first edition of his Victoria
club in the new Pacific Coast Hockey Association. A perennial PCHA all-star,
Dunderdale played twelve PCHA seasons, nine of them in Victoria. No one
scored more PCHA goals than Dunderdale. In 1974, the Australia native was
awarded a tablet in the Hockey Hall of Fame. COURTESY DAVID MACDONALD

Across town that same day, a matter of smaller significance but greater entertainment value took place at the Patrick Arena on Epworth Street. A largest-yet crowd of 3,200 gathered to watch Victoria face off against New Westminster. The home side went down to defeat, 4-2, their season record falling to an even five wins, five losses.

The next day's *Colonist* commended Bert Lindsay's play in the Victoria net as well as that of forward Skinner Poulin. Poulin, even smaller than Smith and Rowe at five feet, six inches and 155 pounds, was twenty-four when Lester Patrick brought him to the west coast. He had played the previous two seasons with the Montreal Canadiens, but Patrick had no need to induce Poulin into breaking a contract: he was a free agent by the time he agreed to Patrick's terms. Poulin scored nine goals in his sixteen games with Victoria. While not the brightest star in the Victoria hockey firmament, he occasionally took a turn in the spotlight.

Readers of the *Daily Colonist* who were also followers of the 1911–12 team knew where to turn for news of their team. The sports section, under the banner heading "The Sporting World," reliably appeared on page nine. Game accounts were richly detailed: an opening summary followed by a comprehensive game account and concluding with a by-the-numbers inventory of goals scored and penalties awarded.

Another sport regularly reported at length in "The Sporting World" was boxing. The February 17 edition featured an image of smug-looking South American champion Taft Williams, in town to challenge local boxers into taking him on.

Meandering through the pages of the *Daily Colonist* delivers a kind of time-travel facsimile: an impression of what concerned Victorians at the time, what they cared about, what occupied them, what they spent their money on. An automobile dealer for many years afterward, Plimley's advertised extensively in the *Colonist*. The Thomas Plimley business, then located at 830 Yates Street, offered the R.C. Hupp roadster, with long-stroke engine, for one thousand dollars. If that seemed too pricey, Plimley's also retailed bicycles: you could have one of those for thirty-five dollars. Another option, offered by the Hinton Electric Company, was the "Silent 'Waverly' Electric" car: "Always at your command for theatre, shopping tour, reception, luncheon or drive." Who knew that electric cars—now in demand by drivers worried about climate change—were available in the Victoria automobile market of 1912?

W & J Wilson—still in business more than a hundred years on—offered suits for twenty dollars. The Bungalow Construction Company pitched Snap bungalows for a mere $3,950. For young fellows dreaming about playing one day for Lester Patrick, the James Maynard Company, at 1313 Douglas in the Odd Fellows Block, offered "Hockey Boots and Skates in All Sizes."

On February 27, Premier McBride brought about the dissolution of the provincial legislative session and called an election for March 28. McBride took no pains to obscure the fact that he was a proud, unrepentant racist; he campaigned on the promise to do his best to make British Columbia a "white man's province." It was not a message McBride need fear would alienate the voters: in the ensuing election, McBride's party won nearly sixty per cent of the popular vote and all but three of the forty-two seats in the legislature.

The same day McBride called the election, the Victoria hockey club (for a short time known as the Capitals) played Vancouver in a game at the Patrick Arena. The Capitals proved an obliging host: they lost to the Terminals, 7-3. As a result of the loss—their third in a row—Victoria saw its season record fall to 5-7.

While the eventual Hall of Famer Tommy Dunderdale was certainly a prize acquisition in the Patrick brothers' pillaging of the National Hockey Association, it is likely that a consensus among hockey cognoscenti was that the brothers had scored an even greater coup in luring Édouard Cyrille Lalonde to say adieu to Montreal and bring his talents to the west coast.

Édouard Cyrille was better known as "Newsy" because he had worked as a youth in a newsprint mill. For a good chunk of the first

Designed by Victoria architect Thomas Hooper, the Patrick Arena, at the corner of Epworth Street and Cadboro Bay Road in Oak Bay, was one of the first artificial ice arenas in Canada. It was the Victoria hockey club's home rink from 1911 to 1926, but it did not endure long after of the demise of western major league hockey: the arena burned to the ground on the night of Remembrance Day, 1929. The fire was believed to have been deliberately started, but no one was ever charged. AUTHOR'S COLLECTION

two decades of the twentieth century, Lalonde was as big a hockey star as there was in the game. As a twenty-year-old in 1907–08, he had tallied thirty-two goals in just nine games with the Toronto Pros of the Ontario Professional Hockey League, a scoring rate of better than three and a half goals a game. In 1909–10, he scored sixteen for the Montreal Canadiens in just six games and then netted nineteen for Montreal the following year.

By 1911–12, Newsy, twenty-four years old, five feet, nine inches and 168 pounds, was just entering his hockey prime. In the February 27 game at the Patrick Arena, Lalonde was Vancouver's leading shooter, scoring three goals, one in each period. He would continue scoring goals at an eye-catching clip the rest of the way. Dunderdale would score an impressive twenty-four that first season, but Lalonde would do even better, scoring twenty-seven.

It was the lure of more money that drew Lalonde to Vancouver, and it was the same lure, perhaps exacerbated by a touch of home-sickness, that drew him back east. He would play just the one season—a glorious one—on the west coast before deciding to return to Montreal to renew acquaintance with his fellow francophones Didier Pitre and Jack Laviolette, both of whom would one day join Lalonde in the Hockey Hall of Fame.

It was not due to his friendly disposition and kind congenial-ity that Lalonde found an early place in the Hall of Fame in 1950. Regarded as one of the nastiest players in the game, Lalonde was widely loathed by hockey foes and even by some of his own team-mates. None of that mattered in 1912: Lalonde's presence in the PCHA materially helped to bring instant credibility to the Patricks' new hockey enterprise.

Three days after Lalonde's hat-trick (three goals), the *Daily Colonist*'s front-page headline on March 2 informed readers of a federal government decision to build a breakwater at Ogden Point, a development that would make the port of Victoria "one of the best equipped on the west coast." Today, more than a century on, the breakwater is one of Victorians' favourite places to take a stroll and enjoy a million-dollar view of Juan de Fuca Strait and the Olympic Mountains on the other side.

Farther from home, another March 2 front-page story reported that suffragists demonstrating in Trafalgar Square in London had "brought consternation" to the city by conducting themselves in most unladylike fashion: they had broken windows in many of "the most famous shops in the world." The demonstrators' actions did not immediately produce the desired result: it would take another sixteen years before women won equal voting rights in the UK.

On page nine, *Colonist* readers could read about the previous evening's game in Vancouver, a 7-3 victory over the Terminals. The

Colonist reported that both Patrick brothers, Lester and Frank, had been injured in the game, but after having their wounds stitched by a doctor, they carried on. It was what hockey-playing men did in 1912.

What generally happened if a player was injured, as they often were? A wounded man was granted a grace period, typically ten minutes, to be patched up and return to the game. To equalize the sides, the opposing team would take a player off for the required time. Substitutions were allowed: each team typically had a spare who could come in to replace a fallen ice warrior, but it was a point of pride—a matter of manly *honour*—that a player should carry on despite his wounds. And that is typically just what happened.

Lester Patrick, member of the Hockey Hall of Fame, class of 1947, wore three caps in Victoria: owner, manager, and player. In team pictures published in the *Daily Colonist* during the first season, Patrick stands at least half a head taller than the other players. In his playing prime, he was six feet, one inch tall and weighed 180 pounds. Starting at age sixteen, Patrick played for a succession of Montreal teams in the early years of the century. In 1906, at the age of twenty-two, he was a Stanley Cup winner with the Montreal Wanderers of the Eastern Canada Amateur Hockey Association (ECAHA). The Wanderers won again the following year. In 1909, Patrick turned pro with the Renfrew team of the NHA.

On March 15, 1915, Victoria defeated visiting Vancouver, 8-7. It was the final game of the season, but the victory failed to save Victoria's bacon: they ended that inaugural season at 7-9—seven victories, nine defeats—and finished last. League champions were the New Westminster lads. The Royals were thus the first team to be awarded the Paterson Cup, donated by and named for Lieutenant-Governor Thomas Wilson Paterson.

An item in the sports page of the following day's *Daily Colonist* leaps to the eye. It is an ad for a "Spectacular Entertainment." Aviator J.V. Cavanaugh, the "Famous Bird Man," would give an exhibition that afternoon at the Victoria fairground. "This is the sight of a lifetime and you should be a witness," the ad shouted. The price for the sight of a lifetime? A mere fifty cents. The ad features an image of the Bird Man's machine, a biplane looking not much evolved from the manned kite Orville Wright had flown for fifty-nine seconds at Kitty Hawk eight years earlier. In another five years, human ingenuity would bring about a quantum leap in the development of powered flight. The skies over the Western Front of Belgium and France would be the scene of battles played out by marvellous new airborne killing machines.

But that was a matter for the near future. In the late winter of 1911-12, the Victoria hockey club had wound up in the league basement, but the Victoria squad distinguished itself in a way that seems truly remarkable in our time: every player on the team—all seven members—played every game, without substitution. That players played sixty minutes of a game was, of course, the norm in 1912. To do so for an entire season was something else entirely. The Victorias had a spare—just one—by the name of Mac McAuliffe, but despite the injuries players sustained during the rough-and-tumble of the game, none of them needed a substitute. Poor McAuliffe never appeared in so much as a minute.

By the Ides of March, the first PCHA season was done, but there was one more thrill in store for west-coast hockey fans. Two years in the future, the premier professional leagues—the NHA in the east and the PCHA in the west—would agree to make the Stanley Cup the prize in an annual showdown between NHA and PCHA champions. There was no such understanding in 1912, not least because the Patricks had burnt every bridge in sight to the NHA owner-operators.

Sam Lichtenhein, owner of the Montreal Wanderers, had lost fully half of his 1910-11 roster to the Patricks' depredations and he was mad as hell about it. Of the twenty-three players who saw action in the inaugural PCHA season, sixteen had been lured away from the NHA. In no way was Lichtenhein prepared to cooperate in organizing a post-season friendly get-together of NHA and PCHA all-stars. But Art Ross, a former Lichtenhein chattel, *was*. And so it came it pass. Though it may have come close to inducing a stroke in poor old Sam, Art Ross liked the smell of money: he expected, correctly, that a good payday would result from a head-to-head NHA–PCHA confrontation. He and the Patricks agreed to an exhibition series to be played on the west coast, two games in Vancouver, one in Victoria. Apoplectic though he may have been, Lichtenhein couldn't stop it.

Despite the erosion the Patricks had caused to NHA rosters, the eastern all-stars arrived in Vancouver brimming with confidence. After all, the eastern crew included Paddy Moran, Art Ross, and Jack Darragh, all of whom would one day be inducted into the Hockey Hall of Fame. Three players of Hall-of-Fame merit might have cinched it for the NHA stars, but for this: the western team had *six*. All but one of the PCHA squad would one day be Hall of Famers: in addition to Victoria's Patrick and Dunderdale, the western all-stars included Vancouver's Lalonde, as well as New Westminster's Ernie Johnson, Hugh Lehman, and Harry Hyland.

The first game, in Vancouver on April 2, was a revelation to the NHA stalwarts: they were hammered, 10-4. All but one of the ten goals was scored by a player who had once worn an NHA team jersey. Sam Lichtenhein must have gone nuts. Two days later, fresh salt air and the charms of the ferry crossing through the beautiful Gulf Islands might have rejuvenated Art Ross's crew but, no, the bloodbath continued at the Patricks' Oak Bay arena. This time the score was 8-2. The east did manage a one-goal victory in the Vancouver return engagement, April 6, but whatever conviction may have existed that the NHA brand was superior now lay in ruins.

Lester Patrick and Tommy Dunderdale could take comfort from the result of the all-star exhibition. What's more, though the Capitals had finished last in their first PCHA season, better things were in store for the 1912-13 edition of the Victoria hockey club.

TWO

1912-13

WORLD CHAMPIONS

O
N DECEMBER 14, 1912, a front-page story in the Victoria
Daily Colonist reported that a conference had been con-
vened in London aimed at seeking a negotiated end to
the war then raging between the Balkan League and the Ottoman
Empire—a preview of the larger European conflagration that would
erupt less than two years later, engulfing much of the world in the
catastrophic Great War of 1914-18.

Elsewhere in the December 14 issue, readers could find something in a lighter vein: an account of a return engagement of some
consequence to Victoria hockey fans. In the opening game of the
previous season, the New Westminster team had come to town
and spoiled the first-ever PCHA game for Victorians, dominating
the home team 8-3. This time, led by Tommy Dunderdale, Victoria
returned the favour, defeating the defending league champions 6-4.
Some four thousand fans—the biggest yet to gather at the Patrick
Arena in Oak Bay—were on hand to savour delicious retribution.

Lieutenant-Governor Paterson made a repeat appearance to
drop the puck in the ceremonial opening faceoff, and thereby "lent
to the occasion an air of distinction." "Never before," the *Colonist*'s reporter wrote, "did such an enormous crowd of enthusiasts

witness the sport in the city, and if it means anything at all, it is a good augury for the season." The sportswriter was prescient.

Opening day of the 1912–13 Victoria hockey season revealed significant personnel changes. Don Smith, the Capitals' second-best goal scorer the first year, had departed for colder, snowier Montreal. Three new names appeared in the Capitals' second-season roster: Goldie Prodgers, Jack Ulrich, and Bobby Genge.

Not yet christened the Aristocrats, the Victoria team was dubbed the *Capitals* in the newspaper's account of the new season's first game. The first star of the game, Dunderdale, "dented the strings three times," but others shone too, including new team member Goldie Prodgers.

During the off-season, Lester Patrick had got up to old tricks. Keen to make the PCHA every bit the equal of the east's premier league, the National Hockey Association, Patrick induced Prodgers to "jump" his contract with the NHA Quebec Bulldogs. Led by future Hall of Famer Joe Malone and with Prodgers in a supporting role, Quebec had been NHA champions and Stanley Cup winners the previous winter. Prodgers' motivation was easily understood: the promise of a bigger payday. He followed the example Dunderdale had set a year earlier; he forsook Quebec City's charms for those of the Garden City.

A native of London, Ontario, Prodgers was just twenty-one when he arrived in Victoria, a five-foot-ten-inch, 180-pound defenceman who would spend only the one season in Victoria before being lured back east to ply his trade for still more money in Montreal. He, too, would eventually decide he owed a duty to King and Country: in 1916, he enlisted in the Canadian Expeditionary Force and went off to war the following year.

It was commonplace in the early years of the PCHA for players to work as on-ice officials. In the opening game of the 1912–13 PCHA season, it was Vancouver players Cyclone Taylor and Si Griffis—both future Hall of Fame members—who filled the ice-arbiter roles: judge of play and referee. Thirteen times, players were "sent to the fence" by judge of play Taylor, most of them three-minute sentences. (At the time, penalized players weren't consigned to a penalty box but were sent off to sit on the fence for two or three minutes. The judge of play could determine the duration of a penalty solely at his own discretion.)

Three weeks later, on January 9, the Victoria team hosted New Westminster for the second time in the young season. Victoria won in overtime, 3-2, its second straight overtime game. A Victoria newcomer, Jack Ulrich, was the man of the hour, scoring the winning goal in the thirteenth minute of overtime. Something unusual had brought Ulrich into the game: Bobby Rowe was hurt badly enough that he was not able to return after his ten-minute grace period and so was replaced by Ulrich. There had been no injury substitutions at all in Victoria's first season, but this was the second time in as many games that Ulrich, the Victoria spare, had had to enter the game to replace Rowe. In *both* games, Ulrich had been the overtime hero, the man who scored the winning goal.

John George "Jack" Ulrich was a most unusual hockey player: he was deaf and did not speak. He had to play a fast, dangerous game without the benefit of sound to let him know when an opposing player bore down for a body check or a teammate shouted for a golden-opportunity pass. A native of Nipissing, Ontario, Ulrich was twenty-four the previous year when he played sparingly for Frank Patrick's PCHA Vancouver team. Appearing in only three of Vancouver's sixteen games, he had somehow managed to score four goals. In December, he crossed the Strait of Georgia, no doubt hoping for more playing time with the Victoria club. He *did* play more in Victoria: five games instead of three, but scored only twice—those two important game-winning overtime goals. "Jack" was the name by which Ulrich preferred to be known, but it is perhaps a reflection of the era in which he played that he was far better known as "Silent"—the name the *Colonist* writer used in his dispatches—or, worse, "Dummy," a name, unsurprisingly, that Ulrich loathed.

How difficult must it have been to be a successful pro hockey player without being able to hear? How rare is such a player? In the century-long history of the National Hockey League, well over six thousand players have competed in at least one NHL game. Of those, only *one* was legally deaf: Jim Kyte, who played 598 NHL games between 1982 and 1996 without being able to hear what was happening around him.

Clearly, Jack Ulrich had also found a way to cope. He played two years for Lester Patrick, managing to get into nine games in 1913-14 before heading east to Montreal.

On January 17, Lester Patrick's Victoria team welcomed brother Frank's Vancouver seven for a game at the Patrick Arena on Epworth Street. Just as the *Daily Colonist* had now settled on *Capitals* as its name of choice for Victoria's team, so it had taken to calling Vancouver's team the *Terminals*, presumably due to the home rink's proximity to the Vancouver docks. The Capitals vanquished the Terminals, 4-3.

Skinner Poulin played "the finest game of his career on the Coast," an outcome the *Colonist* writer credited to the fact that Poulin had just been blessed with the arrival of a "bouncing baby girl."

Once again, current players served as on-ice officials for the game: New Westminster's Jimmy Gardner, the future Hall of Famer, was the referee, his teammate Eddie Oatman the judge of play. Oatman had an easy night of it. "There was absolutely no roughness," the *Colonist* reported, evidently because the boss, Lester Patrick, had ordered his troops to stay out of penalty trouble. The Capitals complied: "Only Tommy Dunderdale and Walt Smaill graced the fence the whole evening," the *Colonist* reported. With the victory over Vancouver, the Capitals improved their record to 4-1, the best in the league.

A few days later, January 22, the *Daily Colonist* blazoned a page two headline: FEAR VIOLENCE BY SUFFRAGISTS: THE GOVERNMENT AND POLICE AT LONDON TAKE EXTRAORDINARY PRECAUTIONS AGAINST OUTRAGES BY FRENZIED WOMEN. Fear of what "frenzied women" might do arose as a result of anger generated by the latest reversal in women's efforts to be recognized as equal human beings with the right to vote. It would take another fifteen years before the male establishment's fear of outrage was finally eased by passage of legislation that gave women the same voting rights as men.

Distraction from anxiety over the events in London was perhaps provided in a story on page nine of that day's newspaper. Under the headline CAPITALS AGAIN BEAT TERMINALS, the *Colonist* reported that with just nine seconds left on the clock, Tommy Dunderdale's goal had secured a 5-4 victory for Victoria over Vancouver at Vancouver's Denman Arena. Victoria's Smaill, Rowe, and Poulin were all credited with excellent work that brought Victoria's season record to five wins against a single loss.

What did a crowd of four thousand pay to attend a Victoria game in 1913? Two dollars would get a fan a box seat close to the action, a reserved seat cost a dollar, and an unreserved seat—if one was left available at game time—was fifty cents. Two dollars in 1913 was not loose change: it was worth about fifty bucks in today's terms, but $50 is still much less than today's average price for a Toronto Maple Leafs ticket—about $370.

The lead story in the Sunday, January 26, issue of the *Daily Colonist* reported that the provincial government had decided to set aside money for the construction of a steel-and-concrete bridge from the foot of Johnson Street to the Songhees lands across the harbour narrows. This happy news merited the lead item in the paper's editorial section that same day. It would take eleven years for the project to be realized and the iconic structure completed. Finished in 1924 and beloved by many Victorians, the "Blue Bridge" served for ninety-four years before it was replaced in 2018.

Elsewhere in that day's newspaper, readers could appreciate a photograph and story noting the fifty-fifth birthday celebrations of a grandson of the late Queen Victoria, a man who would loom large on the world stage in a very short while—the German emperor, Wilhelm II. In a few years, King George V's German first cousin would find his birthdays far less celebrated in the dominions of the British Empire.

The night before, Victoria's four-game winning streak had been halted by New Westminster, 5-2. The Royals had been playing their home games at Vancouver's Denman Street arena, but the *Colonist* reported that the Royals would soon be setting up housekeeping at their new, 3,500-seat artificial-ice arena in New Westminster.

On January 31, Victoria got back on the winning track, defeating the "worn-out" Royals by 7-3. Lester Patrick "was the sharpshooter of the Victoria team" and Tommy Dunderdale "but little behind." At six wins and just two losses, the Capitals were in first place, two games in front of Vancouver.

Four days later at the Denman Street arena, "the redoubtable Victoria seven" improved to 7-2 with a 7-4 win over the Terminals. By this time, visions of sugar plums began dancing in fans' heads, with the *Colonist* writer openly fantasizing about the march to "the famous Stanley silverware." The hero this time was Prodgers. Goldie had been slumping, "unable to bulge the strings," but on this night he ended the drought, recording three goals.

The February 11 *Daily Colonist* was dominated by a large-type headline, a long story, and four photographs reflecting the loss of Robert Falcon Scott and his companions in their quest to reach the South Pole. Judging by the attention paid and the column inches devoted, it was the biggest story of the year in Victoria. Premier Richard McBride addressed the Antarctic tragedy in the legislature and saw to it that the Union Jack fluttered at half-staff on the legislature lawn.

In the evening of that same day the Scott story broke, February 11, the Capitals ran their record to a league-best, 8-2, with a home victory over Vancouver. A crowd of more than four thousand attended the game, the biggest to date. A collision brought about by Vancouver's Cyclone Taylor laid out both Lester Patrick and Walter Smaill. Smaill was knocked unconscious and was out of the game. Patrick, a reliable "sixty-minute man," took over for Smaill; Patrick's cover-point spot was assumed by the spare, Bobby Genge, the Capitals' third new man this season.

Lester Patrick wore multiple hats for his 1912 Victoria Hockey Club: owner, manager-coach, and player. He was a six-time PCHA all-star and was the first former Victoria player admitted to the Hockey Hall of Fame. That honour came in 1947 when, together with his fellow PCHA star, Cyclone Taylor, Patrick was included in the second draft of Hall of Fame inductees. COURTESY DAVID MACDONALD

There is no debating that the Patrick brothers' greatest coup in the PCHA's second season had been the signing of Frederick Wellington Taylor. Though only five feet, eight inches and 165 pounds, Taylor was a hockey titan in his era, his nickname—Cyclone—a marker of the speed and whirlwind flair he brought to the game. In 1910–11, he had skated with Don Smith and Bobby Rowe as members of the Creamery Kings of Renfrew.

Lasting just two years as a franchise in the National Hockey Association, Renfrew's players were the subject of a lottery draft orchestrated by the surviving NHA clubs. The man lucky enough to draw Taylor's name from the lottery bowler was none other than Sam Lichtenhein, owner of the Montreal Wanderers. Alas for poor Sam, the Cyclone didn't want to play in Montreal. If Renfrew was no longer an available work environment, Fred preferred to take his act to the nation's capital, just fifty miles down the Ottawa River. Understandably incensed at being spurned by the crown jewel in the Creamery cast, Sam took the position that Taylor would play in Montreal or he would play nowhere at all. Taylor chose the latter option: he became the first celebrated holdout in hockey history.

As great as Lichtenhein's fury may have been in the first instance, it grew that much worse the following hockey season, when the Pacific coast pirates, Lester and Frank Patrick, persuaded Taylor to abandon the NHA entirely and bring his remarkable talents to Vancouver's ten-thousand-seat stage at Denman and West Georgia.

The Cyclone legend grew only more compelling in Vancouver. Aged twenty-eight the year he joined forces with Frank Patrick, he would play six brilliant seasons at the Denman Arena, lead the NHA scoring parade twice, and finish his PCHA career first in career assists and second in points despite playing more than a hundred games fewer than the league career points leader, Mickey MacKay.

Despite the wounds the run-in with Cyclone Taylor had caused Lester Patrick and Walter Smaill on February 11, the Victoria Capitals were sitting pretty. After ten games of the 1912–13 schedule, Victoria had eight victories and were three games ahead of Vancouver with only five to play. One of the Capitals, Dunderdale, was also far ahead in the individual goal-scoring race, with sixteen goals in ten games—a half dozen ahead of Vancouver's Fred Harris.

Victorians began to count their chickens.

With such a commanding lead, Victoria perhaps grew somewhat complacent: on February 18, New Westminster beat them decisively,

6-1. The setback was only temporary. Three days later, February 21, with Smaill still out of action due to the previous game injury, Genge again assumed his spot in the Victoria lineup. The Capitals overwhelmed the Royals in Victoria, 7-1, running their season record to nine wins in twelve games.

A native of Leeds County, Ontario, Robert Allen "Bobby" Genge, twenty-three, was an anomaly in an era when players typically stood only five and a half feet or so. The Ontarian was all of six feet, four inches and two hundred pounds. He had played the previous year with Port Arthur Lake City of the New Ontario Hockey League, a team that included three future Hall of Famers—Jack Walker, Harry Cameron, and Frank Nighbor. In his first go-round with Victoria, Genge played sporadically, mostly as the team spare, and scored only twice in eight games. But 1912–13 was just the beginning of his Victoria story: he would go on to play eight seasons for Lester Patrick.

With the league championship all but certain, the Capitals and their fans now looked ahead to a matchup with the NHA Quebec Bulldogs for national bragging rights. An item on the *Colonist*'s February 22 sports page reported that the PCHA had "officially" invited the Quebeckers to come to the west coast to play for the "world's title." But there was a hitch. The story made it clear that the PCHA champion would *not* travel to Quebec to play for the Stanley Cup. Neither would the Quebeckers contest a Stanley Cup battle anywhere but in *l'ancienne capitale*. Stanley Cup aside, the PCHA seemed content that the league should face off against Quebec for that vague "world's title," whatever that meant. If the world's title didn't deliver the Stanley Cup, what good was it?

The Capitals could have clinched the league title in their next game, but they flubbed the opportunity. "In the fastest and most brilliant games seen at the arena this season," Vancouver prevailed, 9-6. No one could fault Tommy Dunderdale for the loss: he was the "bright shining light of the Capitals," scoring three goals, all in the third period, while expanding his lead in the individual scoring race to ten.

The 1912–13 Victoria Aristocrats were "world champions" after defeating the NHA-champion Quebec Bulldogs in a post-season exhibition series, but the Stanley Cup was not their reward. The NHA and PCHA had not yet reached an agreement to make the Cup the prize of an annual showdown between the two leagues. From left: Gordon Smaill, Tommy Dunderdale, Lester Patrick, Skinner Poulin, Goldie Prodgers, Bert Lindsay, Bobby Genge, Bobby Rowe, Jack Ulrich. COURTESY DAVID MACDONALD

An intriguing item appeared in the next day's *Daily Colonist*, right beside the game report. In a piece headlined STANLEY CUP DONATED FOR AMATEUR HOCKEY, the anonymous writer argued that the prized bowl—donated, it was said, not by the Governor General himself but by his son Arthur Stanley—was meant to be a prize for hockey *amateurs*, not professionals. Was the article aimed at discrediting the bona fides of the Stanley Cup at a time when it appeared the Cup would not be available for the taking? Perhaps.

The big story on the front page of the next day's *Colonist* was the decision by the government of Richard McBride, champion of a white British Columbia, to commission an imposing statue of Queen Victoria. Created by British artist Albert Bruce-Joy, the sculpture would be completed in 1914 but due to the distraction of the Great War, it was not until after the war that it was unveiled on the legislature lawn. The bronze figure of "Victoria the Good" remains there to this day, a little bit of "olde England" for all the tourists who like to stop and take her portrait.

Elsewhere in its pages, the *Colonist* blamed the previous night's hockey loss in Vancouver on the continuing absence of the injured Walter Smaill. With two straight defeats, the Capitals now stood at 9-5 for the season, and the *Colonist* writer worried a little about "the remote possibility" that the Capitals might manage not to win the league championship after all.

The worry evaporated March 7 at the Denman Street arena, where on a pass from Dunderdale, Bobby Genge scored the game's only goal in a 1-0 victory over New Westminster. It was Bert Lindsay's first goaltending shutout in his two Victoria seasons. With a goals-against average of 3.62, he had reduced his GAA by nearly two a game from the 5.54 average of the year before. The contest was highly exciting, the *Colonist* reported, though marred by excessive tripping. The "sixty-minute man," Lester Patrick, played "lustrously" before being carried off the ice, injured, with only a minute and a half to go. Though scoreless in that final game, Tommy Dunderdale had bagged twenty-four for the season, ten better than anyone else in the league. The Capitals were champions and the *Colonist* celebrated with a picture gallery of all the players spread across the top of page nine.

Now came the best part.

In its early years, the Stanley Cup could be put up for grabs twice or even three times in a hockey season. That had been the case most recently in 1910. By 1914, a new Stanley Cup protocol would be established: the best team in the east—the champions of the NHA, later the NHL—would take on the best in the west for the Cup, but in 1913 that arrangement had not yet been established. Quebec, the NHA champions, had just answered a Cup challenge from the Sydney Millionaires of the Maritime Professional Hockey League. Quebec had demolished Sydney by a 20-5 goals margin in a two-game series, March 8 and March 10.

The Quebec club—popularly known as the Bulldogs—was willing to accept a Victoria challenge just days after dispatching the Cape Bretoners, but only in its own arena. Disinclined to risk losing the Cup on Victoria ice, the Quebeckers *were* nonetheless prepared to travel three thousand miles to southern Vancouver Island for a best-of-three "world championship" exhibition series. Clearly, a so-called world title offered nothing like the prestige and gravitas of the Stanley Cup.

Quebec was an NHA juggernaut that 1912–13 season. With five future Hall of Famers on the roster, including Joe Malone and Paddy Moran, the Bulldogs had won sixteen of twenty regular-season games, six better than anybody else. With the Bulldogs' arrival in Victoria on an eleven-game winning streak, some observers perhaps imagined that the Capitals would present little more trouble than Sydney had delivered just two weeks earlier. They were wrong. On March 24, in a game the next-day *Daily Colonist* headline called "cyclonic," Victoria prevailed, 7-5. Lester Patrick rose to the occasion and Genge, Poulin, and Rowe were "never more effective."

Three days later, March 27, the Bulldogs evened the series, winning the second game, 6-3. The NHA had eliminated the rover position that season, and played six-man hockey. That "eastern style"—six players a side—was the way the March 27 game was played. It suited Quebec well. Being "perfectly at home in the six-man game," Quebec got the jump on Patrick's crew, who were "at sea" in the beginning. Quebec scored the first two goals and made the margin last. That set up a final game for all the marbles.

Would that final game be played eastern-style with six players, or western, with seven? The Solomons in charge decided to divide the baby, playing half the game one way, half the other.

The largest crowd of the season gathered at the Patrick Arena for the third game on Saturday, March 29, with every square foot of standing room occupied. The next day's *Daily Colonist* called the match "scintillatingly brilliant." "Every one of the local men played grand hockey," the *Colonist* reported, "and so did the visitors."

Despite there being no risk of the Stanley Cup changing hands, the game was fiercely contested. Skinner Poulin, "working like a little fiend," got himself entangled with Rusty Crawford, lost some teeth, but carried on. Dunderdale scored the first goal of the game, the only one of the opening period. Lindsay was "sensational" in guarding the Capitals' goal net. Midway through the second period the teams switched to seven a side. Either style suited the Capitals: Patrick, Dunderdale, and Genge all scored for Victoria, with only Tommy Smith responding for Quebec. Going into the third period, Victoria was up 4-1. In the final frame, Patrick and Genge each scored their second goal of the game. The final score: Victoria 6, Quebec 1.

At the close of the game, "[a] roar that shook the building to its foundations rose from more than 4,000 throats, the crowd poured down on the ice, and Lester Patrick and his teammates were surrounded by a madly-delighted crowd." It seemed not to faze the happily deranged Victoria fans that the prize for the victory was just a "World's Championship," not the Stanley Cup.

The opportunity to play for *that* exalted prize would come a year later.

THREE

1913-14

STANLEY CUP SHOWDOWN

O N THE FIRST DAY of autumn in 1911, Conservative Robert Borden brought an end to Sir Wilfrid Laurier's fifteen-year reign as Liberal prime minister of Canada. In British Columbia, Borden's fellow Conservative, Premier Richard McBride, had enjoyed great electoral success on the promise to make BC a "white man's province." Perhaps spotting a winning formula, in 1911, Borden traded on the phrase "A White Canada" and almost perfectly reversed the House of Commons party standings. Laurier's Liberals had beaten the Conservatives, winning 133 seats to the Tories' 85 in the 1908 election; three years later, Borden led the Conservatives to a 132-85 victory.

By December of 1913, two years into his term, Borden appeared determined to make good on his promise of a white Canada. Prominent on the front page of the December 2 Victoria *Daily Colonist* was a headline, HINDU QUESTION BEFORE CABINET. The story under that headline explained that Borden's government was intent on passing measures aimed at "protecting British Columbia from an influx of Hindus."

The government's measures proved effective. A few months later, in the spring of 1914, a ship carrying 376 passengers arrived in Vancouver harbour. More than twenty were Canadian citizens. Others were related to earlier immigrants who had made a success of themselves as new Canadians. After a protracted standoff, the *Komagata Maru*'s passengers—principally Indian Sikhs seeking to make a new home for themselves in Canada—were almost entirely turned away and sent back from whence they came. An event that appalled some Canadians at the time and even more in later years, the *Komagata Maru* incident brought about a formal apology from the federal government, but not until 102 years had elapsed.

A sidebar story in the *Komagata Maru* incident: one of the senior Canadian officials involved in the two-month affair was none other than Cyclone Taylor. In winter, Taylor was a hockey luminary; the rest of the year, he worked as a federal immigration officer and would one day be commissioner of immigration for all of British Columbia. Taylor appears to have had some sympathy for the immigrants, but BC was in the grip of Richard McBride, whose view it was that such sympathy could go to hell.

It is unlikely that anti-Hindu measures were much in the mind of Victoria hockey fans when their beloved Capitals took to the ice against New Westminster for the first game of the 1913-14 PCHA season. Victoria lost the opener, 6-5, but no one could fault Tommy Dunderdale. The future Hall of Famer scored four of the Victoria goals, three in the first period. It was perhaps a significant contributing factor that Lester Patrick was out of action: he watched the game from the sidelines, his injured arm in a sling.

The game introduced a Patrick innovation, the forward pass, at least a limited edition of it. The Patricks—Frank the initiator, Lester somewhat more reluctantly—had decided to divide the ice into three equal-sized segments while establishing a new rule allowing forward passing in the middle, neutral zone. Thus were born the blue lines—two of them—that persist to this day. The *Colonist* reporter remarked on the impact the new rule had on the game, making it faster while providing better attack opportunities; it also required goaltenders to be more vigilant and pay closer attention to attackers.

Victoria's 1913-14 roster was little changed from the one that had defeated Quebec in the "world championship" exhibition the previous March. Perhaps someone in management with the Quebec club had liked what he had seen of Goldie Prodgers. After a single season with Victoria, Goldie headed off to play for the team he had help defeat nine months earlier.

Prodgers' roster spot was filled by Albert "Dubbie" Kerr, a five-foot-ten-inch native of Brockville, Ontario, who had previously played with considerable success for the Ottawa Senators of the NHA. Kerr evidently liked what he saw of Lester Patrick and the west coast: he would spend the rest of his hockey career with Patrick and his PCHA teams.

Kerr delivered a significant impact in his second Capitals game, a 6-2 home victory over New Westminster on December 12. Lieutenant-Governor Paterson once again dropped the ceremonial first puck; he also made unrecorded remarks that impressed both spectators and players. Kerr had missed the 1912-13 season due to injury. The *Colonist* reporter lauded the quality of Kerr's comeback and paid tribute to his skating, stickhandling, and shooting. The newest Capital cemented a favourable first impression by scoring twice, both in the second period.

Things went south in Victoria's next game, December 16. Playing Frank Patrick's crew at the Denman Street arena, the defending-champion Victorians were blown out, 11-3. Frank Patrick had reinforced his Vancouver club, now sometimes recognized by the *Daily Colonist* as the Millionaires, by two more worthies poached from the NHA: future Hall of Famers Didier Pitre and Frank Nighbor. With Cyclone Taylor already on board, the Denman Street denizens were a formidable lot. Taylor scored three of the Vancouver goals, Pitre two, and Nighbor one. If there was a bright light on the Victoria side, it was the ever reliable Dunderdale: he scored twice.

Ten days later, the Capitals took decisive Boxing Day retribution, 9-4, against the Millionaires on their Oak Bay home ice. Once again a crowd of four thousand paid to see the action. As the *Daily Colonist* saw things, Victoria beat Vancouver at its own game, with "speed and bullet-like shooting." The *Colonist* credited Lester Patrick's "strict coaching and instruction" for the reversal of form from the December 16 debacle. Kerr, with four goals, and deadeye Dunderdale, with three, were the Capitals' key marksmen. Despite allowing four goals, Lindsay was credited with having played a "wonderful" game "such as has never been seen here."

After a home loss to New Westminster, the Capitals faced Vancouver again, at the Denman Street arena, on January 6. Led by Rowe's three goals and Dunderdale's two, Victoria took a 6-3 lead into the third period. The final twenty minutes delivered what the *Colonist* described as "one of the most desperate finishes witnessed in Pacific Coast Hockey." When Frank Patrick brought the Millionaires to within one goal, "the building fairly shook as the fans rose en masse." In what the paper described as one of the most exciting finishes on record, Lester Patrick and crew held on for a 6-5 win.

It was not just a hockey game that could attract a large, rapturous crowd in Victoria. On January 15, the *Colonist* featured an ad for a significant event of high culture. In modern times, the word "pavlova" evokes a meringue cake popular among some dessert lovers not worried about calorie counts or heart disease. The dessert is named for Anna Pavlova—or *Pavlowa* as the name was styled a century ago—a Russian ballerina of great renown. In 1914, Victoria was enough of a destination that the doyenne included the BC capital in her North American tour of that year. On January 15, she performed at the Royal Victoria theatre. The 1,400-seat Royal, brand-new at that time, is still a venue today for great cultural events in the city. Sara Bernhardt, Carlos Montoya, Mikhail Baryshnikov, and Luciano Pavarotti are among the luminaries who have strutted their stuff on the Royal stage. The top price for a 1914 hockey ticket was two dollars, only half what one had to pay for the Royal's best view of Pavlova.

The next day's *Colonist* makes it clear not just that Pavlova had enjoyed a successful gig at the Royal but that the reviewer's art of our time is a pale thing compared to its florid 1914 counterpart:

Royal Victoria Theatre

Tonight, Thursday,
January 15

Curtain 8:15

Victoria Ladies' Musical
Club Presents

PAVLOWA

The dancing revelation of
the age, with **M. Novikoff,**
Imperial Russian Ballet,
and complete Symphony
Orchestra

Seats Selling Now

Prices: $4.00, $3.00, $2.00,
$1.50, $1.00

Anna Pavlova, the "dancing revelation of the age." DAILY COLONIST, JAN-
UARY 15, 1914

The exquisite art of Anna Pavlova, which seemed to have reached
the zenith of perfection when she first burst like a meteor on the
theatrical firmament, appears to have broadened with the passing
of the years. Like an exotic bloom that is ethereal in the delicacy of
shading, the petals of her art have unfolded until today the onlooker
is left spellbound at the superb grandeur of the perfect flower.

Whew.

Elsewhere in the January 15 *Colonist*, the caption under a photo of
Bobby Genge informed readers who somehow preferred the sports
section to the cultural page that Genge had played sensational

hockey in the Capitals' Wednesday game at home against New Westminster's Royals. Victoria had gone into the game with a so-so record of three wins and three losses. Their 5-3 victory over the Royals gave Lester's men a winning record for the first time that season.

The headline story in the January 21 issue of the Victoria morning daily reported on the passing, at age ninety-five, of Donald Alexander Smith, better known as Lord Strathcona. The *Colonist* coverage of Strathcona's death reflected the newspaper's high regard for the great man, a feeling widely shared across the country. Born in Scotland in 1820, Strathcona was by turns a successful businessman, philanthropist, builder of the Canadian Pacific Railway, Member of Parliament, High Commissioner to Britain, and much, much more. Two parks—one in BC, the other in Manitoba—honour Smith's memory, as do small communities in three provinces, as well as a fiord, sound, and group of islands in the Northwest Territories.

A less sombre item in that day's paper reported on the previous evening's visit to the Oak Bay rink by the Vancouver Millionaires. In "the most sensational hockey game played on the Coast this season," Vancouver won in overtime, 7-6, on a goal by Cyclone Taylor. Until the disappointing end, "the fans were on their feet in an ecstasy of enthusiasm" that may even have exceeded the Pavlova paroxysms of a few days earlier. In the over-the-top view of the *Colonist* reporter, the game was easily the fastest and best-played one seen that season. The Patrick brothers—Lester for Victoria, Frank for Vancouver—drew praise for their starring roles on behalf of their teams.

In other hockey news, the January 21 sports page also featured images of two strapping young players with the amateur Winnipeg Victorias hockey club: Ralph Baker and Jack Hughes. Among his other achievements, Hughes would go on to coach Team Canada to glory at the 1932 Olympics at Lake Placid, New York. In those games, the Canadians outscored the opposition 32-4 and won the gold medal for the fourth straight time.

A second straight loss, this time to New Westminster, pushed the Capitals' record below .500, but on January 27, Victoria embarked on a winning run. That day Lester Patrick's Capitals took the ferry to Vancouver and beat his brother's squad in the Denman Street arena, 5-3. The game did not give the *Colonist*'s man anything like the euphoria that swept him away in the prior Vancouver-Victoria matchup, but he was pleased with the work of Poulin and Genge and gratified that the Capitals had evened their win-loss record at 5-5.

There was an augury of unhappy events to come in the *Colonist*'s January 28 sports page. A century ago the Allan Cup was just about as big a deal as the holy grail of professional hockey, the Stanley Cup. The previous season, the Winnipeg Hockey Club had won the Allan Cup as Canadian amateur hockey champions.

The Allan Cup-winning Winnipeg team of 1913 featured a future Hockey Hall of Famer, Jack Ruttan, and three more—Jack Aldous, Bert Andrews, and Ollie Turnbull—who had something in common other than Allan Cup bragging rights. All three would set aside their hockey gear to become soldiers in the Canadian Expeditionary Force of 1914-18. Andrews and Turnbull would turn out to be particularly brave officers: both would be awarded the Military Cross for gallantry.

Ruttan, Aldous, and Andrews were fortunate: they would survive their adventures in Flanders and France. Turnbull would not. He was killed in action in November 1916 on the Somme and has a final resting place with sixty-three other Canadians at Bapaume Post Military Cemetery in France. He would not be the only hockey player to die in the war—not by a stretch.

Bobby Genge, his "cyclonic" attacks too much for opposition defenders, scored a hat-trick in the January 30 game against visiting New Westminster. Bert Lindsay, the goaltender, took a nasty cut below the eye but carried on. He was lauded, too. With the win, Victoria pulled to within a half game of the league lead.

Eleven days later, February 10, the Capitals won their third in a row, 5-2, on home ice against Vancouver. In the *Colonist*'s perspective, Bobby Genge was once again the man of the hour, with Lindsay a high achiever, too. This improved the Capitals' won-lost record to 7-5: the *Colonist* began imagining that a second straight league title was in the bag.

Victoria made it four straight in a February 13 match against New Westminster in the Royals' new arena at Queen's Park. The game went to double overtime, with Tommy Dunderdale scoring the winner in the thirty-seventh minute of extra time. Under a headline proclaiming it a "sensational" win, the next morning's *Daily Colonist* called the match "as fast and scientific as has been played in any game on the Coast." At this point, the Capitals were 8-5, two games in front of Vancouver.

A second item on the same page of that day's *Colonist*—brief but significant—reported that National Hockey Association president Emmett Quinn had announced the dates of the showdown between the NHA and PCHA for the "world series" of hockey. In its third season, the PCHA had established its bona fides for good: the PCHA would compete to determine which league's champion got to hoist the Stanley Cup in 1914 and for years to come.

On February 17, Lester's lads crossed the Strait of Georgia and clinched the league title in a 5-4 thriller at Vancouver. For a second straight time, the game went into overtime, Smaill scoring in the eighth extra minute. The *Colonist* reporter reached for new superlatives to describe what he and thousands of others had seen on the Denman Street ice: it was "the fastest and most spectacular game seen in the three seasons of the great Winter sport on the Coast." The outcome was especially gratifying for the Victorians because they had come back from a 4-0 deficit to win. Patrick, Poulin, and Dunderdale reduced the deficit to one in the second period before Kerr scored the tying goal in the third.

Si Griffis, one of Vancouver's brighter lights, missed the game because he was in a hospital bed at Vancouver General. But a "local sporting enthusiast," telephone in hand, kept Griffis continuously informed of the game's ebb and flow. When the tension reached a peak in the third period, Griffis "had great difficulty in restraining himself from jumping out of bed."

The *Colonist*'s next-day sports page mirrored Victoria's excitement. A big photo spread featured all nine of the city's hockey

heroes under a large-type, boldface headline: RETAIN THE
PACIFIC COAST HOCKEY CHAMPIONSHIP.

Back on their Epworth Street home ice for a February 20 game
with last-place New Westminster, the Capitals managed to not let
the excitement get to them: they dominated the Royals 8-3 to bring
their season record to 10-5 with one game to play. With nothing at
stake, that final game proved to be no facsimile of the February 17
thriller. Playing at home, the Capitals were not able to rouse themselves to a stirring finale. "It was plain from the start," the next day's
Daily Colonist reported, "that the Victorians were not in the right
frame of mind." Yes, Lester's lads were league champions, but they
"were unmercifully trimmed" by Vancouver, 13-6. Only Bobby Rowe
came close to playing up to his usual standard.

The *Colonist* conceded that the real star of the evening was
Taylor: the Cyclone scored *five* goals and added one assist. As a
result of that production, Taylor leapfrogged over Kerr and Dunderdale and took the league's individual scoring title. It was likely
of small consolation to the pride of Benalla that Dunderdale scored
late, to level his goals total with Taylor. For the third straight year,
Dunderdale had finished the season with twenty-four goals.

Lester Patrick took a philosophical view of the last-game debacle: "The boys had to get one bad game out of their systems after
travelling at top speed for six successive games, and I'm glad they
did not wait until they got to Toronto"—Toronto, of course, being
where the PCHA champions were headed next to battle for the Stanley Cup they had been denied the year before.

Someone had done her bit to ensure that the journey to Toronto
would be a bountiful one for the Victoria skaters. In a post-game
ceremony in the Capitals' dressing room, "Little Miss Alberta Hurst"
presented each of her hockey heroes with something special: small
steel horseshoes tied with silk in the team's colours. She had embroi-
dered each of the good-luck charms with the player's initials and
admonished them to not let the talismans out of their possession.

Would Alberta's horseshoes have the desired effect?

The 1913-14 Toronto Hockey Club—better known as the Blueshirts—had finished their NHA season tied for first place with the Montreal Canadiens. A two-game, total-goal NHA playoff would determine which team represented the league in the Stanley Cup final against Victoria. Both games ended in shutouts and the home team won each. On March 7, *les Canadiens* prevailed at the Montreal Arena, 2-0. Four days later, the Blueshirts rained on the Montrealers' parade with a 6-0 victory on their home ice.

The Blueshirts were a formidable team. Five of its members would one day be inducted into the Hockey Hall of Fame—team captain, Allan "Scotty" Davidson, George McNamara, and three men whose future endeavours would one day lead them to the PCHA and Lester Patrick: Frank Foyston, Hap Holmes, and Jack Walker.

Lester Patrick's crew took to the Toronto ice for the first game in the best-of-five series on March 14. It had been a fortnight since that that last-game blowout against Vancouver, and the Capitals had had to spend several days crossing the country by train. Perhaps these were circumstances that influenced the first-game result.

In front of a full house of six thousand, Harry George "Hap" Holmes sparkled in the Toronto net as three of the future Hall of Famers looked after all the Toronto scoring in a 5-2 Blueshirts victory: Walker and McNamara had two goals each, Davidson the fifth. The *Colonist* paid tribute to the work of Holmes "who gave one of the best exhibitions of goal-keeping ever witnessed on the local team."

The crowd gave the visitors "a friendly ovation," but when the Blueshirts took to the ice "there was a roar that drowned the music of the band." As the *Colonist* saw it, the event drew a blueblood crowd: "Toronto's best people witnessed the contest and the rink was taxed to capacity." The *Colonist* scribe viewed Skinner Poulin as having been the most effective forward on the ice, and it was Poulin, with Dunderdale, who accounted for the Victoria scoring.

The first game had been played according to the NHA's six-man convention. For game two, March 17, the sides turned to western rules featuring seven men and permitting forward passes in the neutral zone. In its March 17 edition, the *Colonist* ventured that the switch to the seven-man game would give the Capitals the edge later that day, its headline confidently assuring fans that their team was favoured to beat Toronto. Toronto's fans had different expectations.

The next day's *Colonist* gave its readers a richly detailed account of a "sensational" match. The teams again played before a packed house. The game was rough. Late in the action, Genge shoved the butt end of his stick into Roy McGiffin's face above the eye "and laid him out for several minutes." Genge's injurious stickwork slowed McGiffin only briefly. The Oakville native tied the game in the third period, and regulation time ended at 5-all. In extra time, on a pass from the future Hall of Famer Frank Foyston, McGiffin rose to the occasion again, scoring the winner. Game over—Toronto was up two games to none.

Roy McGiffin was the man of the hour, and in a short time to come, he would be something else. After one more season with Toronto, he, too, would set aside hockey gear in order to go to war against Kaiser Wilhelm II's forces. Though Canadian by birth with a made-in-Canada hockey résumé, McGiffin opted to volunteer to do his duty not for King George but for Uncle Sam. He joined the US Army Air Service and became a flight instructor. On August 30, 1918, flying over Call Field at Wichita Falls, Texas, McGiffin's Curtiss JN-4 crashed. He was killed.

Their backs against the wall, the Capitals went into game three, March 19, having to win. With everything on the line, both sides brought their best game to the Toronto Arena. By the *Colonist*'s account, the game was fiercely contested and vicious. The bad feelings gathering during the game erupted in a free-for-all donnybrook in the third period, every player involved. The initiating principals were Bobby Genge and Toronto's young captain, Allan Davidson— who happened to be not just hockey rivals but first cousins. In the battle for the Stanley Cup, close blood kinship counted for nothing. Genge and Lester Patrick were injured badly enough that despite the importance of the occasion they had to leave the game in the second period and did not return until the third.

A key Toronto warrior in this game was Davidson; despite injuries of his own, he "put up a great argument . . . and was in most of the battling." Kerr and Smaill "worked like Trojans" and Lindsay was "miraculous" in goal, but their combined efforts proved not quite enough. Final score: Toronto 2, Victoria 1. Despite little Alberta Hurst's good-luck talismans, the Capitals had gone down three straight in their Stanley Cup challenge. There was no joy in Alberta's house nor anywhere else in Victoria.

That 2-1 game would turn out to be the last one Allan Davidson ever played. Six months after leading the Blueshirts to the Stanley Cup, Davidson enlisted in an infantry battalion of the Canadian Expeditionary Force. In June of 1915, near the French hamlet of Givenchy, Lieutenant A.M. Davidson of the Second Battalion was killed in action. He is one of two hockey greats—the other being Frank McGee—who have no known grave and are remembered on the great Canadian monument to the missing on Vimy Ridge.

Davidson would never know it, but in 1925, *Maclean's* magazine would name its All-Time All-Star team. The right winger on that team was Scotty Davidson.

In the year to come, 1914–15, the Great War would cast more shadows over the NHA, the PCHA, and the rest of the hockey world.

FOUR

1914-15

VICTORIA STUMBLES, VANCOUVER SOARS

B Y OPENING DAY of the 1914-15 PCHA season, December 11, the Great War was already in its fifth month. The number of those in the combined British armed forces—of which Canada was a part—who had died doing their duty to "King and Empire" was already in excess of 38,000.

On the front page of the December 11 *Daily Colonist*, all the lead stories—four of them—dealt with the progress of the war, both on the Western Front in Belgium and France, and the Eastern Front where British ally Russia was taking its part in the war against the armies of Germany's Kaiser Wilhelm II and Austria-Hungary's Emperor Franz Joseph I.

Day after day, the war dominated the news in Victoria. The *Daily Colonist* took pains to keep readers informed of events on both war fronts. The newspaper typically relied on word rather than image to report on the fighting in Flanders and France—battlefield photographs were rare or non-existent—but the *Colonist* did sometimes enhance its coverage with graphic images of war and battle.

In its Sunday edition of December 12, under the headline, DESPERATE FIGHTING TAKING PLACE ON THE YSER CANAL, the *Colonist* featured two illustrations of hand-to-hand fighting by the prolific Italian war artist, Fortunino Matania, an artist who did not believe in pulling punches. His images traded on emotion and were alluring and influential with readers of *The Sphere* in the UK, *Saturday Night* in Canada, and from time to time in the Victoria daily as well.

A prophet's speculation made news in the sports section of the Victoria *Daily Colonist* of December 12. Percy LeSueur, a three-time Stanley Cup winner with the Ottawa Senators of the NHA, had acquired the nickname "Peerless" for his prowess as a puck-stopper. That the nickname was warranted became evident years later when LeSueur was awarded a plaque in the Hockey Hall of Fame. He was inducted as a player, but Percy could just as easily have been anointed for one or another of the several parts he played during a half-century in hockey: coach, manager, broadcaster, and writer.

LeSueur was in the news for his prediction that it was only a matter of time before professional hockey became an international game. Plans were already afoot to establish teams in New York and Boston, he predicted, but it wouldn't be long before a dozen American cities had major professional hockey. Ten years would pass before LeSueur's speculation bore fruit in the east—the arrival of the NHL's Boston Bruins in 1924—but it was not until 1972, fifty-eight years after his confident prediction, that LeSueur's dream of a dozen American teams would finally come true.

Out on the west coast, the innovative Patrick brothers saw to it that year, 1914, that the first major-pro American team was established. The lineup of teams in the PCHA had undergone a far more significant alteration from that of the Victoria roster. Gone were the New Westminster Royals, relocated to Portland, Oregon, where a bigger arena and the prospect of a greater number of paying customers had induced the Patricks and their collaborators into establishing the PCHA's first US-based club. The Portland team was blessed with another of those monikers that leave fans who prefer macho names scratching their heads: the Rosebuds. Yes, the Portland Rosebuds were the PCHA's new arrivals in 1914.

The new season of the Pacific Coast Hockey Association offered a pleasant distraction from the hand-to-hand fighting going on in

Belgium. On December 11, defending PCHA-champion Victoria travelled to Vancouver to take on Vancouver at the Denman Arena. Victoria's team, the one that had won the league title the previous March and battled Toronto for the Stanley Cup, was almost completely unchanged from the season before. Spare part Jack Ulrich had departed to join forces with former Victoria teammates Don Smith and Goldie Prodgers of the Montreal Wanderers. Most fans likely agreed that his replacement on the roster, Bernie Morris, was a significant upgrade. Prospects were looking good—perhaps *very* good—at the start of Victoria's fourth PCHA season.

In 1912, at age twenty-two, Bernard Patrick "Bernie" Morris had demonstrated his hockey ability as a member of the Moose Jaw Brewers—a team nickname a red-blooded hockey fan could value— of the Saskatchewan Professional Hockey League. Brewer Bernie had scored twenty-one remarkable goals in just eight games with Moose Jaw that season. After being brought by Lester Patrick to Victoria in 1914, Bernie would go on to a sparkling ten-year career on the west coast, most of that time with a club yet to be encountered in these pages, the Seattle Metropolitans.

While Lester Patrick was taking a stand-pat approach to the Victoria Capitals, his innovative brother Frank undertook a different plan for the fourth season his Vancouver club would play in the PCHA: a wholesale renovation of the Millionaires roster. Gone for the new Denman Arena campaign were Sibby Nichols, Smokey Harris, and Didier Pitre. The loss of Pitre in particular might have been viewed as a retrograde step, but it was a loss offset by the recruitment of two players who would one day be Hall of Famers: forward Mickey MacKay and goaltender Hugh Lehman. Two other reinforcements—Lloyd Cook and Ken Mallen— would also prove themselves worthy additions to the Denman Arena cast.

The December 8 inaugural matchup of the new season pitted Vancouver against the Rosebuds in their spanking-new arena. The Millionaires turned out not to be accommodating visitors: they spoiled the Rosebuds' home debut, 6-3.

Three days later, December 11, the first showdown between Lester's defending-champion Capitals and Frank's revamped Millionaires unfolded in Vancouver. The next day's *Daily Colonist* led off with stories about the German enemy's violent attack on the small Belgian city of Ypres and about the famine faced by Belgian communities displaced by war. There was lighter news over on page nine, where the *Colonist*'s hockey reporter regaled readers with details of Victoria's season opener.

Loyal Victoria hockey fans could not have been delighted at the *Colonist* account: "Having the edge at all stages of the game, and bombarding the Victoria nets four times to every time the puck came in the direction of Hugh Lehman," Vancouver won, 5-3. The Millionaires could easily have had three times as many goals, the *Colonist* reported, but for "phenomenal work" by Victoria goaltender Bert Lindsay. The reporter was forthright in describing his first-game view of the relative merits of the opposing clubs: "Victoria looked no more like the team that won the title last season than Kaiser [Wilhelm II] did at winning a battle on the continent."

That Frank Patrick's personnel moves might have been astute ones is suggested by this: Vancouver's first and final goals were scored by one of his new men, Mallen. Though it may have been an ugly defeat for his Capitals, Lester Patrick might have taken heart from a coincidence: Victoria's first and final goals were scored by *his* new man, Morris. Perhaps things would look better for Victoria in the next Vancouver matchup.

But before that happened, the Capitals would have a home-and-home pair of games with the Rosebuds of Portland. Playing their second game of the season, in Victoria, December 15, the Rosebuds did unto the Capitals as Vancouver had done unto them: they spoiled the Victoria home opener, 8-4, a score the *Colonist* reported as being "a very fair indication of the merits of the game."

Victoria then had to wait eleven days for a shot at retribution in Portland. But Boxing Day delivered something entirely at odds with sweet revenge. Ordinarily, *Daily Colonist* game reports ran to a few hundred words. On December 27, the *Colonist* report included just forty words. Perhaps having nothing good to say about the Capitals' performance, the *Colonist*'s reporter offered hardly anything at all. The score of the Capitals' first game in the brand-new Portland Ice Arena, also called the Hippodrome, was 8-1. *Colonist* reports typically included a game summary listing goal scorers, penalties, and game officials. In this case, there was no summary at all. Victoria's season record now stood at 0-3: no wins, three losses, the goals-for-and-against ratio, at 8 to 21.

Victoria fans would not have felt buoyed by the news, nor by other events reported in the December 27 Victoria morning daily. A front-page story related that, using "hydro-aeroplanes," British forces had retaliated for attacks on coastal cities by bombing the mouths of the Elbe and Weser Rivers. The war was intensifying.

There was a sidebar war story in a very different vein from the bombing of German rivers. The Christmas spirit had erupted on the Western Front, bringing about a change from the usual mass mayhem and killing. In the aftermath of Christmas, the Victoria *Daily Colonist* reported that someone in town had received a letter from a Lieutenant Ronald Gillespie of the Gordon Highlanders:

> We were up in trenches on Christmas Day, and it was the most extraordinary Christmas I have ever spent. Not a shot was fired, and about 9 o'clock in the morning both sides, by mutual consent, left their trenches and came out between the lines. We shook hands with some of the Germans, exchanged cigarettes, etc., and talked away like blazes. Then both sides buried their dead, men who had fallen between the lines at different attacks—a ghastly business; and all day we walked about as if there was no such things as war... Boxing Day was very similar, and we arranged not to reopen hostilities until 5:30 PM. It seemed very queer to be on friendly terms one day, and the next to be ready to shoot him at the first opportunity.

Very queer indeed. The "Christmas Truce" broke out at many points along the Western Front. Enemy soldiers exchanged gifts, sang carols, and played impromptu soccer matches. The generals on both sides were distinctly unamused by this outbreak of kindness; they issued orders to local commanders that no such disgraceful conduct should ever be repeated. It wasn't. In subsequent years, Christmas was far likelier to provide an opportunity for mounting a terrifying nighttime raid than for singing "O Holy Night" to the enemy.

Back in BC, December 29 delivered a happy prospect for the Victoria players: a chance of beating Vancouver—now called, alternately, either the Terminals or Millionaires by the *Daily Colonist*—on their Oak Bay home ice. The Capitals went ahead 2-0 in the first period on a pair of goals by Dubbie Kerr. Mickey MacKay returned the favour in the second with two goals of his own for Vancouver. The teams each scored once in the third period— Cyclone Taylor for Vancouver, Lester Patrick for Victoria—to send the game to overtime. Then, in what the *Colonist* called "one of the closest and hardest matches ever seen at the Arena," Mickey MacKay completed a three-goal hat trick and sent the Victoria fans home disappointed.

January 8 at the Denman Arena brought a rematch but no satisfaction for the Victoria crew. "Playing superior hockey at every angle of the contest, and scoring enough goals to win several matches, the Vancouver Millionaires waltzed far in front of the Victoria champions," 9-2. Mickey MacKay again led the way for Vancouver with another hat trick. That left the teams with mirror records: Vancouver perfect at 5-0, Victoria perfectly bad at 0-5.

Hockey was not the only respite from war readers could take in on the pages of the *Daily Colonist*. In an age that loved its heroes, there were few greater than Ernest Shackleton. On August 8, 1914— mere days after the outbreak of the war—Sir Ernest and the men of his Imperial Trans-Antarctic Expedition had departed Plymouth in the three-masted barquentine *Endurance*. He aimed to accomplish what Robert Scott had failed to achieve: to reach the South Pole and live to tell all the world about it. Indeed, Shackleton's mission was to go beyond Scott's—to cross the entire continent. *Endurance* had left Buenos Aires October 26, and Grytviken in the South Georgia

Shackleton says !

"The question of the concentrated beef supply is most important—it must be Bovril."

Shackleton knows. He is taking no risks. He chooses Bovril because the food he takes must yield every ounce of nourishment to his men.

Follow Shackleton. Into a single bottle of Bovril is packed the nourishment value of many pounds of beef, and over and above this, Bovril has the peculiar power of making other foods yield up much more of their nourishment to the body.

Now that times are difficult you can be sure of being nourished if you take Bovril.

It-must-be
BOVRIL

Shackleton says, "It must be Bovril." *DAILY COLONIST*, DECEMBER 27, 1914

Islands December 5, just as the Patrick brothers were set to start a new hockey season on the other side of the world.

Then as now, there were admirers and entrepreneurs, too, people who judged there to be business opportunities to be mined in Victoria's admiration for the great Shackleton. "Bovril" is the name of a thick, salty, meat-derived paste that seems to have been included in the *Endurance* larder. If the product was good enough for Shackleton, the Bovril people reasoned, it was certainly good enough for the folks of Victoria, BC. In a *Colonist* ad appearing from time to time as *Endurance* made its way to the Antarctic, a sketch depicts Sir Ernest in Antarctic-suitable headgear and quotes the explorer thus: "The question of the concentrated beef supply is most important—it must be Bovril." To what degree and in what amount had the Bovril people contributed to the financing of the *Endurance* expedition? Generously, one expects.

Daily Colonist readers were as entranced with Shackleton's heroic adventure as everyone else in His Majesty's broad dominions. Though no one not aboard *Endurance* would know about it for a long time, the ship became icebound January 18, 1915, immobilized and helpless. Half a world away, a less momentous ice story was about to play out at the Portland Hippodrome.

A few days earlier, on January 12, Lester Patrick's skaters had finally won a hockey game, 4-3, at home against Portland. A week after that, in the Portland end of another home-and-home series, the Capitals resumed their losing ways, suffering a 10-5 thrashing at the hands of the Rosebuds. It was not a pretty thing. Unsurprisingly, given the Capitals' losing ways, attendance had dwindled at the Epworth Street arena in Oak Bay, but hockey was new in the Rose City, and a crowd of five thousand were jammed to the doors to see the Rosebuds give it to Lester's lamentable lads. In another tellingly brief game account, the *Colonist* reported that the Capitals made a respectable showing of themselves only in the first period, then disappeared. Eddie Oatman led the way for Portland, scoring three goals. With most of his crew underperforming, it was left to Lester Patrick himself to redeem a little respectability for the losing side by scoring twice. The Capitals' season record now stood at one win, six losses.

Half a world away from Victoria, Sir Ernest Shackleton's crew found themselves in circumstances far more dire than those of

Victoria's hockey professionals. Five months and ten days after departing England, Shackleton and the men of the *Endurance* were trapped in Antarctic ice. There they would remain for another nine months and nine days before the *Endurance* was crushed by the ice and the men forced to abandon ship. Fascinated as Victorians and all the world were by Shackleton's endeavour, no one would learn about the plight of the *Endurance* for a long time yet to come.

Closer to home, a marker of the ongoing war materialized in Victoria. The front page of the *Colonist* of January 2, 1915, featured a report of the previous day's visit to Victoria by another knight of the realm, Minister of Militia and Defence Sir Sam Hughes. Perhaps the most colourful, most controversial man ever appointed to a Canadian federal cabinet, Sir Sam was in town to inspect some two thousand troops assembled at Willows Camp, not far from the Patrick Arena. Accompanied by the premier and lieutenant-governor, Hughes inspected what the *Colonist* claimed was the finest military display ever seen in the city.

Though widely commended for building the First Canadian Division in a remarkably short period, Hughes was perhaps even better at another skill: making enemies. Sir Sam eventually wore out his welcome in the federal cabinet; for all the success he had made in building the Canadian Expeditionary Force, he had offended just about every one of his cabinet colleagues. Less than a year after his Willows Camp inspection, Hughes was shown the door by Robert Borden.

Meanwhile, the evening before Sir Sam's visit, the Capitals had finally given *Daily Colonist* readers something to smile about. The Vancouver Millionaires came to town sporting a 6-2 record, likely expecting to make it 7-2 that evening, but Victoria had a surprise in store. The Capitals came out and played like the defending champions they were. In "the finest game of hockey seen this year," Victoria won convincingly, 4-1. Cyclone Taylor was easily the star of the Vancouver seven . . . and "gave an exhibition of brilliant hockey," but in a seven-man game, one hero was insufficient: Skinner Poulin's two goals and one each from Dunderdale and Smaill secured the win for Victoria. Given that he had a victory to write about, the *Colonist* scribe reverted to form: his game account ran to several paragraphs. Might this be the day that the Capitals had turned the tide?

The answer came a week later in the Patricks' Denman Arena. Led by Mickey MacKay's *five* goals, the Millionaires undertook a 12-5 demolition of the team the *Colonist*'s man persisted in calling "the Victoria champions." The champions were now 2-7 with a goals for/against ratio of 27-63. Their season was lost.

They managed to win a February 2 game at home against Portland, 6-5 in overtime. The *Colonist* at last had something to crow about: the Capitals had fallen behind but in a "sensational finish" managed to tie the game in the third period "amid wild scenes of excitement." Dubbie Kerr was again the hometown hero, scoring the winner in overtime.

That might have launched Victoria on a winning run, but it didn't. Instead the Capitals started a new losing streak, falling twice to Vancouver and once to Portland by a combined 19-10 aggregate. The third of those losses, in Vancouver, February 19, was particularly galling. "The Vancouvers stepped out and played the best game of the season," the *Colonist* reported. With four goals, Cyclone Taylor outscored the Capitals all by himself, but he had plenty of help from Mickey MacKay and Frank Nighbor. Vancouver won, 10-3. The "lowly champions" saw their season record fall to 3-10 and their goals deficit drop to 37-82.

Far, far from Victoria, Sir Ernest Shackleton's *Endurance*, locked in the Antarctic ice, reached the southernmost point of the adventurers' journey, latitude 77 degrees south, off Luitpold Land, February 22, 1915.

More than ten thousand miles distant from the scene of the *Endurance* troubles, the Victoria Capitals would manage to win one more game, 4-3, at home against Portland on February 23, before finishing the season with another three-game losing streak. The misery came to an end with a March 6 loss at the Portland Hippodrome. With a roster almost identical to the one that had won the league title at 10-6 the previous year, the 1914-15 team finished at four wins, thirteen losses. Who could explain it?

Tommy Dunderdale fell to sixth place among the league's top individual scorers. The top three—all of whom would one day be inducted in the Hockey Hall of Fame—were Vancouver's Cyclone Taylor, Mickey MacKay, and Frank Nighbor. Dunderdale finished the year first among the Capitals with seventeen goals and ten assists for twenty-seven points, eighteen in arrears of Taylor. Hugh Lehman's goals-against average for Vancouver was 4.2; Bert Lindsay's had crashed to 6.6, despite *Colonist* reports that he had often played brilliantly in the Victoria goal.

What had gone wrong? Perhaps the season was not so much the story of the collapse of Victoria as it was the remarkable rise of Frank Patrick's Vancouver Millionaires. In years to come, Frank's brother would describe the 1914-15 Vancouver Millionaires as the greatest hockey team he had ever seen. At the end of the PCHA's regular season, the Millionaires were about to deliver ample support for Lester Patrick's view.

By 1915, it was securely established that the PCHA was a hockey major league, entitled to a Stanley Cup showdown with the other major league, the National Hockey Association. That year it was the west's turn to host the confrontation that would determine who would get to hoist Lord Stanley's bowl in triumph. The NHA representatives in the best-of-five east-west Stanley Cup playoff was Ottawa.

The Senators were led by Harry "Punch" Broadbent, who would one day be joined in the Hockey Hall of Fame by four of his 1915 Ottawa teammates—Eddie Gerard, Jack Darragh, Art Ross, and goaltender Clint Benedict.

Broadbent was a hockey hero but in a short time he would be another sort of hero, too. Soon after the 1915 Stanley Cup final, Broadbent would, at age twenty-two, enlist in a brigade of the Canadian Field Artillery. By virtue of doing so, he would lose more than three years of his hockey-playing prime, but he would flourish as a soldier, promoted more than once, and ultimately awarded a gallantry decoration, the Military Medal.

Ottawa came to Vancouver with hockey sweaters differing from the norm: the sweaters featured crossed flags, the British Union Jack, and the Canadian Red Ensign, reflecting that Canada and the mother country were nations allied in war.

The trouble for Ottawa in the 1915 battle for the Stanley Cup was that their Denman Street arena adversaries featured the remarkable Cyclone Taylor and five other Millionaires bound for Hall of Fame glory—MacKay, Nighbor, Barney Stanley, Si Griffis, and Hugh Lehman. Six Hall of Famers to five perhaps suggested a close series, but what unfolded wasn't close at all.

On March 22, Vancouver manhandled Broadbent and company, 6-2. That four-goal deficit was the closest Ottawa would get. Two days later, the margin of victory grew to five in an 8-3 Vancouver rout. It grew still worse on March 26 when the demoralized Senators collapsed, 12-3. The aggregate score for the three games: 26-8. It was no surprise to anyone that the individual scoring leader was the amazing Cyclone Taylor, with six goals, followed closely by Barney Stanley's five. Perhaps a little too confident in their prospects for victory, Ottawa had not brought the Stanley Cup with them to Vancouver; the Millionaires had to wait to brandish it in victory.

Two years earlier, the Victoria Capitals had handily defeated eastern-champion Quebec in a "world's title" series, but the Stanley Cup had not been their reward. Now, at last, the PCHA champions were kings of the hill, Stanley Cup champions.

Would they repeat their victory in 1916?

FIVE

1915-16

NEW CAST,
SIMILAR RESULTS

FOR THE 1915-16 PCHA season, the Patrick brothers and their collaborators delivered a significant addition to the league: a second American-based team, the Seattle Metropolitans. That brought the PCHA into international balance, with two American teams and two Canadian. The Metropolitans played their home games in the four-thousand-seat Seattle Ice Arena, a brand-new downtown facility close by the present-day Olympic Hotel.

To stock the new franchise, the Patricks and their associates reverted to old ways. They raided the Toronto team of the National Hockey Association—the squad that had defeated Victoria in the 1914 championship series—for four star players: Frank Foyston, Jack Walker, Cully Wilson, and goaltender Harry Holmes. All but Wilson would one day be awarded a plaque in the Hockey Hall of Fame. If what is good for the goose is good for the gander, the Patricks paid a suitable price for the theft: the NHA retaliated, raiding the Pacific Coast league for four of its players, including three that had been Victoria's own the previous season: Skinner Poulin, Walter Smaill, and goaltender Bert Lindsay.

Obliged to deal with those personnel losses and perhaps inspired by the proceeds of the transformation his brother had undertaken the previous season in Vancouver, Lester Patrick produced a whole-sale renovation of his own for the 1915-16 edition of his Victoria hockey club. The new edition of the Capitals featured a cast of fresh faces. In addition to Poulin, Smaill and Lindsay, the Capitals had to cope in the new season without future Hall of Famer Tommy Dunderdale and Bernie Morris. With all these changes, only three players remained from the Victoria lineup of the previous season: Bobby Genge, Dubbie Kerr, and Lester Patrick.

Perhaps the most significant of Lester's newcomers was Sebastian John "Sibby" Nichols, who had played an important part in the success of Frank Patrick's Millionaires from its inaugural 1911-12 season to the Stanley Cup-winning 1915 peak. A native of Alexandria, Ontario, Nichols had launched his hockey career in Montreal in 1904, where he played until 1910. For the 1910-11 season, he had taken his act six hundred miles east, to Moncton, New Brunswick, where he was a leading light with the Victorias of the Inter-Provincial Professional Hockey League. At age thirty-one, Sibby was no longer a youngster by the time he crossed the Strait of Georgia to play for the elder Patrick brother in Victoria. At five feet, eight inches and 150 pounds, Nichols was a standard-sized pro hockey player of his era.

On the west coast, Nichols somehow found a way to juggle his hockey duties with other obligations. He was a lacrosse player of some distinction who managed to balance a two-part sporting career with responsibilities of another kind. He served for a time in the Canadian Navy, and when the war broke out in August of 1914, Nichols was in Asia aboard RMS (Royal Military Ship) *Empress of Russia*. Two years later, in 1917, he would be a soldier in the Canadian Expeditionary Force, his days as a hockey luminary a thing of the past.

By the start of the 1915-16 hockey season, the war was casting a deep, dark shadow over the city of Victoria, the entire country, and the rest of the British Empire. Almost all the front-page headlines of the December 8 edition of the Victoria *Daily Colonist* addressed war stories. A new feature of the *Colonist* was a daily casualty list of Canadians most recently perished. The newspaper's December 8 casualty list set out seventy-seven names—twenty-two killed, fifty-five wounded. Some of the names included in the grim inventory brought the war close to home. The fallen of the Victoria-based Sixteenth Battalion included Corporal S.R. Thomas, a carpenter and resident of Johnson Street at the time of his enlistment. Private H.A. Charlton, a Vining Street bricklayer, was also listed among the wounded, taken out of action by a growing cause of war casualties, shellshock.

The December 8 *Colonist* provided evidence that the war was women's work too. On page eight, under the headline IN WOMEN'S REALM, the newspaper delivered an extensive report about British Columbia nurses working at the battlefronts. The piece featured an image of Miss C. Campbell, a graduate of the Royal Jubilee Hospital nursing school. Christina Campbell was fated to be one of sixteen nurses killed in action June 27, 1918, when a torpedo fired by a German U-Boat sunk the hospital ship *Llandovery Castle*.

Over on page eleven, the *Colonist* provided some respite from the war. There, the newspaper reported news of the first games of the new PCHA season. The Capitals had ferried to Puget Sound to face the Metropolitans in their new arena in downtown Seattle. But Victorians would not have taken much comfort from the *Colonist*'s game dispatch. The Seattle crowd, 2,500-strong, "worked itself up to a high pitch of enthusiasm" as the Metropolitans narrowly vanquished Victoria, 3-2. The winning goal, scored late in the final period, would have added salt to Lester Patrick's wound: the scorer was Bernie Morris, a Victoria stalwart the previous year.

The Capitals' bright spots in a losing cause that first game were the new goaltender, Fred McCulloch, who was a "star" in goal, and "the magnificent defence" supplied by Patrick and Bobby Genge. Both Victoria goals were scored by newcomers, Ran McDonald and Mickey O'Leary.

Ranald John McDonald was the reward reaped by Lester Patrick in the trade of Tommy Dunderdale to the Portland Rosebuds. McDonald was a twenty-six-year-old native of Cashions Glen, Ontario. Like Sibby Nichols, McDonald was proficient at lacrosse as well as hockey. He had performed well as a New Westminster Royal in his first three PCHA hockey seasons, but he shone particularly brightly in Portland in 1914–15, scoring twenty-two goals in eighteen games with the Rosebuds. Given his age, he was perhaps seen by Lester Patrick as having a better future than Dunderdale, who was two years older and had slipped to seventeen goals with Victoria the season before.

Before the entire history of the Pacific Coast Hockey Association would finally be written, McDonald would have the distinction of being the only man to play for all six PCHA teams. Another, less happy, distinction is that McDonald would miss an entire PCHA season. He was arrested for robbing an arena cashier, a crime perhaps mitigated by a nervous breakdown the player was thought to have suffered at about the same time.

The other Victoria goal was also tallied by a new Victoria cast member, Mickey O'Leary. A twenty-three-year-old Ottawa native of indisputably Irish extraction, Michael Patrick O'Leary had distinguished himself with the Halifax Socials of the Maritime Professional Hockey Association, scoring fifty-eight goals in forty games over two seasons. But that first-game goal in Seattle would turn out to be the only one of O'Leary's PCHA career, a career that lasted only four games. O'Leary is another of the hockey players who would suspend on-ice activities to do their bit in another, bigger game. He enlisted for war duty in the Seventy-eighth Depot Battery, Canadian Field Artillery.

On December 10, three nights after the season opener in Seattle, the same teams faced off again, this time in Victoria. It was clear from the next morning's *Daily Colonist* that the war was front and centre for the paper's readers. The game account appeared under a photograph of forty men of the Victoria-based Fifth Regiment, Canadian Garrison Artillery, set to march off to war.

Elsewhere in the paper, the ad campaign for Bovril carried on. Its manufacturers had already pitched their product as being preferred by the intrepid Antarctic explorer, Ernest Shackleton. "We hear they want more Bovril at the Front," a new ad proclaimed. Another ad perhaps mirrored the war weariness that must surely have afflicted Victorians in the seventeenth month of the conflagration. Dr. Cassell's Tablets, "Britain's Greatest Remedy," offered a solution for "Brain-Fog and Exhaustion."

Meanwhile, at the Epworth Street arena, it was an army officer, Lieutenant Colonel Lorne Ross of the Sixty-seventh Battalion Western Scots, who dropped the puck for the ceremonial opening faceoff. On page five of the December 11 *Colonist*, a two-column piece featured a photo of Colonel Ross wearing a Glengarry cap. The story's headline proclaimed BOMBS AND GUNS ARE EFFECTIVE. "There was nothing so satisfactory," the paper quoted Ross as saying in a Vancouver address, "as being able to drop a 'hairbrush,' 'jam-pot' or other such bomb into a dugout filled with Germans."

As for the hockey game, neither Lieutenant Colonel Ross nor the rest of the Victoria audience could have been satisfied with the outcome on the ice. The home side narrowly lost again, this time by a 4-3 score. Lester Patrick and Bobby Genge were singled out for their excellent efforts, Patrick scoring two of the Victoria goals. Something new appeared in the game account: for the first time—in the team's second game of its fifth season of PCHA hockey—the *Colonist* called the Victoria team the "Aristocrats." That is the name by which the Victoria team of the early years is known today, but the *Daily Colonist* had not employed it before.

It cannot have been an accident that on the same day, December 11, 1915, the practice changed at the *Victoria Times* too. The year before, 1914–15, the *Times*' moniker of choice for the Victoria club was *Champions*—fair enough, given the team's status as defending league champions that season. Neither the morning *Colonist* nor the afternoon *Times* explained why each had suddenly taken to calling the home team the Aristocrats. Presumably someone—likely Lester Patrick himself—had decided that the name suited a collection of hockey bluebloods representing a city that fancied itself a little bit of old England.

Four nights later, December 14, the Victorians won their first game of the season, a contest between Lester's Aristocrats and Frank's Millionaires at the Denman Street arena in Vancouver.

The following day's edition of the *Daily Colonist* featured an account of the hockey game, but something else in that day's paper might have momentarily distracted *Colonist* readers. Under the headline MANACLED CHINESE PARADE STREETS, the paper described the sight of a line of ninety men captured in the raid of a gambling den at the Oriental Club in Fan Tan Alley. Handcuffed in pairs and guarded by a police squad, the men were paraded for public entertainment from the police headquarters to the BC Electric depot on Wharf Street before being conveyed to the provincial jail on Wilkinson Road. The *Colonist* offered details of this newsworthy event:

> Passersby stopped and stared as the long line of manacled Chinamen marched through the streets, and visions of the chain gangs of ye olden times floated across the minds of the spectators. From the standpoint of criminology, it was the most imposing spectacle that the local bluecoats have staged for many years. The public parade in irons would have been something new even for desperate characters. It was absolutely unique in the annals of petty crime.

The *Daily Colonist* had a competitor for newspaper readers' attention in 1912. One might imagine that a parade of ninety men in chains through downtown streets would be a spectacle any newspaper editor would find newsworthy—certainly the *Colonist* editor felt so. But the *Victoria Daily Times* editor did not. The afternoon daily reported on the Chinatown raid, the arrest of the Fan Tan gamblers, and their subsequent conveyance to the local lockup. But one person's news is another's noise: the *Times* delivered no mention whatsoever of the march of manacled men.

With the Fan Tan miscreants safely locked up at Wilkinson Road, the hockey game proceeded securely. The Aristocrats prevailed, 7-5, a result that left the defending Stanley Cup champion Millionaires at the bottom of the league standings with a 0-3 record. The Victoria crew fell behind, 4-1, in the first period, but the Aristocrats opened the second with "a wonderful fund of energy," the *Colonist* reported, scoring four goals in as many minutes. The paper's reporter gave another new team member, "Trooper" Box, much of the credit for the turnaround. Box "was all over the ice, checking like a demon, stealing the puck whenever he wanted."

George Stacey Box entered the world in the autumn of 1892 at the place the hockey-playing Creamery Kings would one day call home: Renfrew, Ontario. It is not recorded how Box acquired the nickname Trooper, but it likely had something to do with the fact that earlier in the year, Box had enlisted in a mounted infantry unit, the Eleventh Canadian Mounted Rifles, Canadian Expeditionary Force. For a time, it appears that Box managed to meet both Lester Patrick's expectations and those of the Canadian military. He played eleven games in the 1915-16 season before soldier trumped player: Box went off to war, missed two complete hockey seasons and all but one game of a third. He survived the war, returned to the west coast, and resumed his career, albeit as an amateur with several Vancouver teams. But for the time being, in 1915 and early 1916, George Box enjoyed his best season of professional hockey.

Three nights following their first win of the year in Vancouver, the Aristocrats hosted the Millionaires in a return engagement, this time in their own Oak Bay home base. The result was a blowout, 8-2, in the Victorians' favour. George Box, establishing himself as "a firm favourite with the fans," had a hand in five of the Victoria goals. The next day's *Colonist* credited others too—Genge, McDonald, and Patrick.

The Victoria victory levelled the Aristocrats' season record at 2-2, while winless Vancouver dropped to 0-4. That would have surprised many observers, given that several of the key players in the Millionaires' dominant Stanley Cup victory earlier in the year still played for the team—Cyclone Taylor, Mickey MacKay, Si Griffis, and Frank Patrick among them. But there were also new faces in the Vancouver lineup in the winter of 1915–16. One of them, Art Duncan, assisted on a Vancouver goal in the December 17 game.

A twenty-four-year-old native of Sault Ste. Marie, Ontario, William James Arthur Duncan was big for his time, at six feet, one inch and 180 pounds. An amateur before 1915, Duncan was in the first of the nine pro seasons he would play in Vancouver. After that first campaign with the Millionaires, Duncan would be distracted by a bigger "game" than PCHA hockey. He enlisted in the Canadian Expeditionary Force, eventually transferring to the Royal Flying Corps, where he distinguished himself as an "ace" fighter pilot. Flying the Royal Aircraft Factory SE5a, Duncan brought down eleven enemy machines between November 1917 and June 1918. His heroics in the air would be recognized by the award of a medal for gallantry, the Military Cross.

Another recipient of the MC—a hometown one—also attracted attention in the December 18 *Daily Colonist*. In a front-page story accompanied by a soldierly portrait, John Gibson Anderson of Esquimalt was reported as having been awarded a Military Cross for gallantry. In time to come, Anderson would make the news again: unlike Art Duncan, Anderson would not survive the war; he was killed in action in November 1917 in the nightmarish Battle of Passchendaele. He is among the 55,000 soldiers without a known grave commemorated on the walls of the Menin Gate at Ypres in Belgium.

For Victorians of German extraction, life in a city billed as "a little bit of old England," the winter of 1915–16 could not have been a comfortable time. One of the eye-catching items in the *Daily Colonist* pages of December 18 appeared under the headline ANTI-GERMAN UNION EXPECTED TO EXPAND. The article described AGU efforts to recruit members from the Rotary Club, Canadian Club, and the local Trades and Labour Council, and itemized the success of its efforts to have enemy aliens interned and ethnic-German businesses boycotted.

Meanwhile, in on-ice battles, eleven days elapsed before Lester Patrick's crew faced their next PCHA foe. The Aristocrats boarded ferry and train to take on the Rosebuds at the Portland

Ice Hippodrome. "More than 4,000 raving spectators" were on hand to watch a contest that took a stretch of overtime to resolve. Portland took a 2-0 lead with two second-period goals by Charlie Tobin, the second assisted by the Aristocrats' former teammate Tommy Dunderdale. Kerr and Patrick answered for Victoria in the third period. It took eleven and a half minutes of overtime to decide the game. The Rosebuds' Fred "Smokey" Harris broke the tie after eleven minutes of overtime. The game, which had started late, did not end until 11:30 that night, and the Victorians nearly missed the train taking them home.

In addition to its account of the hockey game, the December 29 *Colonist* carried the front-page news that Richard McBride would be feted that day at a luncheon in the Empress Hotel for his services to city, province, and Empire. McBride, his popularity dwindling, had resigned on his forty-fifth birthday, December 15. He had been the premier of BC for twelve years. Only one other BC premier, W.A.C. Bennett, would rule a longer time. McBride had a new assignment: the province's representative in London, a role he filled only a year and a half. He died in August 1917 at the age of forty-six.

Meanwhile, for the third time this new season, the Aristocrats' next game was the back end of a home-and-home series. On January 4, the Victorians hosted the Rosebuds at their Epworth Street bailiwick. With Trooper Box, "the brilliant centre," out of action due to a broken collarbone, and Lester Patrick suffering from a wounded knee, the Aristocrats were not the challenge they had been in Portland. They were pummelled by Portland. The *Colonist* 's reporter griped about the judge of play, Charlie Wakely, who was "evidently rather shy of exercising authority" and allowed players to get away with too much tripping and hooking.

Was Lester Patrick given cause to regret his trading away of Tommy Dunderdale? Perhaps. The Australian scored two goals and assisted on a third in the Rosebuds' 10-5 victory. But possibly there were signs of better days ahead: two more first-year Aristocrats did well in the game. Jim Riley scored twice for Victoria, Ken Mallen once.

Kenneth Russell Mallen first came to hockey prominence with the 1904–05 Calumet Miners of the International Hockey League, a circuit notorious for the violence and mayhem of its hockey brand. Mallen played three years in Calumet, scoring thirty-eight times in twenty-four games in 1904–05. The following season, he bailed out after five games in protest over the rough play that defined IHL play. Mallen was a member of the PCHA's New Westminster club during the league's first three years before his contract was sold to the Vancouver Millionaires ahead of the 1914–15 campaign. By late 1915, the scarred thirty-one-year-old native of Morrisburg, Ontario, was a free agent when he signed to play the 1915–16 season with Lester Patrick in Victoria.

James Norman (Jim) Riley of Bayfield, New Brunswick, was a fresh-faced twenty-year-old pro hockey rookie in 1915. At five feet, eleven inches and 180 pounds, he was taller and bigger than most PCHA skaters. Riley played just the one season for Lester Patrick's Aristocrats (1915–16), but he was a PCHA stalwart for eight seasons, all but that first one with the Seattle Metropolitans.

Skilled as he was at hockey, Jim Riley may have been an even better baseball player. He batted close to .300 over nine seasons of higher-level minor league baseball, before briefly making it to "The Show"—major league baseball—with the St. Louis Browns and Washington Senators in 1921 and 1923. After the collapse of the western league in 1926, Riley played a season of NHL hockey with Chicago and Detroit in 1926–27. To this day, he is the only man ever to have played in both the NHL and in major league baseball.

Riley had something else in common with Frank Foyston other than being teammates in Seattle. Each of them served during the war in the Canadian Expeditionary Force. Neither of them did so voluntarily. Foyston and Riley were both conscripted under provisions of Canada's *Military Service Act, 1917*, legislation that nearly tore the country apart as war raged in Europe. In both cases, their duties as soldiers caused only a brief interruption in their hockey careers. Foyston lost the 1917–18 season due to war, Riley the following one.

Would Foyston and Riley have been much moved by a big ad appearing in the *Colonist* of January 5, 1916? The Patriotic Aid Society, headquartered at 1210 Broad Street, urged the people of Victoria to do their bit for the war effort. "Our boys in khaki are fighting or dying," the ad declared, "All they ask is for us at home to do our duty, as they are doing theirs."

On January 11, a week after the home-ice loss to Portland, the Aristocrats travelled to Vancouver to face off against the Millionaires in their Denman Street ice palace. The result was another blowout, this time by a score of 8-3. The Millionaires were led by Lloyd Cook's three goals, and with the victory, Vancouver switched places with the Aristocrats. Vancouver improved its record to 3-4, Victoria falling to the league basement at 2-5. The one-sided loss was bad enough, but the Victoria side also saw their teammate Ken Mallen carted off the ice unconscious after being struck in the head by a hard shot from the future ace flier, Art Duncan. As for the man minding the Victoria goal, having allowed seventeen goals in two games, Fred McCulloch saw his goals-against average spiral to 5.00.

As usual, the front page of the January 12 *Daily Colonist* featured dispatches from the battlefields, but if readers looked, they could find distraction in their morning read. Three columns to the left of the Aristocrats' game account, a story reported on the hardship local birds were suffering from severe winter weather. The piece suggested that readers should "allow their sympathies with the birds to be touched" by putting feed out for their feathered friends. Three columns farther left, the paper reported on a recent meeting of the Victoria Natural History Society. Some things don't change much: more than a century later, an organization with the same name continues to advocate for birds beset by severe winter weather.

On January 14 the Aristocrats gave their home fans something to cheer about: they defeated Seattle, 5-3. In "one of the best and most interesting games seen here this season," Dubbie Kerr was the star of the game. He accomplished an authentic hat trick, scoring three straight goals to lead Victoria to victory.

Four days later, January 18, the Aristocrats ferried to Seattle to take on the Metropolitans for the fourth time. They lost, but narrowly, 5-3. The dispatch in the next day's *Colonist* described the game as a "dashing, scrapping exhibition"; remarkably, it proceeded without a single penalty being called.

Other items in the January 19 *Colonist* delivered a festive season dispatch from the far-off battlefields of Flanders, and a piece touching on a place much more distant than Belgium.

In a two-column story, "How Christmas Was Spent at Front," correspondent Philip Gibson reported that in contrast to enemy combatants' remarkable, unsanctioned, and still-famous Christmas truce of 1914, there were no carols to be heard on the front on Christmas Eve in 1915: [the] "only carol I heard in the trenches was the loud, deep chant of the guns on both sides and the shrill soprano of whistling shells . . ."

Another item in the January 19 *Colonist* suggests that deep concern about catastrophic climate change might not be a strictly twenty-first century worry. *Colonist* readers must have been struck by the headline, RACE MUST FOLLOW EXAMPLE OF MARTIANS. Appearing before a meeting of the Victoria Astronomical Society, the *Colonist* reported that Mr. F.N. Denison, superintendent of the Dominion Observatory on Little Saanich Mountain, showed evidence of the well-defined canals delivering water from the Martian north pole to those living to the south. Mr. Denison had a warning for earthlings: given the rapid departure of moisture from our own planet, it will be necessary to follow the example thought to have been set by Martians, by constructing "world-wide systems of irrigation canals to keep desert areas fertile."

Closer to home, the boys of winter struggled at their Epworth Street arena. On January 21, Victoria lost on home ice, 3-1, to Portland. Four nights later, January 25, they lost again at the Hippodrome in Portland, this time by 7-5. The game provided, the *Colonist* reported, "one of the fastest and most sensational thrills" PCHA followers had ever witnessed. A smaller than expected crowd of 2,500 got to see it, attendance having been diminished by a fierce snowstorm that blanketed the entire northwest.

Neither hockey fans nor birds would have been happy with the storm. SNOW FALLS ALL OVER PACIFIC NORTHWEST, blared a headline in the next day's *Colonist*. The paper made it clear that accumulated January snowfall had left Victorians feeling unamused, but the paper took comfort that things might have been worse. In Alberta and Saskatchewan, people and birds had to cope not just with snow but also extreme cold—temperatures of between minus thirty and minus fifty Fahrenheit. Even ptarmigan, snowy owls, and snow buntings might have found these extremes excessively cold.

Being buried in snow was one thing, but Lester Patrick soon found himself engulfed in another, bigger issue. Late in January, the war was suddenly and seriously a problem, not just for Canadian soldiers fighting on the Western Front but for Patrick and all his Victoria Aristocrats too. On January 29 both the *Daily Colonist* and *Daily Times* reported Patrick's announcement that his Victoria hockey arena would soon close. Strangely, neither paper gave a reason for the closure but the cause would become clear in days to come: the Epworth Street facility would no longer be a PCHA hockey playground. Like nearby Willows Camp, it was to be commandeered by the Canadian army for the purpose of training new recruits required to replace those lost to the wastage of war in Belgium and France.

Mind you, a brand of hockey continued at the arena, at least for a while: the same *Colonist* article informed readers that a large turnout had come to the arena to watch two military teams—the Eleventh Canadian Mounted Rifles and 103rd Battalion— play "an exceptionally fast" hockey game in the Patrick arena. The 103rd prevailed.

In the wake of the news that Epworth Street was no longer their home rink, the Aristocrats' game performance went from bad to very much worse. Their next outing, February 1—their last of the season at Epworth Street—amounted to a demolition. Perhaps Lester's lads were reeling from the news that, like the boll weevil of popular song, they would be looking for a home for the indefinite future. Whatever, inspired by the recent extreme winter weather, the next day's headline writer offered this: LOCAL HOCKEY TEAM WAS SNOWED UNDER. Indeed. The Vancouver champions "played skittles with them to the tune of 16 to 4," the *Colonist* reported. There was "only one team on the ice playing hockey, and the Vancouver men scored as they liked." Fred McCulloch, the Victoria goaltender, was "all at sea, and the net was bulged almost every time the Vancouver players made a shot."

The unfortunate reporter who had to provide copy for the next day's morning paper could find only one thing to feel good about: the band of another military formation, the Sixty-seventh Battalion, attended the game: "The martial airs were much appreciated." In a season gone dreadfully wrong, the Aristocrats' record fell to 3-9— three wins, nine losses.

Having faced a barrage of enemy wrist shots over the eighteen games of the 1915–16 season, McCulloch soon settled on a different pursuit: forty days after his final game in Victoria, he became a soldier in the CEF. At the time of his enlistment, McCulloch could have given "hockey professional" as his "trade or calling," but hardly any hockey pro of the time, no matter how skilled or well paid, could get by solely on his hockey wages: McCulloch described his trade as "clerk." Less than a year after the start of the 1915–16 PCHA hockey season, it was bullets rather than pucks the ex-goaltender had to worry about. Happily, his performance as a soldier surpassed that as the Aristocrats' goaltender. Given an officer's commission, he distinguished himself, winning a Military Cross for gallantry in 1917. He survived and returned to the ice wars afterward but never played another game as a professional.

Occasionally, the *Colonist* managed to find and tell a human-interest sort of war story more likely to make a reader smile than weep. In early February, the newspaper related an account of two brothers, Owen and Alexander Mulcahy of Esquimalt. Years before the war, Alex Mulcahy had departed for Canada's opposite coast, based principally in Halifax. Owen headed north rather than east, working as a surveyor in the Yukon. Years went by without the brothers seeing one another. When war erupted, they enlisted in different military units and went off to England. On a country road in Kent, the brothers crossed paths. Enough years had passed that they did not initially recognize one another, but they sorted it out. Delighted to meet, the brothers "spent a very pleasant time in the Old Country training centre." Happily, war came to an end without either brother's name appearing among the sixty thousand Canadian fallen of the Great War.

In the meantime, while the Mulcahys renewed brotherly acquaintance in England, the Victoria Aristocrats' losing ways continued. On February 4, Victoria was subdued 6-3 in Seattle; four days later it was Seattle 6, Victoria 3; then on February 8, the Metropolitans yet again hammered Lester's downtrodden crew, 8-4.

By now the *Colonist*'s hockey writer had given the homeless Victorians a new, unsanctioned name. No longer referring to them as the Aristocrats, the beat writer had taken to calling them the "orphans." In the February 8 game, it was ex-Aristocrat Bernie Morris who poured salt into the orphans' wounds: Bernie had a hand in all but one of the eight Seattle goals, scoring four and assisting on three more.

On February 11 the losing streak reached seven as the Aristocrats lost by a single goal in Vancouver, 7-6. That defeat brought Victoria's season record to 3-12, just three victories in fifteen games, arithmetic that must have left the Victoria skaters feeling anything but aristocratic.

On February 9, right beside the *Colonist*'s report of the 8-4 drubbing the Aristocrats had endured the evening before in Seattle, there was another report drawing further attention to the intersection of war and hockey. Under the headline EASTERN ATHLETES ENLIST WHOLESALE, the newspaper informed readers that on the urging of one Lou Marsh, the entire Toronto Riversides team of the Ontario Hockey Association's senior division had enlisted in the Canadian Expeditionary Force.

Lou Marsh was a talented athlete in several sports who by this time was a referee. The Riversides were tied for the league lead with the Toronto Argonauts—the hockey version—at the time Referee Marsh persuaded them all to set aside sticks and skates in favour of rifles and boots. The enduring legacy of Lou Marsh is that he would go on to be the man honoured in the naming of a trophy awarded annually to Canada's top athlete.

As for the young hockey players persuaded to become soldiers, one of them was Gordon Henry Applegath, twenty-one on the day he enlisted in the 180th (Sportsmen) Battalion. Applegath was given an officer's commission; he would go on to deliver distinguished service as a soldier. Applegath was awarded a Military Cross for gallantry; then, in late August 1918, during the Last Hundred Days of the war, Lieutenant Applegath, now twenty-three, was killed in action near Wancourt, France.

In the less dangerous battles in PCHA rinks, Lester Patrick's lads finally won a hockey game. Playing in Seattle on February 18, the Aristocrats vanquished the league-leading Portland Rosebuds, 5-2. Sibby Nichols led the way for Victoria, scoring twice. Then, two days later, the Rosebuds took revenge at the Hippodrome, 4-1. Perhaps reflecting the aggravation the Aristocrats' season had generated, the *Colonist*'s game report comprised just a single paragraph, one that contained a striking element. A normally even-keeled, responsible man, Lester Patrick was so aggravated by the game's judge of play—and perhaps other irritations left unreported—that he threw his stick into the crowd, hitting a woman on the head. Perhaps nothing else could have displayed so clearly how infuriating the 1915-16 season must have been for the proud, supremely competitive future member of the Hockey Hall of Fame.

Their season standing now at 4-13, the Aristocrats had only one game left to endure before their season drew to a close. On February 25 they played Vancouver in the Seattle rink. They managed not to snatch defeat from the jaws of victory. The Aristocrats scored the game's first seven goals and then, with a 7-0 lead, they almost gave the game away before holding on for a 7-6 win. The *Colonist* again supplied a game account of just one paragraph, and it was the Millionaires, not the Aristocrats, who were singled out for praise. By storming back from a seven-goal deficit, the Millionaires had "won the admiration of every fan in the house." It was a fitting end to a miserable season.

The Portland Rosebuds finished the season at 13-5, well ahead of both Vancouver and Seattle. Victoria finished last, its 5-13 record the perfect inverse of Portland's. The Stanley Cup showdown, played in Montreal—the first featuring a US-based team—was a close, fiercely contested affair. The fifth and final game went ahead March 30, the Canadiens winning, 2-1. It was Goldie Prodgers who scored the winning goal for *les Canadiens*. Tommy Dunderdale scored the sole Rosebuds marker. No one needed to point out to Lester Patrick that both players were former Victoria Aristocrats.

SIX

1916-17

EXPROPRIATION AND EXILE

CONTRASTS ABOUNDED FOR Lester Patrick's hockey team in the opening days of the 1916-17 PCHA season, some wel-come, some not.

The Aristocrats had lost their first two games the year before; the new season got off on the right foot with two victories—a 5-4 win in Portland over the Rosebuds and a 6-4 conquest of the Vancouver Millionaires on home ice. But in the early days of the new season, home ice was no longer the Patrick Arena on Epworth Street. Lester Patrick perhaps expected that the eviction the Aristocrats endured in February at the hands of the Canadian military might be a temporary arrangement. He might have hoped that the army could find a way to accommodate a few hockey games in winter while serving the facility's new principal role as a base for training new soldiers in the arts of war. It was not to be.

Instead of the broad waters of Juan de Fuca Strait as a backdrop, the exiled Aristocrats played within wrist-shot range of the Spokane River in 1916-17, a less-than-pristine tributary of the mighty Columbia.

The Spokane arena—affectionately dubbed the Elm Street Barn by local wits—lacked some of the amenities the Aristocrats had enjoyed in Victoria. But in one way, it may have been superior for a segment of the audience: non-smoking hockey fans didn't have to breathe fouled air as they watched their hockey heroes in action. The new arena was well ventilated: it didn't have a roof.

Deprived of a Victoria home base, Lester Patrick had settled on Spokane as the best available locale for his hockey team in the winter of 1916–17. The Patricks—the brothers Lester and Frank together with their father, Joe—took a key part in covering the costs of refurbishing an existing arena. Enough time and resources were available to have the team play on artificial ice, but not to have the players protected from rain, snow and other unpleasant elements. The players would notice differences in the Spokane climate from what they had enjoyed in Victoria. The average December low temperature in the BC capital is four degrees Celsius; in Spokane it is minus five.

Originally a league of three Canadian-based teams and no American ones, the PCHA had changed in six years: now there were three American teams and only one remaining Canadian one, Frank Patrick's Vancouver Millionaires.

Five of the players who had underperformed as Victoria Aristocrats in 1915–16 migrated with Lester Patrick to Spokane: Dubbie Kerr, Ran McDonald, Sibby Nichols, Ken Mallen, and Bobby Genge. "Aristocrats" may have seemed a suitable name for the hockey team of a Canadian city fond of its royal affinities, but it wouldn't suit eastern Washington State, where mining and farming were prevalent in 1916. The Spokane players wore sweaters featuring an S overlaying an H—for Spokane Hockey—but the team wasn't given an official nickname. It was a local boy, struck by the yellow-and-purple colours of the team logo, who dubbed his new hockey heroes "Canaries." The name stuck. The Victoria Aristocrats had morphed into the Spokane Canaries. Perhaps the name was an augury, canaries being less intimidating than falcons, hawks, or eagles.

Back in Vancouver Island's Garden City, it was evident to readers of the Victoria *Daily Colonist* that the former Aristocrats no longer enjoyed partisan advantages and privileges. The newspaper's account of the Canaries' December 5 home victory over Vancouver was just one paragraph long. Previously, *Colonist* dispatches provided a narrative of a game's main events and a statistical summary itemizing goals scored and penalties assessed. The *Colonist* provided none of those details the next day.

It now seemed clear that the *Colonist* had shifted allegiance not to the former Aristocrats, but to the PCHA's sole remaining Canadian team. The *Colonist*'s account of the December 9 game in Vancouver pitting the Canaries against the Millionaires reverted to form with a full game account, only now it was Vancouver's success being documented. In a game featuring hockey "of all kinds, good, bad and indifferent," the Millionaires prevailed, 9-6, despite the efforts of former Aristocrat Ran McDonald, who "starred for Spokane and was the fastest man on the ice."

Allowing nine goals might have led some readers to imagine that the goaltending sieve, Fred McCulloch, was still safeguarding the Canaries' goal but, no, McCulloch was now a soldier in the Canadian Expeditionary Force. In his place stood Norman Boswell "Hec" Fowler. Though a native of Peterborough, Ontario, Fowler had established his goaltending credentials in Saskatchewan, mostly in Saskatoon, over eight amateur seasons starting in 1908. His new role as Canaries' netminder was Fowler's first experience of playing for pay, his initial season as a hockey professional. Fowler's hockey career was interrupted in 1918 for reasons both similar to and different from those that applied to Fred McCulloch: he became a soldier, but while McCulloch had volunteered for the Canadian Expeditionary Force, Fowler was conscripted.

Neither Spokane nor any other American city was at war in December 1916, but in the British Columbia capital, the European conflagration was, more than ever, the everyday preoccupation of the Victoria *Daily Colonist*.

The casualty list in the December 10 edition of the *Daily Colonist*—the catalogue of Canadians killed, wounded, and missing—ran to two columns. The paper published a call for young men between the ages of eighteen and twenty-five to help satisfy the demand for fliers in the Royal Naval Air Service. One of the Vancouver Islanders who would answer that call was Raymond Collishaw of Nanaimo. By war's end, Collishaw would be credited with sixty victories over enemy fliers—one of the greatest numbers scored by any ace pilot.

Also on December 10, the *Colonist* published a long piece illustrating one of the consequences of war: with men away fighting and dying in the front lines, women had taken over functions that would never have been theirs beforehand. The article was accompanied by five images of women working in munitions factories—making bomb fuses, assembling eight-inch shells, painting eighteen-pounders.

For readers grown weary of war, *Colonist* advertisers offered distractions. Pantages Theatre—familiar nowadays as the McPherson Playhouse—offered Victorians the Biggest and Best Six-Act Bill Ever Here. Headlining the vaudeville attractions was "Hardeen the Handcuff King." Escape artists were a great attraction in the second decade of the century and Hardeen, though now entirely forgotten, may have been as renowned an escapist in his time as the great Harry Houdini. There were other entertainment options, too. One could pay as little as twenty-five cents to see a pantomime production of *Puss in Boots* at the Royal Victoria Theatre, or take in a local production of Rudyard Kipling's *The Light That Failed*. Or the celebrated silent-film star Theda Bara in *Carmen*, showing at the Columbia Theatre.

On December 16, the *Colonist* reported on the imminent visit of Robert Borden, Canada's prime minister. By late 1916, the war had already been going for twenty-eight months, and Sir Robert had a major problem. Soldier recruitment had seriously declined, and the government was having difficulty persuading young men to step forward to do their bit for King and Empire. Everywhere he went in late 1916, Borden's mission was to do whatever it took to secure Canada's promise to have half a million men in uniform for the Empire's war effort.

Apart from the daily casualty lists, other war-related items were routine in the paper: a frequent advertisement from the 143rd Battalion CEF took up almost half of three columns and urged Victorians in extra-large type to GIVE US HIS NAME. "Nearly everyone knows of One Man who should be in Khaki today," the ad proclaimed. "Reinforcements must go forward or our Canadian soldiers may lose what they have gained." Helpfully, the ad provided a coupon that citizens could complete to provide a man's name and address. One need not identify oneself, the ad clarified: "You may sign this Coupon or not, as you wish."

Elsewhere in the December 27 edition, readers could see an augury of the conscription crisis that would engulf the country in 1917. A Government of Canada notice informed *Colonist* readers that under authority of the federal War Measures Act, men between the ages of sixteen and sixty-five were obliged to complete National Service Cards. The ultimate purpose of this initiative was to build an inventory of men who could be called upon to be soldiers whether they wanted to serve or not.

On the same page as the Government's National Service notice, the *Colonist* advertised another escapist attraction. Just a fortnight after Hardeen the Handcuff King, the Pantages Theatre availed Victoria audiences another escape artist. Mr. Herbert Brooks was "the most wonderful man who ever visited the city." The artist's audience-pleasing trick was to have himself locked in a twenty-seven-inch-by-sixteen-inch steel chest and escape from it in six seconds.

That same day—December 27—the *Colonist* supplied a non-commercial item that would have caught many a reader's eye. Nearly twelve decades after the famous—or infamous—naval mutiny led by Fletcher Christian against Captain William Bligh of HMS *Bounty*, the story of the mutiny continued to attract and fascinate readers. That very year, 1916, featured the release of an Australian film—a silent one, of course—*Mutiny on the Bounty*, starring George Cross and Wilton Power.

Under the headline SHIP TAKES GIFTS TO PITCAIRN ISLAND-ERS, the *Colonist* reported that the steamer *Port Hardy* had departed New York for Australia by way of remote Pitcairn Island. The *Port Hardy* cargo included gifts for two hundred descendants of the *Bounty* mutineers still living at Pitcairn. Mutinous and despised as their ancestors may have been, present-day Pitcairn was, the *Colonist* reassured its readers, "a law-abiding and Christian community. The Bounty Islanders are extremely pious, read the bible regularly and neither smoke nor drink."

Meanwhile, much closer to home than Pitcairn Island, Lester Patrick and his Spokane Canaries were managing to win about as often as they lost. On Boxing Day, with a 3-3 record—three wins against as many losses—they took on the defending-champion Portland Rosebuds in the open air at Spokane. It was a good game for the Canaries: they won, 6-2. The following day the *Daily Colonist* celebrated Dubbie Kerr as star of the game—he had a hand in five of the six Spokane goals—and also praised Hec Fowler for his excellent work in the Spokane goal net.

In the first game of 1917, on January 5, Dubbie Kerr was again the home-ice hero as the Canaries beat Seattle, 5-1. Paying customers witnessed a fistfight between Sibby Nichols and the Metropolitans' Frank Foyston, a bout that cost each of them twenty minutes in penalty time. The victory nudged Spokane into first place in the league standing, at least for the moment.

Four days later, January 9, the Mets took revenge, 3-1, on their own ice in downtown Seattle. Across Juan de Fuca Strait, the *Daily Colonist*'s game coverage shrunk from a paragraph or two to nothing at all. The paper's sports page provided coverage of local events and details of efforts to organize a heavyweight fight between champion Jess Willard and the French fighter Georges Carpentier. But there was no dispatch whatsoever about the Spokane–Seattle hockey game.

Another item on that day's sports page mirrored what was front of mind for many Colonist readers. Under the headline More Athletes Fall on Western Front, the newspaper reported on the latest casualties of war from the sporting world—boxers, swimmers, rowers, rugby and track stars, et al.

On January 10, the day's war-casualty list took only half a column—a mere seventy-six names—a light day by comparison to so many others.

Perhaps inspired by a desire to put earthly matters in perspective and hint that our little planet is less than a mote in the eye of the cosmos, the *Colonist* reported on the musings of one Sir William Dyson. Sir William invited earthlings to contemplate the existence of stars a thousand times more powerful than our own very ordinary star, the sun. He singled out Arcturus, a red giant star whose light, even travelling at 186,000 miles a second, we now know takes thirty-six years to reach the rods and cones of human eyes. But even among these out-of-this-world contemplations, the war was never far from mind: "Starlight will reach the battlefield tonight which shot out from the stars while the Franco–German war was in progress," the *Colonist* pointed out, and the "light which is leaving the same stars tonight will not reach the earth until the war is over and gone, only a memory upon the scarred mind of man."

Meanwhile, just the tiniest fraction of a light-second from Victoria, the Spokane Canaries continued their win-one, lose-one habit. In the latest battle of the brothers, Frank Patrick's Millionaires doubled Lester's Canaries, 6-3, on January 20 in Vancouver. According to the *Colonist*'s hockey scribe it was "one of the fastest games of the season." "It was real hockey," he wrote, "the kind that makes the fan say he will never miss a game."

Immediately below its Spokane–Vancouver account, the *Colonist* had another story for hockey enthusiasts. At a time when military-based hockey teams were in action all over the country, the Victoria daily reported that the 223rd Battalion (Canadian Scandinavians) had taken the league lead in the Winnipeg Patriotic League. No one could have known it at the time, but the most accomplished of the 223rd men would eventually become the greatest player Lester Patrick ever signed to play in Victoria. More on him later.

In eastern Canada, just as there was a new team in the PCHA, there was one in the National Hockey Association, too. It may have been the unlikeliest major-league hockey team of all time: the 228th Battalion Northern Fusiliers. One or more of the deep thinkers among the army's top brass came up with an idea for aiding Sir Robert Borden's recruiting efforts. What if a hockey team comprising men who were both soldiers and talented hockey players were to compete gloriously in major-league hockey? Would such a team inspire young men to flock to recruiting stations and "join the colours"? Thus was born the khaki-wearing 228th Battalion hockey team in late 1916.

The Patrick brothers and others would have disagreed, but the NHA was viewed by many observers as providing the world's best professional hockey. The 228th men were admitted to a circuit that included two Montreal clubs—*les Canadiens* and the Wanderers— as well as the Quebec Bulldogs, Ottawa Senators, and the Toronto Blueshirts. The skating soldiers did not embarrass themselves in the early going—not in the least. They won their first four games by an aggregate 40-13 margin. The victories included a 16-1 thrashing of the Bulldogs, whose roster just happened to include three men destined to be enshrined in the Hockey Hall of Fame: Joe Malone, Rusty Crawford, and Joe Hall.

For its part, the 228th included three faces familiar to fans of the PCHA, including two former Patrick hirelings: Goldie Prodgers had played in Victoria for Lester Patrick in 1912–13; Art Duncan— the future ace flier—was a Vancouver Millionaire in 1915–16; the third, Eddie Oatman, was a four-year veteran of the PCHA wars who had distinguished himself with twenty-two goals for New Westminster in 1913–14 and another twenty-two for Portland the following season.

As a hockey player, Eddie Oatman did himself proud with his army comrades. After a dozen games, he led the team in scoring, with seventeen goals and twenty-two points. Then the soldier mandarins decided the army needed soldiers more than it did hockey players. The 228th played its last game February 10, after which the battalion was soon loaded onto a ship and sent off to war.

Oatman and one other player, Gord Meeking, balked. They proclaimed that the army had agreed they would enlist for the sole purpose of playing hockey, not exchanging rifle fire with enemy soldiers. A very public furor erupted, but it was the army that blinked, not the players: Oatman and Meeking were excused from their duties. Oatman returned to Portland and resumed his career as a Rosebud, untroubled by military obligations. As events transpired, both Oatman and Meeking would one day play for Lester Patrick in Victoria, but that is a story for later pages.

Meanwhile, back on the west coast, the Spokane Canaries were reverting to the same losing habits they had established in Victoria the year before. On January 23 the Canaries lost their second straight game, 8-5, to Vancouver. One of Lester Patrick's first-year players, Lloyd Cook, scored one of the Spokane goals and set up another.

In 1916–17, Lloyd Tramblyn Cook—better known as "Farmer" to his nearest and dearest—was a twenty-six-year-old in his third season of pro hockey. He had played two years in Vancouver before being loaned by Frank Patrick to his brother for Lester's 1916–17 season in Spokane.

Like the Patricks, the Cooks were a family rich in hockey DNA. Lloyd Cook had played for the Taber Chiefs of the Southern Alberta Hockey League from 1910 to 1913. Sometimes during this time, fully half the Taber team were Cooks: in 1912–13, the Chiefs featured four of them: Lloyd and his brothers Leo, Wilbur, and Arnold. Lloyd Cook was the best of the lot: he would play nine seasons in the PCHA through 1924 before briefly joining the Boston Bruins for their inaugural NHL season, 1924-25. Before hanging up his skates for good, Cook would play twenty-four seasons of hockey. He was a long-time hockey coach, too, from 1919 to 1933.

The *Daily Colonist* of January 24 had other news of interest to sports fans. Jack Munroe of Boularderie Island, Cape Breton, was a heavyweight boxer of considerable renown. He had been one of twenty fighters featured in a sports card set, the 1909 American Caramel series. He had fought world champions Jim Jeffries and Jack Johnson. His boxing heyday behind him, the Cape Bretoner was an early volunteer in the Canadian Expeditionary Force. On January 24, the *Colonist* reported that Munroe was back in Canada, "invalided" home, his right arm having been shattered by a German sniper's bullet.

Munroe would never again throw a knee-buckling right hook, but he was more fortunate than some other soldiers.

The January 24 *Colonist* reported on the fate of Piper John Park of the Sixteenth Battalion, Canadian Scottish, a formation partly raised in Victoria. Piper Park had gone missing in action October 9 during the fighting for Regina Trench in the months-long Battle of the Somme.

Park, twenty-five years old, was not the only Sixteenth Battalion piper lost that day. Another British Columbian, James Clelland Richardson, aged twenty, is today much better remembered than his comrade piper. Richardson was posthumously awarded the Victoria Cross. The pipers were just two of the 191 Canadians who died October 9. Richardson's "final resting place" is in a military cemetery, Adanac—*Canada* spelled backwards—in the vicinity of where he was last seen alive. He is one of 1,071 Canadians buried there. As for Park, his body was never recovered and identified; he is among more than eleven thousand Canadians without a known grave commemorated on the towering Canadian monument to the missing on Vimy Ridge.

Back at home, in an up-and-down season, the Canaries went into their February 2 home game against Seattle with a 7-8 record. A win over the 10-6 Metropolitans would even Spokane's season standing at eight wins, eight losses, and perhaps offer improved prospects for the season's remainder. They may have hoped for glory, but what the Canaries got instead was a kick to the gut: they lost the game by the remarkable score of 14-1. The *Daily Colonist* gave the game just two short paragraphs with few particulars, but the Spokane *Spokesman-Review* felt obliged to deliver more generous details of the debacle.

For the first seventeen and a half minutes, Canaries' fans were treated to "the best hockey ever played on Spokane ice." Then the wheels came off: Seattle scored four times in less than two minutes. They netted three more in the second period to go into the third period with a 7-0 lead.

"The third period was a slaughter," the *Spokesman Review* reported, "If he [goaltender Hec Fowler] had let down for a minute Seattle would have scored 20 times instead of 7." Seattle was ahead 14-0 when Lloyd Cook's brother Leo scored the lone Spokane goal with thirty-five seconds left in the nightmare. It was the worst drubbing in the six-year history of the PCHA. Lester Patrick's aggravation must have been compounded by the fact that six of the Seattle goals were scored by former Victoria Aristocrats: Bernie Morris and Jim Riley had one apiece; Bobby Rowe had a hat trick and then scored one more for good measure. Morris was taken out of action in the second period by something indicative of the Canaries' aggravation: Bobby Genge swung his stick with intent and seriously damaged Morris's knee.

Attendance had not met Lester Patrick's expectations, and the events of February 2 could not have helped to remedy the problem. How could customers be expected to pay to watch hometown skaters capable of losing by 14 to 1? Lester's lads did rebound in their next game, February 6, against Portland. In what the *Spokesman-Review* called "the most sensational and exciting game of the season played on Spokane ice," the Canaries prevailed by 4-3 in overtime on Leo Cook's second goal of the game.

Not quite the talent his brother was, John Leo Falconbridge Cook nonetheless enjoyed a long career in hockey. Starting in 1910 with the OHA Simcoe Travellers, Leo would play six seasons of professional hockey in the PCHA and Western Canada Hockey League from 1916 to 1923. His hockey career came to a dramatic end in

1930, when he was handed a lifetime ban for striking a referee in a California Professional Hockey League playoff game.

A referee in the February 6 Spokane game might have felt similarly endangered. The match featured a new two-referee system that produced mayhem when—four times during the game—one referee overruled the other to the Canaries' disadvantage. For a while it seemed the offending referee might come to grief at the hands of incensed fans, but he managed to get out of the Elm Street Barn alive and undamaged.

Victory notwithstanding, the February 6 game turned out to be the last the Canaries would ever play at their open-air facility on Elm Street. Fan attendance had fallen below a thousand a game, not enough to cover expenses, so Lester Patrick chose to have his Canaries play all their remaining games in their opponents' home rinks. In 1916 the Aristocrats had been forced by a decision of the Canadian army to take to the road for their final games. A year later, it was Patrick's own decision that led to the same result.

The Canaries were humbled again in their next game, February 10 at Vancouver. Though not 14-1 this time, the deficit was only a little better. Before a Denman Street crowd of three thousand, the Canaries stumbled and fell, 8 to 1. The *Colonist*, so supportive when Lester's men had played well in Victoria, showed no sympathy now that they were a bunch of losers from Spokane.

In Victoria, there were bigger issues to worry about than the poor performance of the Spokane Canaries.

The front page of the *Daily Colonist* of February 11—almost every story—dealt with the ongoing world war. In addition to far-flung events in France, Austria, and Mesopotamia (in present-day eastern Iraq), the *Colonist* took pains—as it did every day— to bring the war closer to home by reporting on Victorians and Vancouver Islanders caught up in the war's clutches.

The paper reported that Mrs. E. Pascoe of Caledonia Avenue had received word that her son James had been killed on the Somme. The Pembroke Street parents of another Victoria soldier,

Private J.E.B. Crawford, had informed the *Colonist* that their son was in a London military hospital recovering from wounds and neurasthenia—shellshock. Three Copas brothers—Fred, Edwin, and Roy—were scions of a thriving grocery business, Copas & Young, located at Fort and Broad Streets in downtown Victoria. The Copas boys had volunteered to do their bit for King and Country. Frederick Copas, twenty-one, would be killed in action three months later, on Easter Monday, April 9, on the shattered slopes of Vimy Ridge.

One of the more intriguing stories of February 11 had to do with a letter received by Mrs. James McFeat of Pendergast Street, Fairfield, from her son, Sapper A.H. McFeat of the Royal Engineers. In the letter to his mum, Sapper McFeat, wrote, "I have just had my first night in the trenches and, oh, what an experience!" Young McFeat explained that he had come up to the front line just the morning before. Along the way, he and his comrades had passed numerous graves of French soldiers marked by simple wooden crosses, some with the dead soldier's helmet placed on top.

At considerable length, McFeat's letter told his mother about his adventure working a "sap"—a tunnel forty feet underground—toward the enemy line. Comparing the present "game" to the baseball and football matches he had played in Victoria, the son told his mother, "Well, this is the best game I ever took part in." Eventually Mrs. McFeat received a different sort of missive, one informing her that the game had not ended well for her boy. Archibald Hood McFeat was killed in action fighting in the Fifth Battalion, Cheshire Regiment, March 23, 1918.

The Spokane Canaries' February 6 win over Portland turned out to be their last of the season. They lost all their remaining games—12-8 and 11-5 to Vancouver, 9-7 and 7-0 to Seattle, 9-1 to Portland. By season's end, Hec Fowler's goals-against average had ballooned to 6.20, a figure even worse than Fred McCulloch's had been the year before. Dubbie Kerr's twenty goals were seven better than any other Canary managed to score. Spokane had scored eight-nine goals in its twenty-three games while giving up 143. They were

SEVEN

1917-18

RETRENCHMENT

B Y LATE 1917, the ongoing world war had already eroded the operations of the Pacific Coast Hockey Association. Player numbers had been diminished by voluntary enlistment of players who decided that serving King and Empire was a greater duty than entertaining fans of professional hockey. The Victoria Aristocrats had lost their home base when the Canadian army commandeered the Epworth Street arena in the spring of 1916. A year and a half later, the war in Europe still raging, and there was no chance that Lester Patrick could have his Victoria arena back.

In 1917 the war's impact intensified. Nineteen-seventeen delivered a series of events of great consequence, not just for PCHA hockey players but for Canadians and Americans generally. The United States' entry into the war in April was a milestone event having huge impact on the way the war would unfold and conclude. It was also a year in which the Canadian Expeditionary Force—the Canada Corps—would come to be recognized as an elite military formation, the "shock troops of the British Army."

At Easter time, over the four-day period April 9-12, 1917, the Canadians seized the supposedly impregnable enemy fortress dug into Vimy Ridge. Earlier Allied attempts to take Vimy had failed. The Canadian victory at Vimy launched a view that has cemented into national myth over the ensuing decades: that the birth of the nation occurred not on July 1, 1867, in the halls of Westminster, but on the shattered slopes of Vimy in April 1917.

In August, the Canadians captured Hill 70 in a battle their commander, Arthur Currie of Victoria, felt was even more monumental than Vimy.

In the autumn of that year, the supreme British commander, Douglas Haig, turned to the Canadians again, this time to succeed where earlier Allied efforts had failed: to capture a low-lying Belgian ridge east of Ypres, a place called Passchendaele. The Canadians succeeded once more. The cost of these successes in lives lost was enormous: more than three thousand killed at Vimy, another two thousand at Hill 17, four thousand more at Passchendaele.

In contrast to what was imagined at the beginning of the war, by 1917 young Canadian men had a much better idea of what they would be getting into if they volunteered to become soldiers. They were no longer the wide-eyed innocents they had been three years before. In 1914, boys and young men flocked to recruiting stations, fearful the war might be over by Christmas and their chance at glory lost if they didn't enlist right away. That had all changed by the time of Hill 70 and Passchendaele. Recruitment had withered, and without taking extraordinary measures, the government knew it could not keep its commitment to have half a million men in uniform for the Empire.

In 1917, the government of Sir Robert Borden turned to coercion to remedy the problem: conscription. In late August, just days after the third anniversary of the war's start, the *Military Service Act, 1917* (MSA), became Canadian law. Whether they wanted to fight or not, Canadians between the ages of twenty and forty-five became liable to be drafted as soldiers.

The country nearly blew apart as a consequence. There was wide resistance in Quebec, from trade unionists across the country, and from western farmers who needed their sons to keep the nation fed. There were other opponents: pacifists, people motivated by religious conviction, and immigrants for whom Britain was not the beloved Old Country.

The Victoria *Daily Colonist* of November 11, 1917—a year to the day before the guns of the Western Front were finally stilled—held up a mirror to the times. As always, the *Colonist*'s front page was completely concerned with the war, but interior pages were war-focused too. The latest advance at Passchendaele had progressed eight hundred yards. A large contingent of wounded and disabled soldiers returning home included twenty-seven from Victoria. The Nanaimo police were poised to round up MSA defaulters.

The paper's main front-page headline on November 11 was this: VICTORY LOANS ON SALE IN VICTORIA TOMORROW. A notice at the bottom of page one, "To the People of Canada," signed by Minister of Finance Thomas White, announced that the federal government needed to raise $150 million through its Victory Loan program to support "[the] heroic deeds of our brave men in the field."

Ads urging Victorians to support the Victory Loan program appeared throughout that day's newspaper, at least four of them on page two alone: W & J Wilson, Wm. Cathcart & Co., J.E. Painter & Sons, et al. At a rate of fifteen cents each, the boys and girls of George Jay School worked toward the goal of raising enough for the purchase of a fifty-dollar Victory bond. On page fifteen, there appeared a large image of eighteen-month-old Doreen McGregor standing on children's toy blocks spelling the words "Buy Me a Victory Bond." Thousands of Victorians were set to march in a Victoria Parade set for that day, a Sunday.

Not everyone was on board. The *Colonist* reported that at a political rally in Vancouver, two socialist candidates seeking a parliamentary seat in the impending election railed against the *Military Service Act, 1917*, the Victory Loan, "and practically every achievement" of the nation's war effort. Some two hundred people attended the meeting. They passed the hat afterwards, yielding $34.10, substantially less than the amount targeted by the George Jay schoolchildren.

But there were a few items in the *Colonist* of November 11 having nothing at all to do with war. "America's Sweetheart," the film star

The Daily Colonist.

No. 312—FIFTY-NINTH YEAR   VICTORIA, BRITISH COLUMBIA, FRIDAY, DECEMBER 7, 1917   PRICE FIVE CENTS

CONDITIONS IN HALIFAX UNEQUALED IN WAR ZONE

Shattered City of 2,000 Dead and Unnumbered Wounded Waste of Smouldering Ruins

RENEW FIERCE DRIVE FOR ITALIAN PLAINS

Teutons Gather Up Fresh Forces With Object of Forcing Defenders From Positions Among

TWO THOUSAND KILLED BY EXPLOSION ON SHIP IN HARBOR AT HALIFAX

"Conditions in Halifax Unequaled." DAILY COLONIST, DECEMBER 7, 1917

Mary Pickford, of Toronto, was available for viewing onscreen in the movie *Rebecca of Sunnybrook Farm* at the Royal Victoria. Admission could be had for as little as ten cents, not including amusement tax.

There was something else that day that might have been largely overlooked. Taking up only a few inches of column space, the 1917–18 schedule of Pacific Coast Hockey Association games appeared on page nine—just the schedule of games, with no additional text. The schedule contemplated a season in two parts—a first half and a second—in which four teams would play twenty-four games each. The plan was that the first-half winner would take on the second in a post-season playoff. The four teams were the same as those competing the year before: Vancouver, Spokane, Seattle, and Portland.

Before the new PCHA season took flight, other events commandeered the spotlight. On the morning of December 6, with a major snowstorm on the near horizon, the war came home with a vengeance to the people of Halifax, Nova Scotia. In the Halifax Harbour Narrows, a Norwegian ship, the SS *Imo*, and a Belgian-French cargo ship, the SS *Mont-Blanc* got in each other's way.

The *Mont-Blanc* was loaded to the gunwales with high explosives on their way to war. The explosion resulting from the ships' collision was the greatest man-made one ever until it was surpassed twenty-eight years later by the atomic bomb at Hiroshima. In one part of the city, virtually every home was destroyed, blown to rough kindling. More than two thousand died and many more were seriously injured. In Victoria, on the other side of the country, the explosion was even bigger news than events on the Western Front. CONDITIONS IN HALIFAX UNEQUALED IN WAR ZONE, the *Colonist* headline shouted.

Just ten days later, December 17, Canadians voted in the federal election, confirming that a majority of the country supported Robert Borden and conscription. The federal election of late 1917 was the most divisive in the country's history. Borden's Unionist coalition—his Conservative caucus and a bloc of supporting Liberals—was pitted against Sir Wilfrid Laurier and most Quebec Liberals. The Unionists won the election, but at the cost of alienating a big minority of the country.

With that election result, the government was now armed and determined to remedy its soldier-recruitment problems. Young men all over the country not already in uniform were pressured to register under the *Military Service Act, 1917.*

That was one of several complications that interfered in the well-laid plan the PCHA had announced five weeks before. Already deprived of Trooper Box, Art Duncan, Fred McCulloch, and others, the Patrick Brothers now needed to worry about the additional impacts the war would have on PCHA rosters. As events unfolded, eight more PCHA players would be lost to PCHA teams due to conscription.

The Patricks also had the problem of Spokane itself. Fans in the Lilac City had underperformed as paying customers. Gate receipts had not come close to covering costs. Faced with multiple obstacles, the Patricks decided to retrench. The Spokane Canaries were folded after their single less-than-glorious season. The plan had been for the new campaign to commence December 7, with four teams. Instead, the season began three weeks late, December 28, with three. Instead of a twenty-four-game schedule like the one played the year before, the revised schedule had each team playing just eighteen games. Now instead of three Canadian clubs, only one, Vancouver, remained to deliver west-coast professional hockey in league with American teams in Seattle and Portland.

The nine men who had played as Spokane Canaries in 1916–17 scattered in multiple directions. By the start of the new PCHA season, Sibby Nichols was serving voluntarily as a soldier in the Canada Corps. Ran McDonald and the Cook brothers, Lloyd and Leo, suited up for Frank Patrick's Vancouver Millionaires. Lester Patrick and goaltender Hec Fowler joined the defending Stanley Cup champions, the Metropolitans, including the future Hall of Famers Foyston, Walker, and Holmes, in Seattle. Three of the 1916–17 Canaries—Albert Kerr, Ken Mallen, and Bobby Genge—had called it quits and would not play anywhere at all in 1917–18.

In the first game of the 1917–18 season, December 28, Vancouver travelled to Portland, where the Millionaires lost to the Rosebuds, 4-2. The game merited no attention whatsoever in the pages of the next day's Victoria *Daily Colonist*; not a word. In Portland, the *Oregon Daily Journal* reported that fog rising from the ice had sometimes made the players almost invisible to paying customers, but Tommy Dunderdale, the ex-Victoria Aristocrat, could see well enough to score the game's first goal for Portland, and the Rosebuds went on to win, 4-2.

Meanwhile the December 29 *Colonist* reported on the outcome of a game in far-off Winnipeg that revealed a good deal about the war's impact on the game of hockey. Under the headline SMAILL STARS IN MILITARY HOCKEY, the Victoria paper reported that "old Walter Smaill" had led the Winnipeg Somme to a 5-1 victory over the rival Ypres in the season opener of the WMHL—the Winnipeg Military Hockey League. All three of the teams in the WMHL were named for iconic Canadian battles of the war. "Old Man

Smaill," who had turned thirty-three a few days earlier, had been an important member of the Victoria Aristocrats from 1911 to 1915.

There was real hockey talent among the ranks of WMHL soldier-skaters in the winter of 1917–18. One of Smaill's Somme teammates was Jack Ruttan, who would one day be awarded a place in the Hockey Hall of Fame. Another was Emory "Spunk" Sparrow, member of the Canadian amateur champions of 1916, the Sixty-First Battalion team, winners of the Allan Cup.

As reported in the *Daily Colonist*, Walter Smaill and his Somme comrades won the league opener over the Ypres, but they would win only two more games thereafter and finish last for the season as a whole. The Ypres team compiled the league's best record for 1917–18, with eight wins against just two losses. While Walter Smaill had volunteered to be a soldier, two of the opposing Ypres players had not. Dick Irvin, another future Hall of Famer, and Stan Marples, both of them Portland Rosebuds the year before, had been conscripted under the *Military Service Act, 1917*.

It was Irvin who led the WMHL's scoring parade in 1917–18, with a remarkable twenty-nine goals in the nine games he played. In addition to Marples, Irvin's Ypres teammates included his brother George and someone else, Halldor "Slim" Halldorsson, who would become one of two players of Icelandic extraction to win both the first Olympic hockey gold medal for Canada, in 1920, and another important championship later on in Victoria.

Yet another Canadian Icelander destined for 1920 Olympic glory, Kristmundur (Chris) Fridfinnson, was a member of the third WMHL team, the Winnipeg Vimy. One of Fridfinnson's Vimy teammates in 1917–18 was one John Wilfred Loughlin. After the war was finally over and the Epworth Street arena back in Lester Patrick's hands, Wilf Loughlin would take his turn in the Victoria hockey spotlight.

The *Colonist* found stories to tell having nothing to do with battles, either the on-ice variety or the other sort. On December 30 the *Colonist* reported that the Ladysmith branch of the IODE—Imperial Order Daughters of the Empire—would hold a concert that evening at the Rialto Theatre to benefit victims of the Halifax disaster. Perhaps inclined toward temperance, some of the IODE ladies might not have been troubled by another story in that day's edition: local breweries faced prosecution under the province's new Prohibition Act.

The reduced PCHA schedule in 1917–18 brought Frank Patrick's Millionaires against his brother's Metropolitans nine times during the regular season. The first showdown unfolded January 4 in Vancouver. In the second season, deprived of a hometown Victoria team, the *Daily Colonist* gave the game short shrift, just two paragraphs. By contrast, the *Vancouver Sun* delivered three columns worth of game detail. The *Sun* mused that some fans perhaps imagined that at age thirty-three, Cyclone Taylor's best days might have passed him by. But it was the Cyclone who tied the game at 2-2 in the second period and it was he who won it for the Millionaires in extra time.

It would turn out to be a remarkable year for the scarred, prematurely bald veteran of seventeen hockey seasons. Twice before, Taylor had scored twenty-four goals in a season, but he had slipped more recently. There was no slippage at all in 1918. Playing all eighteen scheduled games for the Millionaires, Fred Taylor would lead the league in both goals, thirty-two, and points, forty-three, outdistancing Seattle's Bernie Morris by twelve goals and eleven points.

While ignoring the previous night's game in Vancouver, on January 5 the *Colonist* did publish one item of interest to readers who still cared about the PCHA. Despite the absence of several players from the previous year, the piece ventured that "local sharps" were predicting that the league would be better balanced and more competitive in the new season. Though the defending Stanley Cup champion Seattle team had lost Eddie Carpenter and Jack Walker, the pundits felt that the champions would be bolstered by the acquisition of Lester Patrick, "one of the greatest defence men in the game." The same *Colonist* piece listed the skaters who would play for each team. The total for the entire PCHA was just twenty-one players, about the same as the regular roster of a single NHL team in our time.

In Victoria, the war was never far from mind. By early 1918, it had become commonplace for the *Colonist* to resort to pejorative terms in describing the enemy. Germans were "savages" on land and "pirates" at sea. A front-page story, SAVAGES AGAIN BOMBARD PADUA, reported on the civilian casualties and damage to the old Italian city resulting from an enemy bombing raid.

Soldiers' duty could be just as lethal at home in Canada as it was in front-line trenches: six soldiers had been killed in a train collision near Montreal. In conscription news, Victoria police were busy searching for thirty-four conscripts who had failed to report to the city's Willows army camp as required under the MSA.

In the enduring call to help the war effort in whatever ways people at home might accomplish, retailers found opportunity. The Kellogg's people urged Victorians to conserve wheat by turning to their delicious brand-name corn flakes for breakfast. Wrigley's, the chewing gum manufacturer, urged "the girl he left behind" to keep her military man supplied with pep-inspiring Juicy Fruit gum.

A front-page story in the *Colonist* of January 12 reported that seven men of the Canada Corps had been awarded the greatest of gallantry decorations, the Victoria Cross. One of the seven was Victoria's own George Randolph Pearkes of the Mount Tolmie neighbourhood. Unlike so many others awarded a VC, Pearkes would survive his heroics and go on to become defence minister in the government of John Diefenbaker and later, BC lieutenant-governor.

Another front page story of January 12 shed light on why conscription might have been viewed as essential in the eyes of federal cabinet members. The *Colonist* reported on the wastage figures for the second half of December. "Wastage" was the term used to describe men killed or wounded seriously enough to be taken out of action. In the second half of December, the number of those killed and wounded exceeded the number of new recruits by 2,764. Conscription efforts intensified.

The Victoria *Daily Colonist* gave the Vancouver–Seattle game of January 11 four whole paragraphs. "Brother Frank Patrick's seven gave the Seattle Mets a tough time of it," the *Colonist* reported, but "Lester's aggregation ... sent the Vancouver squad home with a five to two licking." The Victoria daily paid almost as much attention to another hockey game. In a WMHL match in Winnipeg: in "the most sensational game of the season," Vimy edged Somme, 7-6.

Elsewhere in its January 11 edition, the *Colonist* displayed a big advertisement featuring the image of a woman in form-fitting bathing suit. A native Australian like Tommy Dunderdale, Annette Kellerman was a pioneer of multiple parts. She was one of the first women to give bathing pantaloons the heave-ho in favour of a one-piece swimsuit. She was also the first famous actress to appear nude in a Hollywood picture. The film was *A Daughter of the Gods*, a million-dollar production by movie mogul William Fox that Victorians could see for themselves at the Dominion Theatre. Not just a swimmer and actress, Ms. Kellerman was also a writer and a star of vaudeville—another of the famous persons of the century's second decade who are now just about completely forgotten.

If Annette Kellerman wearing no clothes was not to one's taste, there were plenty of other silent-film options on offer in the capital city. The Royal Victoria offered demure Mary Pickford in *The Little Princess*; Gladys Coburn was in *The Primitive Call* at the Columbia; or if an action movie was your preference, William S. Hart—the John Wayne of his time—starred in *The Cold Deck* onscreen at the Variety ("If it's good it's at the Variety").

At least for the time being, Victoria theatre operators needn't worry about competition for the entertainment dollar from professional hockey, but the *Colonist* continued to give its readers brief accounts of events in the PCHA. On February 14, the paper reported that the Seattle Metropolitans had strengthened their grip on first place with a 3-1 win over Vancouver.

In other Valentine Day's news, the *Colonist* reported that the Victoria police were back in action in Chinatown. A raid on a suspected opium den at 549 Fisgard Street netted nine miscreants. A tenth man escaped police clutches by leaping across the eight-foot gap of Fan Tan Alley. "The leap was a daring one," the *Colonist* allowed: "…had the fugitive missed it his life was forfeit."

Featured attractions on the entertainment page included an appearance in Victoria by a man Winston Churchill described as Scotland's greatest-ever ambassador, the world-famous star of vaudeville and music hall, Harry Lauder. Sir Harry's biggest hits included "Roamin' in the Gloamin'," "A Wee Deoch-an-Doris," and, of course, the immortal "I Love a Lassie."

He may not have been a gallant soldier, but forty-eight-year-old Harry Lauder was a hero of another sort, someone who raised huge sums for the Empire's war effort. He was in town to address a joint luncheon of the Canadian and Rotary Clubs at the Empress Hotel. That evening he delivered a song-and-comedy performance at the jammed-tight Royal Victoria. There he was rewarded with waves of laughter that "nearly split the ceiling." Laughter notwithstanding, Lauder's serious purpose in all his February 14 Victoria efforts was to raise money for the treatment of soldiers maimed by war.

Lauder was doubtless the major Valentine's Day attraction in the city, but another big star appeared just a few blocks away, at the Pantages. She was Minnie, the "the largest elephant on the stage today." Minnie shared the Pantages stage with a dancing horse and a performing pony. Such was the diversity of the city's amusement options in 1918.

Despite the distractions offered by Harry Lauder and Minnie the elephant, the *Daily Colonist* did not allow Victorians to forget that Europe was still torn by war. The Bolshevik revolution in Russia was nearing its last dramatic moments. Vladimir Lenin had already taken Russia out of the war, and on February 28 the *Colonist* reported that Russia had completely capitulated to the peace terms dictated by Germany and the Fatherland's Central Powers partners. Under another end-of-February headline, TURKS MASSACRE MORE ARMENIANS, the *Colonist* reported on recent developments in Turkey's efforts to be free of its Armenian minority. The eventual toll of what is today widely recognized as a genocide would reach one and a half million people.

Still another headline—Savages Torpedo Hospital Vessel—reported yet more grief. Readers learned that at least 160 had perished in the sinking of the hospital ship *Glenart Castle*. The victims included wounded soldiers, doctors and orderlies. More than two dozen hospital ships were sunk in the war, most by German torpedoes. The greatest toll of lives lost resulted from the torpedoing of a Canadian ship, the *Llandovery Castle*, in late June 1918. That sinking cost 234 lives, including those of fourteen nurses, illustrating that it was not only men who paid the ultimate price for doing their duty in the war. Fifty-six Canadian nurses died too. Nor was it only men who were decorated for gallantry. On March 5, the *Colonist* reported that a local nurse, Kathleen Little, a 1913 graduate of the Royal Jubilee nursing school, had been awarded the Royal Red Cross for distinguished service.

Meanwhile, though it was insignificant news by comparison to larger events, in the final regular-season contest between the Patrick brothers, March 6 in Seattle, Lester's Metropolitans prevailed in overtime against Frank's Millionaires by 4-3. Seattle completed the season two days later in Portland and despite a loss to the Rosebuds in that final game, Seattle finished first in the league standing at 11-7, eleven victories in their eighteen games.

Two of the PCHA's five leading scorers were former Victoria Aristocrats Bernie Morris and Tommy Dunderdale, but the top scorer was the Millionaires' remarkable Cyclone Taylor, who had finished with thirty-two goals in eighteen games, an even dozen better than anybody else.

What followed was a two-game, total-goal playoff between first-place Seattle and the runner-up Millionaires. In what the *Vancouver Sun* called "one of the most fiercely-fought ice hockey games the Northwest has ever witnessed," the first game, March 11 in Vancouver, finished in a 2-2 draw. Vancouver's scoring hero was not Taylor this time but his teammate Mickey MacKay, who scored both Vancouver goals.

As the *Sun* saw it, the second game at Seattle two days later, "will go down in history as one of the classic games of Western America." Mickey MacKay was again a hero, threading a pass to "steady old Barney Stanley" for the game's only goal. Though he came out on the losing end, the *Sun* singled one of the Metropolitans for highest praise: "Lester Patrick worked harder than any man on the ice and deserved the rounds of applause he received."

This meant that it would be Vancouver, not the defending champions from Seattle, who would compete for the grand prize, the Stanley Cup. Vancouver's foes would be the first champion of the league that had arisen from the ruins of the NHA—the Toronto Arenas of the new National Hockey League.

The final showdown was played March 20 through March 30, entirely on Toronto's home ice, the Mutual Street arena. Games alternated between NHL and PCHA rules. The latter featured seven players rather than six, and allowed forward passing. Not surprisingly, the rule differences mattered: the Arenas won the games played under NHL rules while the Millionaires prevailed in those played under PCHA standards. Unluckily for Vancouver, the NHL rules applied in three of the games in the best-of-five series. Toronto won three games to two, but no one could blame Fred Taylor for Vancouver's defeat. The Cyclone scored *nine* of his team's twenty-one goals.

By the spring of 1918, the Great War had wasted the lives of Canadian soldiers in their tens of thousands—and devoured untold millions of dollars in the nation's resources. For reasons shared with every other Canadian, Lester Patrick must have fervently hoped that the war would soon come to an end. But after two years in the wilderness and two years of banishment from the Epworth Street arena, Patrick would just as surely have had reasons entirely his own for wanting the war to be over.

EIGHT

1918-19

HOME AGAIN

THE MODERN-DAY VICTORIA *Times Colonist* does not publish on Mondays. That was also the case a hundred years ago. But Monday, November 11, 1918, was a special day warranting a special edition of the *Daily Colonist*. The extra edition comprised just four pages. The page-one headline was a single word, in three-inch type, PEACE. The Great War had finally come to an end 1,560 days after it had begun in mid-summer 1914. More than sixty thousand soldiers of the Canadian Expeditionary Force had perished, a small fraction of the ten million from all nations who died in the fighting.

The second page of the day's special edition reported that revolution, famine, and anarchy were among the growing legacies of the war in central Europe. The page was filled with stories describing particulars. Jubilation might have been the principal emotional response to the war's end, but other issues ensured that relief and gratitude were offset by unhappier emotions. The November 12 edition of the *Colonist* reported on the arrival in Vancouver of the SS *Princess Alice*. A "Ship of Death," *Alice* carried the bodies of 157 victims from the sinking of another vessel, the CPR passenger liner, *Princess Sophia*, which had foundered on a reef near Juneau, Alaska, with the loss of all 364 people on board.

With the war just ending, another world-wide calamity relentlessly built to a climax. By November of 1918, every day's issue of the *Colonist* reported on the local toll taken by the influenza pandemic that had begun earlier in the year and would go on to kill throughout 1919 and well into 1920. A century later, no one has a precise number of the people who died of "Spanish flu" and its associate killers—chiefly pneumonia—but the estimates run as high as fifty million, ten million more than the number thought to have died as a direct result of the war itself.

In a full-page editorial on page one of its November 12 edition, the *Colonist* lectured readers on their after-peace civic obligations, chief among which was the duty to buy Victory Bonds to help the nation deal with the costs of war and recovery. Advertisers—the New England Market, Gordons' Clothiers, Maynards' Shoes, et al.— urged the same thing.

The *Colonist* of November 12 reflected the prevailing mood of the preceding days and many more that would follow. The local medical health officer urged men to step forward to help nurses overwhelmed by the burden of looking after influenza-stricken patients. The pandemic's victims included Sister Mary Josephine, a St. Joseph's Hospital nurse. Another nurse, Florence Pearson, was one in a long list of those who had succumbed at Nanaimo. Another victim was Charlie Swain, a baseball player who had starred with the Victoria and Vancouver clubs of the Northwestern League. Charlie's brother Ira had died two weeks earlier, of influenza. There were many more.

With the war finally over, there were celebrations too. A few hundred residents of the Mount Tolmie neighbourhood gathered around a bonfire on Tolmie's summit to sing and rejoice—and to burn an effigy of Queen Victoria's grandson, the deposed German Kaiser Wilhelm II.

Amid the influenza gloom and the expressions of joy in the Kaiser's downfall, there were signs that good things might be restored. One prospect certain to delight at least a segment of the city's population was that after an absence of more than two and a half years, professional hockey would return to the Patrick Arena on Epworth

Street. With the war over, the arena could revert to the purpose for which it had been built in 1911, the playing of hockey by the professionals of Lester Patrick's Victoria team in the Pacific Coast Hockey Association.

On December 10, more than six hundred people accepted Patrick's invitation to come for a skate at his arena. Some in the throng offered evidence that the war was not entirely a thing of the past. Skaters included soldiers stationed at nearby Willows Camp, men of Canada's Siberian Expeditionary Force who would soon travel to Vladivostok to do battle with the Bolsheviks now in charge of the country transformed from Russia to the Soviet Union.

Three days later, on December 13, the *Colonist* voiced optimism that Lester Patrick was well on his way to building a strong Victoria team for the new PCHA season. Victoria was back in, but another club, the Portland Rosebuds, had suspended operations for 1918-19. With the addition of one team and the subtraction of another, the PCHA would remain a three-club circuit for the first post-war pro hockey season on the west coast. The balance had shifted again: now there were two Canadian clubs and just one American, in Seattle.

With Portland at least temporarily out of the league, unemployed former Rosebuds were available for hire by the other clubs. Over the course of several days in mid-December, the *Colonist* reported on Lester Patrick's recruitment successes. Eventually, he would sign seven Rosebuds, including one, Tommy Dunderdale, entirely familiar to Aristocrats' fans in Victoria. Even at the advanced hockey age of thirty-one, the pride of Benalla was still an accomplished hockey professional. He had led the Rosebuds as a goal scorer the previous season, with fourteen in eighteen games.

On December 17, the *Colonist* let readers know that Patrick had signed Eddie Oatman, the same Eddie Oatman who, two years earlier, had balked at doing anything but play hockey for the 228th Battalion Northern Fusiliers of the NHA. The Victoria daily described Oatman as "one of the greatest players to be found in America." Oatman and Dunderdale had both finished among the

Eddie Oatman played hockey for three decades, from 1909 to 1939. For six years in the 1920s, he was a leading light with Lester Patrick's Victoria hockey club. Oatman is not a member of the Hockey Hall of Fame, but he should be. COURTESY HOCKEYGODS

top five PCHA scorers in 1918. Lester Patrick was exultant about getting the duo to play in Victoria. "If we don't cinch the world's championship this year," the *Colonist* reported Patrick as saying, "I'll eat my hat."

The Aristocrats played their first home game January 3, 1919— 1,067 days after their previous game at the Epworth Street arena. The Aristocrats lost to the visiting Seattle Metropolitans, and it wasn't close: Seattle won by 7-1. The *Colonist*'s reporter stated that the Metropolitans were superior "in every department of the game." Compounding the misery for Lester Patrick, four of Seattle's goals were scored by former Aristocrats, two each by Bernie Morris and Bobby Rowe. On the bright side, it was one of the former Rosebuds, Alf Barbour, who scored the sole Victoria goal.

James Alfred Barbour had a nickname other than "Alf." A trained and practising pharmacist, Barbour's alternate nickname was "Doc," presumably because in the view of his hockey-playing comrades, there couldn't be much difference between prescription dispensers and doctors. When permitted by his pharmacy practice at Blairmore, Alberta, Barbour had played hockey in the winter of 1910–11 with the Taber Chiefs, four of whom were Cook brothers—Lloyd, Wilbur, Arnold, Ernie and Albert. Indeed, other than Barbour himself, only one other Taber Chief at the time was someone *not* named Cook. Seven years after his adventures with the Cooks, Barbour had played a significant role in the success of the Rosebuds, scoring a dozen goals in seventeen games playing with Oatman and Dunderdale for Portland the previous season.

Other news items vied for attention in Victoria on January 3. The *Colonist*'s front page featured a message from Sir Arthur Currie, commander of the Canada Corps in the last eighteen months of the war. In it, Currie took pride that his Canada Corps were freely acknowledged as "the hardest-hitting force in the armies of the world's history."

Currie was perhaps a bit biased, but the Canadians did earn a reputation as a fighting formation that perhaps only the Australians could rival. In his post-war memoirs, the British prime minister during the war, David Lloyd George, wrote that he would have given Currie command of the entire British army had the war dragged on into 1919—a substantial tribute to a man who was not a professional soldier but someone who had spent two decades in Victoria prior to 1914 as a teacher, a realtor, and a part-time soldier.

Another British knight was also in the news in early January. Sir Harry Lauder, the song-and-comedy vaudeville star, was in Halifax en route to Montreal seeking to make peace with Quebeckers over derogatory remarks that some had taken as critical of French Canadians' contribution to the war effort.

Back on the ice, Lester Patrick would have taken no greater comfort from the Aristocrats' second game than he had done from the first. The Aristocrats ferried to Vancouver, where they were drubbed by brother Frank's Millionaires, 6-1, on January 6. Five thousand paying customers at the Denman Street arena were happy to see the ageless Cyclone Taylor score three of the Vancouver goals, with two more coming from Mickey MacKay.

Once again it was a reconstituted Rosebud who scored the lone Victoria goal. Charles Stuart (Charlie) Tobin, had been an important cog in the Rosebud machine during his four years in Portland. With sixty-one goals and ninety points in seventy-eight games, he is still the all-time Rosebuds' career leader in all three categories.

The front page of the following day's *Victoria Colonist* was dominated by the news that former US president Theodore Roosevelt had died at age sixty, partly as a result of health issues contracted from his various adventures in steamy jungles far removed from Washington, DC. Other front-page news related that Canadian soldiers still in Europe were growing increasingly angry about the time it was taking the army to repatriate them. The anger would grow in the weeks ahead, culminating in riots that would leave several soldiers dead in circumstances that could not be blamed on the enemy they had crossed the Atlantic to fight.

In their third game, on January 8, the Aristocrats were once again limited to a single goal, but in this case that was all they needed for their first win of the season. Playing in downtown Seattle, the Aristocrats beat the Metropolitans by 1-0. According to the next-day's *Daily Colonist*, Victoria hockey fans "went wild with excitement" when word arrived by wire that their team had won. Lester Patrick had not boarded the steamer to Seattle with the other Aristocrats because he was sick at home with influenza. Eddie Oatman, just recovered from flu himself, shone for the Aristocrats, but it was defenceman Ernie Johnson, yet another ex-Rosebud, who scored the game's only goal.

supposed to play a twenty-fourth game, in Vancouver, but Frank Patrick cancelled the game. Seattle had already clinched the league title: why bother playing a pointless final game against the hapless Spokane Canaries?

Any doubts that the best of the Pacific Coast Hockey Association were the equal of the NHA were put to rest by what happened in the Stanley Cup final, in Seattle. The Montreal Canadiens won the first game in the best-of-five series, March 17. The loss motivated Seattle: the Metropolitans stormed back to win three in a row by an aggregate 19-3 margin. The final game was 9-1. For the first time in its twenty-four-year history American-based hockey players—every one of them a Canadian—had their names inscribed on the Cup.

For three of the Metropolitans, it was a second Stanley Cup triumph. Frank Foyston, Jack Walker, and goaltender Harry "Hap" Holmes had won the first time as Toronto Blueshirts in 1914. The trio would accomplish it again a third time in the years ahead, a story yet to be told.

Earlier in March the Victoria *Daily Colonist* had reported an item that would have great consequences not just for the PCHA but the whole world. British intelligence agents had intercepted a telegram in which Germany had made an offer it hoped Mexico could not refuse: if the Mexicans entered the war on Germany's side, Mexico would be given Texas, New Mexico, and Arizona when the war was won.

Mexico did not enter the war, but eleven days after Seattle's Stanley Cup victory, another country did.

By the time he signed to play for Lester Patrick in late 1918, Thomas Ernest Johnson, better known as "Moose," was a thirty-two-year-old veteran of seventeen hockey seasons. A native Montrealer, Johnson had won the Stanley Cup four times by age twenty-four. In 1911, he had been among the prized players the Patrick brothers targeted in their raid for the cream of talent in the National Hockey Association. He had played in all seven of the preceding PCHA seasons, three with New Westminster, four in Portland. Moose had plenty of hockey left in him: he would play three more seasons in Victoria, and was still a hockey professional in 1931 at the advanced age of forty-five. Johnson would eventually be an early inductee in the Hockey Hall of Fame, together with western-league stars Mickey MacKay and Bill Cook, Hall of Fame Class of 1952.

Tommy Murray, the goaltending star of the January 8 game, had been custodian of his team's goal when the Winnipeg Monarchs won the Allan Cup as Canadian amateur champions in 1915. The Winnipeg Amateur Hockey League flourished between 1908 and 1915 and produced a lode of hockey talent. Murray's 1915 Monarchs teammates included one, Dick Irvin, who would one day also become a member of the Hockey Hall of Fame, and two more—Stan Marples and Clem Loughlin—who joined him with the Victoria Aristocrats in 1919. Born in the US, Murray would eventually play five seasons of PCHA hockey before returning to his native land for five more with Los Angeles Richfield Oil of the California Professional Hockey League.

Apart from the news of the hockey victory in Seattle, there was other news in the January 9 edition of the *Daily Colonist*. Preparations for the conference mandated to settle the terms of the post-war peace were underway in Paris. The talks would continue throughout the winter and spring and the first days of summer in 1919 before the June 28 conclusion at Versailles.

In London, Labour Members of Parliament took their place for the first time as His Majesty's Official Opposition. In Montreal, Sir Harry Lauder appeared to have made peace by clarifying it had

ERNIE JOHNSON

Ernie Johnson, 1960–61 O-Pee-Chee hockey card series. Ernie Johnson was an established star with the Montreal Wanderers of the National Hockey Association when he was induced by the Patrick brothers to leave Montreal and join the New Westminster Royals of the brothers' new Pacific Coast Hockey Association in 1912. Over the next eleven seasons—the final four with Victoria—he was a PCHA all-star seven times. In 1952, Johnson was inducted into the Hockey Hall of Fame. AUTHOR'S COLLECTION been "shirkers and slackers," not *Quebecois*, he had targeted in criticism about those who had failed to pull their weight in the war.

The newspaper continued to list names of soldiers who had died across the Atlantic, but now they were falling not to bullets and bombs but to influenza and pneumonia.

If *Colonist* readers needed relief from such serious matters, they had options other than hockey for finding it in Victoria. Admirers of Douglas Fairbanks—the George Clooney of his time—could see him onscreen at the Columbia, where they could look forward to watching him taking on "Wolf, Mountain Lion and Rattler in a Desert Adventure," *The Lamb*. If that seemed a bit too edgy, film enthusiasts of gentler disposition could opt for the Princess Theatre, where Miss Eva Hart was starring in the pantomime *The Old Woman Who Lived in a Shoe*. The cost of a seat at the Princess ranged from twenty-five to seventy-five cents, proceeds in aid of the Red Cross.

Across town at the hockey barn in Oak Bay, the Victoria Aristocrats made it four in a row: for a fourth straight time, the team Lester Patrick had assured fans would be world champions managed just a single goal. This time the Aristocrats stumbled, 4-1, to Vancouver. According to the *Colonist*'s following-day account, the Aristocrats needn't hang their heads in disgrace. With influenza no longer a factor—at least for now—the Victoria team was fit and fast, but the Millionaires' goaltender, "Old Eagle Eyes" Hugh Lehman, had simply been too good. Reliable Cyclone Taylor and Mickey MacKay led the scoring for Vancouver, with just-as-dependable Tommy Dunderdale replying for Victoria.

On January 11, the *Colonist* delivered a front-page catalogue of influenza casualties in other cities—7 more deaths in Winnipeg, 18 in Vancouver, 336 in Seattle since December 10. The day's Ottawa's casualty list included seven more soldiers' names, most of them felled by influenza or pneumonia.

In what had become a daily routine, the *Colonist* published human-interest stories focused on soldiers who had come home— soldiers like Private Albert William Sage, who had returned to his wife on Hillside Avenue to meet his twin children for the first time. And, of course, there were stories about soldiers who *wanted* to come home but were still languishing on the wrong side of the Atlantic, soldiers like the five sons of Mrs. Jane Dorman of Linden Avenue.

In local political news, candidates for election to city council wrangled about how, or whether, to proceed with construction of a new Johnson Street Bridge. Sick and tired of talk, Victorians wanted the politicians to *do* something. But those demanding action would have to wait five more years before the "Blue Bridge" that would serve Victorians for close to a century was finally completed in 1924.

On January 17, the Aristocrats finally broke their goal-a-game habit with a 3-1 victory at home against Seattle. The *Colonist* game account ran to two columns and waxed enthusiastically about Frank Patrick's view that Victoria would be the PCHA team to beat in 1919. Charlie Tobin was once again the game star, netting two goals of his own and assisting on the third by Alf Barbour. Evidently still not fully recovered from his flu battle, Lester Patrick watched the game from the stands.

Other stories competed for attention in the next day's *Colonist*. Rosa Luxemburg, the famed Marxist, philosopher, economist, and antiwar activist was murdered at forty-seven in Berlin. The SS *Olympic*, sister ship to the *Titanic*, landed five thousand Canadian soldiers in Halifax. Feeling great pressure to repatriate more of the thousands of soldiers still in Europe, the government published a half-page notice—the third in a series—detailing its demobilization plans.

In a small item that would have meant something to residents of the city's Fairfield neighbourhood, the *Colonist* reported that Shoal Bay had been renamed McNeill Bay. The name change, sanctioned by the Geographical Names Board of Canada, was a triumph of citizen action; the neighbourhood had petitioned Oak Bay Council to make the change a year before. The new name honoured Captain William Henry McNeill, master of the Hudson Bay Company steamer SS *Beaver*, and one of the original landowners of Oak Bay.

On January 22 the Aristocrats embarked on a three-game winning streak: after another 1-0 win in Seattle, they edged Vancouver 3-2 and Seattle 2-1 at home in Victoria. The *Colonist* billed the January 24 victory over Vancouver "easily the most exciting played this year on local ice." It was once again Ernie Johnson who scored the winner for Victoria, a victory that left Victoria tied for first with Seattle. On the last day of February the Aristocrats' one-goal win over the Metropolitans made the Aristocrats the league's top dogs, at least for the time being. Perhaps Lester wouldn't need to eat his hat after all.

In the *Colonist*'s account of Victoria's February 28 performance, "every man engaged was playing all the hockey he knew." The men who secured the victory for the Aristocrats were the old reliables, Dunderdale and Johnson, each of whom scored a goal.

Meanwhile, as Victoria hockey fans savoured the team's win streak, other matters drew headlines in the *Daily Colonist*. In the morning of January 24, SS *Empress of Asia* delivered returning soldiers to Victoria. It had been a long voyage—twenty-three days from Liverpool and eight thousand miles via the Panama Canal.

Supposed to stop at the William Head quarantine station for several hours, *Empress of Asia* kept on going, only to be forced to anchor off Royal Roads while officials came on board to carry out their required inspections. The delay was met with "loud yells of disgust from the men aboard." The returning soldiers could see their loved ones—fifteen thousand strong—gathered on and near the city's outer docks. "[All] along the shore the people of Victoria waited impatiently to see them. Never before has the city turned out such a tremendous crowd to witness a single event."

But everyone had to wait hours more for the yearned-for reunion. The total number aboard the ship was 1,373, including six nurses. Some 243 were able to disembark at Victoria late in the afternoon, the others having to endure a further wait as the ship proceeded to Vancouver. By now, with the Armistice seventy-four days in the rear-view mirror, the war still exacted a toll. Thousands of soldiers still waited in Europe, several dying every day of debilitation and disease. Every day the *Colonist* reported stories of local people dead from influenza and pneumonia.

There were other markers of the war's impact. It was problematic enough that soldiers and citizens had turned to alcohol to ease the misery inflicted by war. Now there was something else: a report from a London medical institute indicated an enormous increase in drug dependency. COCAINE CRAZE BECOMING MENACE, shouted the headline in the *Colonist* story detailing the ravages of cocaine, opium, and morphine in both men and women.

Victoria's cinema houses provided escape significantly safer and cheaper than opium or cocaine. The Columbia offered a twin bill: Douglas Fairbanks in *Down to Earth* and Fatty Arbuckle in *The Bell Boy*. The alternative at the Romano was Priscilla Dean in *The Brazen Beauty*. The cost to see a matinee screening was as little as a dime, just a nickel for children.

Someone else had done his bit to take minds off the lingering effects of war and pestilence. On February 1, just below the account of the previous evening's home victory over Seattle, the *Colonist* reprinted letters from officers serving in the Esquimalt Military Hospital. They thanked Lester Patrick for the generosity extended to their hospital patients: Patrick had given recovering soldiers 100 tickets for the home game against Vancouver and another 150 for the upcoming Friday game, February 7, also against Vancouver.

Though the Aristocrats had been hammered, 9-1, by Seattle two days before, in the Friday-night match on February 7, Victoria rebounded mightily. The *Colonist* called it "without doubt the most exciting game of the season"—evidently, one "most exciting game" followed another. Mickey MacKay delivered the only goal in a 1-0 Vancouver win. The 150 soldiers attending compliments of Lester Patrick might have been disappointed in the game result but not in the action and quality of play brought by both sides. Tommy Dunderdale sustained a bad cut over the eye in a collision with Mickey MacKay. Dunderdale returned after repairs with "about half a yard of the club doc's plaster on his head, but played as if a little blood-letting had increased his vigor." With Bobby Genge suddenly feeling unwell, likely due to the flu, Lester Patrick, still subpar, "had no choice but to get into the game himself." He did just fine.

Two days later, February 10, the pandemic generated one more compelling story. The Aristocrats travelled to Vancouver for another tightly contested game. This time they won, by a 2-1 margin. The hero of the game for the Aristocrats was someone not even on the team roster. In an arrangement that could not possibly happen today, Frank Patrick lent his brother the services of Vancouver spare Alex Irvin, brother of Dick, the future Hall of Famer. The player loan was necessitated by the fact that Victoria didn't have enough players of its own to put a full team on the ice. Four Aristocrats—Johnson, Genge, Loughlin, and Barbour—were all in hospital being treated for influenza. Alex Irvin took over for Johnson then, on an end-to-end rush three and a half minutes into extra time, scored the winner for the elder Patrick brother and the few Aristocrats not in hospital.

After a string of exciting, well-played games, the Aristocrats produced a Valentine's Day stinker on their home ice. In a game the *Colonist* called the poorest of the season, Seattle pummelled Victoria, 8-2. Former Aristocrat Bernie Morris scored five of the Metropolitans' goals. The Aristocrats perhaps had legitimate grounds for their performance: they had been "shot to pieces" by influenza, with Genge, Loughlin, and Johnson still out of action.

In a game evidently as rough as it was ugly, the *Colonist* complained of too much slashing and tripping in the February 14 blowout. Two fights broke out, both featuring Tommy Dunderdale in the Victoria corner. In bout one, Dunderdale, "playing with a chip on his shoulder," took on Roy Rickey. That yielded three-minute penalties for each combatant. Bout two pitted Dunderdale against his former teammate Bobby Rowe. The *Colonist* grumbled that Rowe needed reminding that it is unforgivable to hit a man when he is down. The paper described a scene in which Rowe sat on his opponent, punching his head against the ice. The referee saw things differently: he awarded both fighters ten-minute penalties.

Not all the on-ice events offended the finer sensibilities in the audience. In the first intermission, Seattle coach Pete Muldoon put on an exhibition of "fancy" skating—much appreciated by the fans—with his "pupil," Miss Venita Engel. ("Fancy skating" was what we now call "ice dancing.")

Five days later, February 19, Bernie Morris went on another tear, scoring three goals in a 4-1 Seattle home win over Victoria. The Aristocrats were again weakened by the absence of Johnson and Genge, and Patrick was still playing under the weather.

On February 21 Victoria fans at last got something worth their eighty-five-cent admission price. "It would seem impossible," the *Colonist* reported in its next-day lead, "to pack a hockey game more full of excitement than that played at the Arena last night." The Aristocrats won, 3-2, over Vancouver in a game that set a new over-time record. Clem Loughlin scored the winning goal thirty minutes, twenty seconds into overtime. He accomplished the feat despite this being his first game back after a "hard tussle" with influenza.

The Victoria fans enjoyed a bonus: the debut of Clem's kid brother, Wilf, playing his first game as a pro at age twenty-two. The Millionaires' boss, Frank Patrick, was among those who lauded the play of the younger Loughlin. No amateur he'd seen was likelier to flourish in pro hockey than Clem's six-foot-two younger brother.

John Wilfred Loughlin was born February 28, 1896, not long before Wilfrid Laurier commenced his fifteen-year run as Canada's seventh prime minister. Wilf would go on to play six seasons for Lester Patrick in Victoria and would be an all-star by 1921.

The February 21 win was a highlight moment for the Aristocrats. It brought their season standing, 7-8, to within a single game of a level record of wins and losses. The players had all survived the pandemic and those who had been worst afflicted were on the mend. Unhappily for Victoria fans and the man who had promised to eat his hat, the victory would turn out to be the Aristocrats' last of the season.

The account of the overtime conquest of Seattle took up three columns of the *Colonist* sports section but of course many other matters clamoured for readers' attention. On February 6, a front-page item reported significant news in the influenza story: army doctors in England had identified the lethal virus. On February 17, Wilf Loughlin's namesake, Wilfrid Laurier, leader of the Opposition, died at age seventy-eight. Laurier was still highly regarded by Canadians: tens of thousands crowded Ottawa streets for his funeral procession on February 22.

An event in Halifax on February 19 mirrored the temper of the times. Right beside its front-page account of the plans for the Laurier funeral, the *Colonist* reported that for a second straight night, returned soldiers had rioted in the Nova Scotia capital. Halifax was the principal port of entry for soldiers coming home, a place ready-made to feel the brunt of soldiers' aggravation and resentment. In the *Colonist*'s view, the soldiers had disgraced themselves by breaking windows and pillaging shops, including one operated by a widow whose two sons were still at the front.

It wasn't just in the port of Halifax that angry soldiers rioted. Discord grew deadly in early March when Canadian soldiers—as many as fifteen thousand of them—decided that they had had enough of waiting in crowded, miserable conditions at Kinmel Park, North Wales. Cold, underfed, unpaid, and denied the opportunity to leave the camp, the Canadians went on a rampage. The *Daily Colonist* showed little sympathy for the rioters, calling them a disgrace to themselves and their country. Disgraceful or not, suppression of the riots exacted a fresh toll among men who had survived enemy bullets and bombs: five were killed, twenty-three wounded. Another twenty-five were eventually convicted of mutiny, some sentenced to up to ten years penal servitude.

On Canada's west coast, far from the Kinmel rioting, hockey fans perhaps sought distraction at the Patrick Arena. They, too, would be disappointed: the Aristocrats lost their final five games of the season. Their 7-8 standing of February 21 fell to 7-13 by March 10. Rather than lead his squad to a world championship, Lester Patrick instead saw his Aristocrats finish in last place once again. Not one of the Victoria players finished among the league's top ten scorers. The Cyclone, tireless Fred Taylor of Vancouver, led the way with twenty-three goals and thirty-six points in twenty games. With eleven goals and sixteen points, the best of the Aristocrats, Eddie Oatman, hadn't been half as productive as Taylor. Tommy Dunderdale, the future Hall of Famer who had never scored fewer than fourteen goals in any of his seven previous PCHA seasons, had just five in 1918–19. Was Tommy over the hill?

Lester's crew could only watch from the sidelines as Vancouver and Seattle once again met in the PCHA playoff to determine which team would represent the league in the Stanley Cup showdown. Seattle reversed the previous year's outcome, defeating Taylor and his Millionaires, 7-5, in a two-game, total-goal series.

The ensuing Stanley Cup final, played entirely in Seattle, would set a precedent no one celebrated. Between March 19 and March 30, the NHL's Montreal Canadiens and Seattle played five games in the best-of-series, each team winning twice, with one game tied. In early April, Joe Hall, future member of the Hockey Hall of Fame, died of influenza at age thirty-seven. With Hall dead and several other players ill, the series was cancelled—the only time in history that a Stanley Cup series started but was not completed. In 1919, there was no winner.

Lester Patrick was among the throng paying tribute to Joe Hall. "I cannot tell you how deeply grieved I am," the *Colonist* of April 6 quoted Patrick as saying. "Joe had a heart as big as a house, and was a prince of good fellows."

People would continue to die of influenza in the weeks and months ahead, and the social fabric in Canada would continue to fray in the aftermath of war. Eventually it would be more than soldiers venting their anger at their lot in life. Between mid-May and late June of 1919, the city of Winnipeg would be paralyzed by a general strike driven by inequality and the poor conditions prevailing among the city's working class, and by returned soldiers who had arrived home to circumstances nothing like the ones they had expected to find.

The number joining in the strike reached thirty thousand. As happened at Kinmel Park, the event culminated in bloodshed. On

June 21, armed men of the Royal Northwest Mounted Police rode on horseback into the crowd of demonstrators. The police fired more than a hundred rounds. Two demonstrators died, and up to thirty were wounded. The violence effectively ended the strike but not the hard feelings in which it had germinated. Those would endure.

Back on the west coast, Victoria's hockey professionals escaped the fate that had befallen Joe Hall. Later in April, the *Daily Colonist* reported that stricken members of the Montreal Canadiens and Seattle Metropolitans were out of danger. The Victoria Aristocrats seemed out of the woods too.

For Lester Patrick and so many others, the year had been something of an *annus horribilis*. Might the ever-optimistic Patrick have perhaps bought himself a new hat and imagined that brighter days were on the near horizon?

NINE

1919-20

BOLDLY INTO THE ROARING TWENTIES

B Y THE END of the decade, it was hard for positive thinkers to imagine that large-scale human conflict was strictly a thing of the past. The lead story in the Victoria *Daily Colonist* of December 27 informed readers that the Bolsheviks in charge of the Soviet Union had made gains against the international alliance intent on undoing the Russian Revolution.

Twelve months earlier, in December 1918, more than four thousand Canadian soldiers of the Siberian Expeditionary Force had departed Victoria for Vladivostok. The multi-nation campaign against the Bolsheviks endured until June of 1920, but the Canadians withdrew from the Siberian intervention in April of 1919. Twenty-four Canadians who died in Russia in late 1918 and 1919 lie for evermore in Russian war graves, most of them in or near Vladivostok.

Another faraway conflict clamored for attention. In Ireland, by means often leading to violence, republicans led by Sinn Fein sought freedom from British rule. There was an augury of trouble in the Middle East too. Under the headline ZIONISTS FLOCK INTO PALESTINE, the *Colonist* reported that a great tide of immigration was sweeping into Palestine, a tide drawn by the prospect that the long-sought dream of a Jewish homeland was about to be realized.

Though the Armistice had been signed more than thirteen months earlier, Canadian soldiers continued to die. In the seventy-two hours between Christmas and December 27 of 1919, sixteen soldiers who had survived the war breathed their last, almost all of them victims of influenza and its attendant killer, pneumonia.

In Victoria the IODE—Imperial Order Daughters of the Empire—organized a Christmas party for 150 soldiers' orphans and widows. Santa Claus made an appearance at the event and was instantly surrounded by a throng of little people. The jolly old fellow proceeded to distribute a pile of gifts before the kids capped the excitement with a flurry of games: London Bridge, oranges and lemons, and "the ever-popular drop the handkerchief."

Soldiers still in the land of the living were in the news too. Every week hundreds of returning soldiers applied for land grants and loans under the federal *Soldier Settlement Act*. The *Colonist* reported that 33,000 had been approved for land grants and another twenty thousand for loans amounting to more than fifty million dollars.

There was news for people having a scientific bent. An American geologist, William Allanson Bryan, claimed to have evidence of a lost continent. Dr. Bryan was persuaded that a four-thousand-mile-long continent once stretched from South America to the Hawaiian Islands. If the world could have a submerged Atlantis, why not a "Pacifis" too?

In Victoria, those preferring entertainment to edification could go to the Columbia Theatre to see D.W. Griffiths' *Birth of a Nation*, a film still famous a hundred years later for its cinematic mastery and its unashamed racism.

The Victoria daily presented its news from the world of sports under a bold new banner, Sporting News. On December 27, the *Colonist* had good news for fans of the Victoria Aristocrats. Lester Patrick's men had won their home opener against Seattle. With all four thousand seats in the Epworth Street arena sold and occupied and another four hundred customers in the standing-room sections, the Aristocrats had prevailed, 2-1, over Seattle.

There were cast changes in the Victoria lineup. Charley Tobin had packed his gear bag and joined the Aristocrats' adversaries in Seattle. After three seasons as a PCHA pro, Stan Marples, a prairie lad, had returned to amateur hockey to become a leading light of the Moose Jaw Maple Leafs of the Saskatchewan Senior Hockey League. Alf Barbour had reverted, too: he and Mickey MacKay—another player destined for the Hockey Hall of Fame—went to Alberta to reinforce the Calgary Columbus club of the senior amateur Big-4 Alberta Hockey League, an aggregation alleged to be amateur in name only.

Alex Irvin, the player borrowed from Frank Patrick to help fill the gaps caused by influenza, moved on, too, eventually to another Big-4 club, the Calgary Canadians. There was one more change: Tommy Murray, the man who guarded the Victoria goal in 1918–19 was out. In his place stood Hec Fowler, the goaltender Seattle had relied upon to get to the Stanley Cup final the previous March. Fowler was familiar to the Aristocrats: most of them had been his comrades in 1916–17, the year the Aristocrats were bumped out of the Epworth Street arena and forced to become Spokane Canaries for a season.

One familiar face and one new one took over the remaining vacancies in the Victoria roster. At age thirty, Dubbie Kerr was persuaded to come out of retirement for one last season as a Victoria Aristocrat. The fresh face belonged to Harry Meeking, the kid brother of Gordon Meeking, the willing skater but reluctant soldier who had played NHA hockey with the 228th Battalion Northern Fusiliers in 1917. In the dispatch describing the Aristocrats' first game of the new season, the *Colonist* lauded the collaboration of Eddie Oatman and Meeking.

Harry Arthur Meeking had played three seasons in Toronto before spending 1918–19 with the Glace Bay Miners of the Cape Breton Hockey League. The younger Meeking would become a fixture in Victoria: his 1919–20 debut would be followed by six more seasons at the south end of Vancouver Island.

An item at the foot of the December 27 sports page provided a brief, by-the-numbers review of the PCHA's first eight seasons.

Vancouver had been league champions three times, Victoria twice. The other clubs—New Westminster, Portland, and Seattle—had one title each. The amazing Cyclone Taylor, now thirty-three, had been the league scoring champion five times in his seven seasons on the west coast. Could he do it again?

On December 29, the Aristocrats ferried to Vancouver to play the Millionaires at the Denman Street arena. In a game the *Colonist* described as one of the most sensational ever played on the west coast, Lloyd Cook needed just twenty-four seconds of overtime to win it for Vancouver. Evidently the Aristocrats were a good draw on the far side of the Strait of Georgia: seven thousand fans paid to see the action.

The *Colonist* covered games played in other leagues, too. In Toronto, another crowd of seven thousand paying customers saw the NHL's Toronto St. Patricks conquer Quebec, 7-4, and Ottawa won 2-0 over the Montreal Canadiens. At a time when amateur hockey still commanded just about as much attention as the professional game, the *Colonist* reported on the action in the Winnipeg Senior Hockey League. The WSHL was a worthy proving ground: several league alumni went on to long careers in professional hockey, and a few made it all the way to the Hockey Hall of Fame.

In addition to the ongoing conflicts in Russia and Ireland, the front page of the December 30 *Colonist* reported on the investigation into the events of the preceding April in the Punjab city of Amritsar. Commanded by a British general, R.E.H. Dyer, troops had fired on a crowd of unarmed demonstrators, killing more than four hundred, including forty children. The massacre rocked moderate Indians and fuelled agitation for Indian independence, a goal that would not be realized until 1947.

In Dublin, more than four thousand miles west of Amritsar, rioters wrecked cars and fired shots in protest over the latest aggravation perpetrated by Ireland's Westminster rulers.

In Canada, repatriation of thousands of soldiers needing gainful employment continued to be an important public issue. A new order-in-council required that the workforce of shipyards employed under federal contracts had to comprise at least sixty per cent returned soldiers.

Given all the troubles abroad and at home, Victoria hockey fans would have taken heart from their team's second home game of the season on January 2, a convincing 7-4 win by Lester Patrick's Aristocrats over brother Frank's Millionaires. The *Colonist* paid kudos to the brilliant work of Wilf Loughlin, "whose beautifully expert stickhandling proved an insoluble puzzle to the Vancouver defence." The twenty-three-year-old Loughlin may have been brilliant, but it was one of the old guys, Tommy Dunderdale, who made the game's biggest splash. For years, Dunderdale had been a dependable twenty-goal scorer in the PCHA, but in 1918–19, at age thirty-one, his output had shrunk to just five goals in Victoria's twenty games. On January 2, Dunderdale turned back time and somehow became the Tommy of old: he scored four goals, boosting his league-leading total to seven in just three games. Not even Cyclone Taylor had been so prolific in the early going.

On January 9 a goaltender's duel unfolded at the Patrick Arena. Seattle's Hap Holmes already had three Stanley Cups to his credit, and a place in the Hockey Hall of Fame was in his future, but on this occasion Holmes was upstaged by his opposite number. Hec Fowler stopped every Seattle shot on goal and the Aristocrats won, 2-0. Dubbie Kerr satisfied the Victoria crowd that a two-year retirement had not eroded his skills: he scored both Victoria goals.

Tommy Dunderdale continued his revitalized ways. On January 13 Victoria returned to Vancouver, where they took retribution for the defeat inflicted a fortnight before. The Aristocrats won, 4-3, the same score by which they had lost in late December. Dunderdale was again a star of the show. He was "sensational" as the *Colonist* saw it, and scored a goal despite the inconvenience of a bad cut across the forehead that required five stitches.

On January 22, ex-Aristocrat Charley Tobin scored the first goal in Seattle's 3-1 home-ice win over Victoria. The victory left all three

PCHA teams with matching 4-4 records. A better result came out of Victoria's next game, a 4-1 win against Vancouver two days later at the Epworth arena.

Citing "spectacular stickhandling, and some of the best team work any Coast team has ever shown," the *Colonist* described the Aristocrats' performance as "brilliant." Tommy Dunderdale scored two more goals and assisted on a third by Wilf Loughlin, thereby increasing his scoring-race lead over Cyclone Taylor. Now thirty-six, Lester Patrick was devoting himself more to managing and coaching than playing, but on this evening he took to the ice again—and shone. Patrick "several times made one of his old-time rushes up the ice." The victory pushed the Aristocrats into first place, at least for the time being.

Elsewhere in the *Colonist*, there were items to absorb readers who did not count themselves hockey fans. In 1920, just as there was a sports page, there was also a women's section in Victoria's newspaper of record. A feature of the women's page was a regular column, "Taming My Husband," in which one Kathleen Fox sought to offer women humorous, whimsical advice on the best ways of ensuring that their spouses were compliant, cheerful, and more easily managed.

The *Colonist* kept readers reliably informed of the troubles in Ireland, Turkish atrocities in Armenia, and agitation by London "reds" to persuade their countrymen that the Soviet example was the model to follow in Britain. But the *Colonist* offered solace too. Vaudeville fans could go to the Pantages to see Prince Joveddah de Rajah, India's most distinguished "Seer in Telepathy and Occult Science" give a most remarkable demonstration "in which questions are answered in connection with your past, present or future, in business or love." With the assistance of Princess Olga, Prince Joveddah offered a special matinee the following Friday for ladies only.

Over at the Princess Theatre, children and adults who had not been able to get tickets for the scheduled run of *Alice in Wonderland* could capitalize on one of three extra performances. This "most delicious of all pantomimes" was a surefire tonic for the world's chronic skepticism, the Princess vouched.

How many *Colonist* readers were lured by an ad placed by the manufacturers of the famous Marmola prescription, which promised that users could eat candy but miraculously shed weight without telltale wrinkles or flabbiness to show where the fat had come off.

In hockey news out of Winnipeg, the *Colonist* reported that a series was to be organized for the benefit of the widow and children of Joe Hall, the Montreal Canadien who had played his last game in Seattle the previous March.

A front-page story in the *Colonist* of January 24 reported that the city had been rocked by an earthquake at 11:10 the previous night. The quake "created great excitement" in theatres and restaurants, sending patrons into the streets. Opinion was divided over the cause: was it really an earthquake, or was it a big explosion at the James Island munitions plant? The *Colonist* did not report a seismic reading for the very good reason that Charles Richter had yet to invent it—that would not happen until 1935.

On January 26, another big Vancouver crowd, six thousand strong, paid to see the latest installment in the Victoria–Vancouver hockey rivalry. The game turned out to be one that Don Cherry might have celebrated in one of his "Rock 'em Sock 'em" segments.

Tommy Dunderdale and Vancouver's Jack Adams—another future Hall of Famer—had vexed each from the opening faceoff, but in the third period the gloves came off and the combatants went toe to toe, which led to more generalized mayhem. One of the men on the ice, big Ernie "Moose" Johnson, surprised the *Colonist* observer by *not* joining in the general mayhem. Ordinarily no shrinking violet, Moose "lamped the action"—stayed out of it—and turned pacifist, retiring to the dressing room. Eddie Oatman felt no such compunction. When referee Mickey Ion attempted to pour oil on troubled waters, Oatman's left hook landed squarely on Ion's nose.

Assaulting a referee is something that simply does not happen in our time, but a hundred years ago hockey mores were different.

Dunderdale, Adams, and Oatman were all ejected; Oatman was "taxed" twenty-five dollars for the left hook. Vancouver won the game, 7-5.

He could have no premonition of it in 1920, but Ion was also destined to be honoured by a plaque in the Hockey Hall of Fame. He has the distinction of having been referee-in-chief of two major professional leagues, both the PCHA and the NHL. He was inducted into the referees' wing of the Hockey Hall of Fame in 1961, when he was still alive and spry enough to enjoy the tribute.

On January 30, the Aristocrats lost again, this time at home to Seattle, 4-2. By contrast to the January 26 donnybrook in Vancouver, this was a tranquil affair: Ion didn't have to call a single penalty. Five days later, February 4, in a return engagement in Seattle, the Aristocrats made it three losses in a row, shut out by the Metropolitans, 3-0. Frank Foyston was once again the hero for Seattle: "the Flash" scored twice, narrowing Tommy Dunderdale's lead in the individual scoring race.

Lester Patrick provided some consolation for Victoria fans. The man who would come to be known as "the Silver Fox" was back on the ice. "The old Roman was a wonder on defence," the *Colonist* reported, "and if the visitors had displayed the pepper of the veteran skipper, the Mets would have had a tougher evening." Patrick was the star for Victoria, injury notwithstanding. After sustaining a badly cut lip and another wound to the cheek, Lester called it a night.

Meanwhile, in developments not covered in the *Colonist*'s sports section, human conflict continued to draw headlines. In Russia, the Bolsheviks made gains against their capitalist enemies, closing in on the Ukrainian city of Odessa. In Berlin the Reich Finance Minister, Matthias Erzberger, survived an assassin's bullet—this time. One of the signatories of the 1918 Armistice, Erzberger was reviled as a traitor by German right-wingers. While the assassination attempt in January failed, another the following year did not: the assassins succeeded in August 1921, as Erzberger savoured the serenity of a walk in the woods.

Once a citizen of Victoria—and commander of the Canada Corps—Arthur Currie was back in the news. On February 2, the *Colonist* reported that Sir Arthur had said no thanks to urgings that he offer to take over as leader of Robert Borden's Unionist coalition. Later in January the *Colonist* reported that a new Currie oil portrait by a promising artist, Nora Raine Southwell, would be displayed in the city.

In local news, the not-yet-built Johnson Street Bridge continued to draw headlines. City councillors considered construction options that ratepayers could afford. Pursuing subliminal influence, the *Colonist* slipped shorthand messaging into the sports section: "We have talked Johnson Street Bridge for a quarter of a century—let's build it."

In early February, the *Colonist* reported that the convention of BC boards of trade had approved resolutions calling on the provincial government to ban "Orientals or undesirable aliens" from being allowed to own land.

Just a few days later, the Conservative member for South Okanagan, Mr. James William Jones, stood in BC Legislature to support the motto "British Columbia for the white race." The Honourable Mr. Jones called on the provincial government to demand that Ottawa seek authority to restrict or exclude "Oriental" labourers and artisans from Canada. Mr. Jones was re-elected by the voters of South Okanagan when he stood again later that year, and again in 1924 and 1928.

Debt-averse voters might have been alarmed by a February 8 *Colonist* report that as a consequence of the war, federal debt had ballooned to $1.9 billion, a little more than $200 per capita. How appalled would Canadians of 1920 be at what has happened since? The figure has grown to some $768 billion, well over $20,000 per capita.

By February 9, the Aristocrats' season record had fallen to 5-8—three games in the red. For the fourth time that season, the team travelled to Vancouver to take on the Millionaires. Victoria won, 3-2, Oatman scoring twice, Dunderdale once. But in the *Colonist*'s account of the game, the Victoria hero was the ancient Lester

Patrick. Not only did the Victoria boss "infuse his protégés with pep throughout the game, but his work was a revelation to the younger fry on the ice." When the final whistle blew, Patrick's stick "went skyrocketing in the air," propelled by Lester's exultation.

Four days later, the Aristocrats brought their season record to 7-8 with a 6-1 thrashing of Seattle at the Epworth Street rink. Victoria Skates Rings Round League Leaders, bragged the *Colonist* headline the next morning. Dunderdale scored three of the Victoria goals, Oatman two. The paper credited Patrick too, for the effective team work the Aristocrats displayed.

Despite his three goals, the *Colonist* chastised Dunderdale for being more concerned about padding his own scoring numbers than getting his teammates involved. A meeting between Bobby Rowe's stick and Harry Meeking's forehead delivered Meeking a nasty cut. As the Victoria rookie left the ice in search of sticking plaster, Mickey Ion, the referee, took exception to the injured player's "unparliamentarily language" and fined him ten dollars. Otherwise, Ion had a fairly easy night: he didn't call a single penalty.

As Harry Meeking brooded over the injury of a nasty cut compounded by the insult of a fine, *Colonist* readers could fret about bigger issues. Apart from the foreign enemies seeking to wreck their infant revolution, Russians had to worry about a major typhus outbreak. In Dublin, the British military rounded up several members of Sinn Fein in their ongoing campaign to foil those agitating for an independent Irish republic. In London, Conservative House leader Bonar Law argued that protecting the Christian races being massacred in Armenia was one of the most vital subjects the leaders attending the Versailles peace conference needed to confront.

A small item in the February 10 issue of the *Colonist* reflected that memorializing Canadians who had been lost in the war was a matter of growing importance. The Royal Architectural Institute of Canada had met at the Chateau Laurier in Ottawa to discuss building national memorials in already-mythic battlefields such as Passchendaele, St. Julien, Courcelette, and Bourlon Wood, among others. Architects and artisans would have plenty of work to do in the years ahead: over the ensuing decade, thousands of war memorials would be designed and installed in communities from one end of Canada to the other.

Closer to home, the question of how to deal with the flood of returned soldiers continued to worry politicians. BC Premier "Honest John" Oliver took pains to assert that the financial burden of resettlement was Ottawa's, not Victoria's.

Hockey fans continued to seek respite in troublesome times by enjoying the successes of their Aristocrat hockey heroes. Inevitably there were disappointments. Just five days after their resounding win over Seattle, the Metropolitans turned the tables on their Victoria adversaries. On February 18, the Mets scored a convincing 6-0 victory in the comfort of their downtown home. The teams played to a scoreless draw through two periods and then the Aristocrats were buried in an avalanche of goals.

The *Colonist* called the game the roughest of the season. Two former Aristocrats, Jim Riley and Charley Tobin, delivered most of the damage. Not only did he score three of Seattle's goals, but Riley—"a chip on his shoulder all through the battle"—was a relentless intimidator, too. After being tripped by Dunderdale, Riley "lunged at Tommy's attic." Riley—"the Long Irishman"—somehow found a way to score three goals despite fifteen minutes of penalty time.

The rough stuff continued two days later in Victoria. In the final period, Dunderdale and Vancouver's Gordon Roberts "got into a fracas." To punish Tommy for a slash across the legs, Roberts landed "a sequence of uppercuts" to Dunderdale's head. In the *Colonist*'s view, it was Roberts who had the best of the exchange, but in addition to tossing Dunderdale for the rest of the game, Mickey Ion fined him ten dollars. Roberts suffered only a ten-minute penalty. Happily for the hometown fans, Victoria won the game, 3-1.

Roberts, another future Hall of Famer, had a telling nickname, "Doc." In addition to his hockey talents, he was a surgeon and pediatrician. While playing for the Montreal Wanderers of the NHA from 1910 to 1916, Roberts had multi-tasked, managing to earn a degree in medicine from McGill University. After his playing days were done, Dr. Roberts went on to a forty-year career in medicine.

On February 23, the Millionaires took a measure of revenge and a good deal more in a 10-4 rout of the Aristocrats on their own Denman Street ice. Roberts, clearly as skilled at scoring goals as he was at landing uppercuts, scored three Vancouver goals and assisted on a fourth.

Four nights later, the Aristocrats remedied their aggravation in a 3-2 win at home against Seattle. The *Colonist*'s witness called it the most sensational game of the season. It was also the only home game of the year settled in overtime. Jim Riley seemed in a sour mood once again. After objecting to a slash from Riley, Harry Meeking "squared off and went at it with his fists." Mickey Ion sent them both off for the rest of the game and fined them twenty-five dollars to boot. Dunderdale managed to stay out of penalty trouble: he scored the game's first goal and its last, in the eighth minute of overtime. Final score: Victoria 3, Seattle 2.

On March 3, the *Colonist*'s hockey writer reached new hyperbolic heights as the Aristocrats contested "the greatest game of the 1920 season" in Seattle. Lester Patrick's crew "came down from the north with fire in their eyes" and battled Seattle in the "roughest, toughest, fightingest sixty minutes" anyone had seen in years. Alas for Victoria, the fightingest game ended in a 2-0 loss, both Seattle goals scored by former Aristocrats Tobin and Riley. But with two games left to play, the good news was that Victoria still had a chance to reach the league's championship playoff.

On March 5, the Aristocrats did what they had to: they won their final home game of the season, 3-2 over Vancouver. The *Colonist* delivered its game report under the headline ARISTOCRATS SCORE A SPLENDID VICTORY. Once more, the scoring was dominated by Eddie Oatman and Tommy Dunderdale. Oatman scored twice, Dunderdale once. There was one last fight to report, too. Retaliating for a blow to the head from the stick of Doc Roberts, Harry Meeking was sent off for three minutes at a crucial point of the game, but the Aristocrats weathered the storm.

Splendid though the game had been, not all the on-ice thrills in this final home game were delivered by the players. "Fancy" skating—the sort we know today as ice dance—was a regular feature of game intermissions. On March 5, the audience gave loud applause to the fancy-skating champions of Alberta, Miss Mary McHugh and her brother Harold of Calgary.

Needing one more win for a shot at the playoff, the Aristocrats went to Seattle only to be humbled by the Metropolitans, 5-1. The *Colonist* offered no excuses: Lester Patrick, "the old Roman of the Aristocrats," may have felt that fate had played a cruel trick, but everyone else felt the Seattle victory was deserved.

In a twenty-two-game season, the Aristocrats finished last at 10-12, a game behind Vancouver and two in arrears of Seattle. It might not have comforted Lester Patrick, but Victoria fans could take some consolation that Tommy Dunderdale had pulled off something like a miracle. After a five-goal season the year before, Dunderdale had managed to increase his goals tally more than five-fold. With twenty-six goals and thirty-three points, old Tommy finished first in the scoring parade, four ahead of Frank Foyston and eight better than teammate Eddie Oatman. The great Cyclone Taylor finally seemed mortal: at the old-for-hockey age of thirty-five, infirmities had limited him to just six goals in ten games.

For the third straight year, Victoria was out of the league's playoff, while Seattle and Vancouver were in. In a two-game, total-goal playoff series, both games ended in shutouts, and in both games the fates favoured the visiting team. On March 12, Vancouver won 3-0 in Seattle. Three days later in Vancouver, the Metropolitans saw the Millionaires' three and raised them by three more: Seattle won in a walkover, 6-0.

It was the eastern league's turn to host the Stanley Cup showdown. Between March 22 and April Fool's Day, Seattle played the NHL champion Ottawa Senators five times. The games were supposed to have been played in Ottawa, but the Senators' home rink, Dey's Arena, did not have artificial ice. When unseasonably warm weather left the ice too soft for hockey, the series shifted to Toronto.

Seattle lost the first two games, then won the next two. None of the first four games had been a blowout. The teams played the fifth and final game of the best-of-five series at Toronto's Mutual Street Arena. Seattle's bright light was the one easily predicted: Frank Foyston scored six of Seattle's eleven goals in the series, but Frank Nighbor—the same Frank Nighbor who had played two seasons for Frank Patrick in Vancouver, 1913–15—also had six, and his teammate Jack Darragh another five. Ottawa won the final game convincingly, 6-1. For the second time in six seasons, the Senators were Stanley Cup champions.

Back in Victoria, Lester Patrick may have fallen into a funk after one more losing season. His mood would have lifted had he known that before another season began, he would persuade an Icelandic Canadian to come to Victoria, a man who would prove to be the greatest among all the players who wore a Victoria sweater in the years of the Pacific Coast Hockey Association.

TEN

1920-21

GOLD MEDALLIST
COMES TO TOWN

I N THE YEAR 1920, the officials authorized to determine such matters awarded the Olympic Games to Belgium. The decision was motivated in part to make amends for the suffering inflicted on the Belgian people by the calamity of the Great War. There, of course, had been *no* Olympics Games four years earlier: the 1916 Games, scheduled for Berlin, had been cancelled because the nations that might have played games were instead distracted in a collaborative effort to annihilate one other.

In 1920 the losing side in the war—Germany, Austria, Hungary, the Ottoman Empire, Bulgaria—were banished by the side that had won. The 1920 Games were the first featuring the Olympic Oath, the first to release a large flock of doves to symbolize peace, the first to fly the Olympic Flag. There was another first of particular consequence to Canadians: the first Games to include ice hockey. Seven nations participated in the hockey event: Belgium, Czechoslovakia, France, Sweden, Switzerland, the United States—and Canada.

The opening round of the hockey tournament exposed a power imbalance. The winning nations outscored the losers in the quarterfinal games by an aggregate 52-0 score. Sweden beat the host Belgians 8-0. Canada walloped the Czechs 15-0, and the

Americans—several of whom were Canadian-born players who had honed their talents in Canada—humiliated the Swiss by 29-0, a scoring rate of a goal every two minutes or so. Things got tighter in the semifinal round: the Swedes blanked the French, 4-0, while the Canadians edged their American friends, 2-0. Thus far in the tournament, the losing sides had failed to score a single goal. That finally changed in the gold-medal game: Sweden scored once while the victorious Canadian side waltzed to a 12-1 victory.

While the first ice hockey gold medal was Canada's to celebrate, another country could take as much pride in the triumph. All but one of the men on the winning side were sons of immigrants who had come to Canada in the 1890s from the North Atlantic island nation of Iceland. The Canadians' names mirrored their ethnicity, names such as Fridfinnson, Halldorsson, Johannesson, and Friðriksson.

Fair hair and blue eyes notwithstanding, the boys with the odd-sounding names had been victims of discrimination in their hometown, Winnipeg. They ate unfamiliar food, went to a strange church, and spoke English with a distinctive inflection. Because other boys wouldn't play with them, the Icelandic Canadians took to playing hockey among themselves. Soon enough, they were better than anybody else. In 1920, playing together as the Winnipeg Falcons, the first-generation Canadians won the Allan Cup, becoming the best amateur team in the country. Having accomplished that, the Falcons won the right to represent Canada at the Olympics in Antwerp.

The leader of the Canadian side was one Sigurður Franklin Fredrickson. It was Fredrickson who scored seven of the dozen Canadian goals in the gold-medal final game, April 26.

After winning Olympic gold and before returning home, the Canadians travelled to Paris and to the battlefields of the war. For some, it was a return visit. Before winning hockey gold, some of the team had been soldiers in the Canadian Expeditionary Force. One of those was Frank Fredrickson. Initially an infantryman in the 223rd (Canadian Scandinavian) Battalion, at age twenty-one

The 1920 Olympic Games at Antwerp were the first to feature ice hockey. The Canadian team—almost all of them sons of Icelandic immigrants—won the gold medal handily. The team captain and scoring leader was Frank Fredrickson. This is the image attached to the Canadian passport Fredrickson took to the Antwerp Games. AUTHOR'S COLLECTION

he had found time to lead the 223rd team in the 1916–17 season of the Winnipeg Amateur Patriotic League, scoring seventeen goals in just eight games.

Fredrickson transferred to the Royal Flying Corps, where he distinguished himself as a flier, instructor and test pilot. He survived a ship-sinking by German torpedo. He survived an airplane crash, and then another. He came through. After the Olympics he went to the land of his forebears to spend the summer of 1920 introducing Icelanders to the joy of flying.

After his Icelandic adventure, Fredrickson was at a crossroads. At age twenty-five, what was he to do next? He was considering a career as a military pilot when an entrepreneur named Lester Patrick reached out to offer him $2,500 to play a season of professional hockey with the Victoria Aristocrats. Fredrickson mulled it over, but perhaps not for long. He said yes to Patrick's offer. It was a momentous decision for the gold medallist and for Lester Patrick too.

Two days before Christmas, the afternoon *Victoria Daily Times* published a sports-page item under the headline Fredrickson's Signing Real Christmas Present. "Happy as a school boy just released on his Christmas holidays," an exultant Lester Patrick was quoted as promising that Fredrickson would be a great acquisition. "He has everything in his favour, youth, speed, stick-handling, a wicked shot and great ability to penetrate a defence." In his ardour to persuade Victoria fans that in Fredrickson they could look forward to a "stocking-full" of happy hockey news, the boss perhaps went a little overboard. The *Times* gushed about Fredrickson's "brilliant war record" in France, where he "saw much fighting with the scouts."

The facts were not quite so glorious. The life expectancy of a frontline fighter pilot having been something in the neighbourhood of two weeks, Fredrickson's Royal Air Force commanders felt they could make better use of his abilities by making him a test pilot and flying instructor, and it was out of an air base in Scotland, not France, that Flight Lieutenant Fredrickson did his RAF duty. The *Times* got one more thing wrong: the image of Fredrickson accompanying the piece was not of "Freddie" at all but his good friend and Winnipeg Falcon teammate Konnie Jóhannesson.

The arrangement to have Fredrickson play in Victoria was not consummated until late in 1920. Between December 22 and December 27, without Fredrickson, the Aristocrats played their first three games of the new season. They lost them all. The first game was a 7-2 drubbing at the hands of Seattle. The *Daily Colonist*'s hockey writer critiqued the home team for being in poor physical condition and for "carrying much surplus poundage." Only one

Aristocrat was credited: thirty-five-year-old Moose Johnson, "who has been playing hockey since the fall of Quebec," was a tower of strength.

The Victorians lost again to Seattle on Christmas Day, 4-3, and to Vancouver on December 27. In that game the Millionaires had taken a 2-0 lead into the third period when Lester Patrick, now thirty-seven, decided to insinuate himself into the action. The appearance of "the skilled general brought cheers of approval from the spectators," but it was not enough; Victoria fell, 6-3. The final paragraph of the *Colonist* dispatch must have loaded more than a little pressure on the new arrival: there is no doubt, the *Colonist* observed, that the arrival of the Falcons star "will give the Aristocrats just what is needed."

Apart from the addition of the gold medallist, Patrick took a stand-pat approach to the 1920-21 season. Dubbie Kerr retired again—this time for good. Patrick did add a second brother act to the Aristocrats roster, to go along with the Loughlins. Harry Meeking's brother, Gord, who had played with Eddie Oatman for the NHA 228th Battalion team in 1917, joined his younger brother in Victoria; he had only a slight impact, however, scoring just a single goal in his nine games as an Aristocrat. It would turn out to be the elder Meeking's only season in Victoria.

Frank Fredrickson reached Victoria in time to play the first game of his professional career on New Year's Day 1921. With his new team trailing by 3-1 in the third period, Fredrickson scored on a pass from Oatman to make it 3-2 and then set up his boss, Patrick, for the tying goal. The Aristocrats scored two more to make it 5-3, their first victory of the season. Who felt more exultant, Fredrickson or Patrick?

Victoria narrowly lost its next game, on January 5 in Seattle, by 2-1 in overtime. "Reinforced by the services of Frank Fredrickson," the *Colonist* reported, the Aristocrats looked a different team from the one that started the season. They were unlucky to lose.

Another close game followed on January 7 at Victoria's Epworth Street home base. The Aristocrats turned the tables on Seattle, blanking the Metropolitans, 2-0. "The star of the game was easily Fredrickson." the *Colonist* reported, "and the big skipper of the Olympic champions was doing two men's work... and could give several of the old professional veterans a lesson or two on team work and unselfishness."

In the new year, as Frank Fredrickson made his initial impressions on the fans of the Victoria Aristocrats, larger events took up column space in the pages of the Victoria *Daily Colonist*. In Brussels, delegates met to sort out details of the reparations Germany and its Central Powers allies would have to pay in war damages. In Korea, under Japanese rule since 1910, allegations were made that the Japanese were using terrorism as one of their administrative tools. But the big international story as seen by *Colonist* editors was the ongoing, increasingly bloody conflict in Ireland, where Republicans resorted to violence to bring about their dream of independence—and the British employed violence of their own to resist them.

The Dublin Easter Uprising of 1916 had led to the execution of fourteen nationalists in May that year. Rather than suppressing nationalist fervour, the executions inflamed it. Almost every day during the 1920–21 PCHA hockey season, the *Colonist* published front-page stories about the ongoing violence in Ireland. The *Colonist*'s editors left no doubt as to whose side they were on. In dispatches about events in Dublin and elsewhere, the *Colonist* described the Republicans as "thugs," "fiends," and "murderers."

In more mundane matters at home, the Victoria daily reported on a civic issue that appears to have been as significant a century ago as it is in our own time. As the new year approached, the *Colonist* reported that Victoria city council was set to embark on an ambitious program of sewer improvements. Then, as now, city council wanted senior governments to help pay the cost, but one of the city's motivations was unique to the post-war period: the project would provide work for returned soldiers and other unemployed men.

On December 24, a Christmas party was held at Craigdarroch Castle. At the time, Craigdarroch was not the tourist attraction it is today but the home of maimed, sick, and "bedfast" soldiers. "That the generous heart still beats, and the sacrifices of the war years are not forgotten" was proven, the *Colonist* reported, by the numerous gifts bestowed on the bedridden soldiers. One of the kind women on hand to support the event was Mrs. Bobby Genge, spouse of the rugged Victoria defenceman who had played hockey throughout the war and thus managed to avoid the damage afflicting the men at Craigdarroch.

Despite the presence of the golden Icelander in the Victoria lineup, the Aristocrats lost another three in a row between January 10 and January 19. The first two were close, the third a blowout at the hands of the Metropolitans in Seattle.

In the January 10 game, at Vancouver, Victoria lost to the Millionaires, 5-3. In just his fourth PCHA game, Fredrickson was already a major draw, not just in his own rink but on the road too: eight thousand customers paid to see his Denman Arena debut. "Not since the never-to-be-forgotten night when Cyclone Taylor broke in," the *Colonist* reported, "has any individual player received a reception equal to that accorded to Frank Fredrickson." The *Colonist* called it the speediest, most exciting game of the young season, and from the beginning "sixteen thousand eyes were glued on the big man from the champion Falcons." The Millionaires' Mickey MacKay vied with Fredrickson for first-star recognition, but Fredrickson outscored his fellow future Hall of Famer by two goals to one.

TOUGH LUCK! began the *Colonist* account of the Aristocrats' January 14 game in their home rink. "Outskated, outgeneraled and outplayed" in the first period and a half, the Vancouver Millionaires resorted to rough stuff, as the *Colonist* saw it. Weather-beaten Tommy Dunderdale had entered the game and "treated the fans to some of his old bursts. Dunderdale outmaneuvered Old Eagle Eyes, Vancouver goaltender Hugh Lehman—another player destined for the Hockey Hall of Fame—on a goal the *Colonist* called a "beauty." Soon after, Dunderdale was laid out on the ice with nasty cuts about the face. A donnybrook erupted at this point, a costly one for Victoria. Referee Mickey Ion sent Lester Patrick off for ten minutes and

Eddie Oatman for the rest of the game. Dunderdale re-entered the fray "with his face all done up in plaster." Lehman was the man of the hour for Vancouver, "stopping shots rained on him by Fredrickson, Oatman," et al. Wilf Loughlin scored twice for Victoria, one on an assist from Fredrickson, but it was not enough; Vancouver won, 4-3.

The next game was something else entirely. Victoria took the ferry to Seattle, where the Metropolitans had them for lunch by a 9-2 score. The *Colonist* called it a "rampage." Almost everyone on the Seattle side participated in the deluge. Old foes Frank Foyston, with three goals, and Bernie Morris, with two, led the way in the Aristocrats' humiliation. Fredrickson set up Wilf Loughlin for a pretty goal, and the new man "looked just as good as ever tonight despite the terrific beating his team was taking." In spite of Fredrickson's artistry, the Aristocrats went into their next game with an ugly 2-7 season record.

The United States had joined the Great War in 1917. Though he was Canadian, Bernie Morris had earned his livelihood in Seattle for two years, so the American authorities eventually called on the Canadian hockey player to set aside skates and hockey stick and take up arms as a soldier in the American Expeditionary Force. Bernie Morris demurred. He missed parts of two hockey seasons for the very good reason that by 1918, he was a resident of the infamous federal prison on Alcatraz Island in San Francisco Bay. That was Bernie's reward for evading the US military draft. He served his sentence, then resumed his hockey career. His experience at Alcatraz might have soured Bernie on west-coast charms but, no, Morris resumed his career where it had left off, in Seattle.

Back in the comfort of their Oak Bay bailiwick, the Aristocrats redeemed themselves January 21. "No better hockey has been seen in the league this season," the *Colonist* reported in its next-day account. Wilf Loughlin scored the opener for Victoria just sixty-five seconds into the action, but it was Frank Fredrickson who managed all the Victoria scoring thereafter. Fredrickson collected an authentic hat trick—three straight goals—two of which were aided by Dunderdale, the third accomplished all by himself.

The game was not one of the friction-free variety. When Fredrickson and the Millionaires' Alf Skinner were "invited to take a seat" by referee Mickey Ion, "the good-natured Icelander was retiring to the bench without arguing the matter when Skinner took a crack at him." A fan objected to Skinner's conduct and "took action" against him, whereupon Skinner's teammate, Jack Adams, started in slashing at the spectators. Such conduct—assaulting the paying customers—is unthinkable in our time but was not unheard of a century ago.

Other sports competed with hockey for attention under the *Colonist*'s Sporting News banner. Basketball, boxing, soccer, rugby, tennis, billiards, and badminton all took turns in the spotlight. In its January 22 edition the *Colonist* reported on another sporting event that must have attracted readers' attention. The ladies' section of the Sixteenth Canadian Scottish shooting team had accepted a challenge from the young men of the Winchester Junior Rifle Corps—and won. Miss Dover and Miss Richardson were particularly invincible in the spoon shot.

As always, there was no shortage of amusements other than hockey to entertain the city's cultivated population. Long before television—or even radio—competed for attention, Victoria's several theatres offered the best in modern screen and live attractions. One could choose live vaudeville at the Pantages, or *In Walked Jimmy* at the Princess. Five theatres competed for moviegoers' dollars. On January 22, options included *Shipwrecked Among Cannibals* at the Columbia, *Blackmail* at the Dominion, *Dr. Jekyll and Mr. Hyde* at the Romano, or *The Amateur Wife*, starring Irene Castle, at the Variety. The greatest excitement might have been reserved for the great Anna Pavlova and her Ballet Russe, scheduled for a return engagement—one night only—at the Royal, January 24.

The *Daily Colonist* continued to keep readers informed of contentious events in the larger world. Virtually every day, the Victoria daily delivered its slant on events in Ireland. The *Colonist* delighted in the news that a planned Sinn Fein attack on the Tower of London had been thwarted. On January 8 the paper reported that the toll of those slain in 1920 by "Irish thugs" had reached 261, including 165 policemen, 53 British soldiers, and 43 civilians. The editors did not disclose the number of Republicans killed in the same period, but on January 22 the *Colonist* reported that a police ambush had yielded one Republican wounded and six captured.

Disputes on a lesser scale occurred in Canada, too. On January 22, the newspaper informed readers that unemployed men were making trouble in Montreal. A restaurant had been "stormed" by unemployed ex-servicemen as demonstrations erupted in various parts of the city. By police order the headquarters of the unemployed servicemen was shut down for an afternoon. A city official blamed the disorder on "an undesirable element . . . many of them with Bolsheviki ideas."

In 1920–21, famine devastated China. Among the agencies looking to provide relief for the stricken Chinese was the local Victoria branch of the YMCA. The organization launched a drive aimed at raising fifty thousand dollars for Chinese relief. In its January 21 edition, the *Colonist* reported on a resolution passed by the local branch of Veterans of France. The former soldiers protested the YMCA initiative on the basis that since "charity begins at home," the YMCA should direct its benevolence to helping unemployed former soldiers who are "suffering from distress, and, in some cases, in actual want."

The resolution may not have achieved the results its advocates wanted: several days later, the YMCA reported that its kindness campaign was making good progress.

Meanwhile, provincial fruit growers, gathered in convention at Nelson, endorsed a resolution calling on the Dominion Government to place severe limits on the ability of Asians and "Orientals" to own land in British Columbia. Such limits were necessary, supporters of the resolution argued, to ensure "that during such a time of unemployment, nothing should be thrown in the way of our own citizens."

Though it had ended more than two years earlier, the war continued to cast shadows. A story out of New York told of a man, Daniel P. Sullivan, appearing in court to face a charge of "soliciting alms"—panhandling. On being sentenced, Mr. Sullivan, "homeless and overcoatless" in the New York winter, asked whether he might say a few words. The alms solicitor approached the bench and explained in a whisper that he had not previously been a beggar or someone caught up in the toils of the law. "I begged for a few cents," he said, so that he could have a bite and a place to sleep before going over to Staten Island for a job in the morning. The magistrate asked what was wrong with his voice. The man explained that he had been gassed and wounded while serving as a soldier in the Canadian Expeditionary Force. He had come to New York for work, but no one would hire him. The magistrate clearly had a heart: he suspended the sentence and then proffered some bills to Mr. Sullivan. The defendant wouldn't take them—until it was agreed that the money was a loan.

A story under an Ottawa dateline addressed a matter less weighty than bloodshed in Ireland or mass starvation in China or poverty on the streets of New York. Rather, it was one that revealed more than a little about the tenor of the times in Canada. The item, just three paragraphs long, reported that some citizens of the national capital were offended that a woman "old enough to know better" had appeared on a principal Ottawa street wearing a daringly cut-away skirt "exposing her knees."

Inspector McLaughlin of the city's morality squad disappointed complainants by pointing out the absence of any law barring such exposure. The inspector doubtlessly frustrated more than a few by stipulating that "as long as her body was covered," no woman could be arrested for baring her knees. This was early 1921; skirt lengths would rise higher as the Roaring Twenties progressed, no doubt scandalizing the upright folks who felt that Inspector McLaughlin was not trying hard enough to deal with shameless flappers.

As the good folks of Ottawa fretted about skirt lengths, the Victoria Aristocrats took to the ice again on January 24 before another big crowd in Vancouver. With more than eight thousand in attendance this time, spectators were treated to a game said to be the fastest of the season. Cyclone Taylor, now thirty-six and near the end of his glorious run in Vancouver, "was given a tremendous reception by the fans." In the second period, Taylor and Fredrickson staged a pas de deux for the puck. "For several breathless seconds, the two held the fans motionless while they circled and stickhandled with rare skill." On this occasion, it was old age and treachery that prevailed: "Taylor escaped and carried out one of his sensational rushes." Vancouver won this chapter of the Millionaires–Aristocrats rivalry, 5-2, but Fredrickson only embellished his brand: he scored both Victoria goals.

On January 27, the Aristocrats savoured payback against the Seattle Metropolitans for the ignominy the Mets had visited upon them nine days earlier. "Easily the best hockey of the season," the *Colonist* pronounced in the next day's issue. Apart from the blood-thirsty minority who prefer the rough stuff, the Victoria crowd appreciated "the cleanest and headiest hockey played here this season." Seattle's defenders checked Fredrickson closely but the attention devoted to "the big Icelander" worked to the advantage of the veterans Dunderdale and Oatman, who teamed up to score two of the Victoria goals in a 5-3 win.

The Aristocrats won another against the Mets, February 2, in Seattle. On goals by Fredrickson and Dunderdale, the Aristocrats were tied 2-2 at the end of regulation time. It took more than a period and a half of extra time before Fredrickson set up Wilf Loughlin for the winning goal in the twelfth minute of the second overtime period. Luck was a factor in the Victoria win, as Seattle's ace, Foyston, did not play due to injury. The game "waxed exceedingly rough," according to the next-day *Colonist* dispatch. Usually mild-mannered Bobby Rowe, the ex-Aristocrat, aimed "a mean smack at Tommy Dunderdale's turret." The referee, Mickey Ion, assessed a flurry of penalties but "a lot of the necktie checking" escaped Ion's trained eye.

Their second straight win brought the Aristocrats a little closer to evening their win–loss record, but in this see-saw season, bad fortune followed good; on February 4, they lost to the Millionaires at home and again, three days later, in Vancouver. The February 4 game began with Mickey Ion laying down the law: the referee wanted good clean hockey to be the main attraction for paying customers, not violence and mayhem. The referee's instructions may have mattered, a little. As Ion was looking elsewhere, Mickey MacKay took a slam at Fredrickson's back, and "sundry little pokes and jabs" went unnoticed. Fredrickson was at his best: the fans "fairly shrieked with delight" at a display of skating and stickhandling foiled only by Lehman's expert goaltending. The Icelander scored the game's first goal and choreographed another by Dunderdale. Wilf Loughlin added a third, but three were not enough: Vancouver won, 4-3.

The seven thousand fans attending the February 7 game in Vancouver "got more than their money's worth" as the Aristocrats and Millionaires "battled through three of the fastest, cleanest periods which have been staged this season." The *Colonist* lauded Fredrickson, Oatman, and Johnson as all being in their best form. But the Millionaires were clearly in good form too: they won, 5-2, with Fredrickson and Oatman scoring one apiece for Victoria.

One of the Vancouver scorers was Art Duncan. The six-foot-one-inch native of Sault Ste. Marie, Ontario, had something other than hockey talent in common with Frank Fredrickson. They both would have long careers as players before proceeding to shorter ones as NHL coaches. They could both legitimately claim to have had worthy service as airmen in the Great War. Fredrickson was a sufficiently talented flier and communicator that his commanders agreed his best role was as test pilot and flying instructor. The officers decided that air warrior was the better fit in Duncan's case. Though he would never make it to the Hockey Hall of Fame, as Fredrickson would, Duncan was decorated for gallantry and is one 194 Canadians who earned the status of flier ace in the war—men credited with at least five victories over enemy fliers in aerial warfare. As mentioned earlier, Duncan flew the Royal Aircraft Factory

SE5a, one of several machines Fredrickson flew while based at Gullane, Scotland, during the war.

Two victories followed two losses for the Aristocrats. On February 11, at home, Victoria hung a 3-1 defeat on Seattle. The fans warmly welcomed the Metropolitans when they skated onto the home ice. In contrast to the Millionaires of Vancouver, the Mets typically played "good clean hockey." The lads from Seattle lived up to their reputation: Mickey Ion didn't have to call a single penalty, not one. It was "fine, scientific hockey all the way," two "almost equally perfect machines opposed to each other." Fredrickson delighted the crowd whenever he got the puck. The two Franks—Fredrickson for Victoria, Foyston for Seattle—each scored goals in the first period. The first, by Victoria's Frank, came on a pass from Wilf Loughlin to the Icelander, "who whipped it in like a flash of lightning." Foyston's was the only Seattle goal; Victoria won, 3-1.

On February 16 the Aristocrats delivered "the greatest hockey they have ever played in Seattle." The *Colonist* complimented the play of Oatman, Fredrickson, and Meeking, but reserved its highest praise for Moose Johnson, whose work on defence "will go down in the pages of Victoria hockey history." That was just the beginning of the kudos. "If the Moose stopped one Seattle rush at the blue line he stopped a hundred," the *Colonist* enthused. Harry Meeking was no slouch either: he scored three of the Victoria goals in a 4-3 victory.

Other hockey players were in the news February 17. Under the headline LADY PUCKCHASERS ARRANGE SCHEDULE, the *Colonist* reported that arrangements had been finalized for a six-game tournament of ladies' hockey. Teams representing each of the PCHA cities would compete between periods of PCHA games and a further fifteen minutes "after the male puckchasers are finished."

The Aristocrats' one-step-forward, one-step-back habit continued: having won two in a row, the Aristocrats proceeded to lose two more. On February 22 the *Colonist* blamed a combination of bad luck and Hugh Lehman's marvelous goaltending for a 2-0 home-ice loss to the unloved Millionaires of Vancouver. Three nights later, February 21, the first-place Millionaires inflicted more misery on Victoria, this time in their own Denman domain. The Aristocrats played like tigers, the next-day *Colonist* headline asserted, but the tigers came out on the short end of a 5-1 score. With the loss, Victoria's season fell to 7-12; they had a solid grip on last place in the PCHA standings.

If Victoria's sports fans were soured by another Aristocrats defeat, other items reported in the February 22 *Colonist* might have provided distraction. A winter sport other than hockey commanded attention. No professional basketball was played on Canada's west coast in 1921, but plenty of the amateur variety was regularly reported in the Victoria daily. The game scores in the winter of 1921 suggest that basketball of a hundred years ago must have been very different from the modern game. The present-day population of the south-Island community of Jordan River is about a hundred people. Perhaps it was greater in 1921, certainly big enough to support *two* basketball teams. The Jordan River "B" quintet had managed to win a squeaker against Tod Inlet by a score of 13-11, while team "A" walloped Shawnigan Lake by 33 to 13. There was ladies' basketball, too. The V.I. Ladies "B" hoopsters took on the Mothers squad in a strenuous game "greatly appreciated by the numerous spectators." The Mothers won, 18-13.

Meanwhile, back on the ice, the pair of losses led to another pair of wins for the Victoria Aristocrats. On February 24, Victoria once again hosted the Seattle Metropolitans. The Mets' goaltender, Hap Holmes, destined for a place in the Hockey Hall of Fame, was on this occasion bested by Hec Fowler, a man for whom no Hall of Fame plaque awaited. Holmes allowed three Victoria goals—all by Frank Fredrickson—while Fowler was stopping every Seattle shot fired his way.

In a season packed with highlights, the 3-0 victory of February 24 surpassed them all for the Aristocrats' rookie. As "clever and clean as it always is when Seattle comes here," the game began with a gesture beyond imagining in our time. The referee, Mickey Ion, looked forward to his thirty-fifth birthday the following day. Before the opening faceoff, Ion was "duly presented with a birthday cake." The birthday cake safely stowed away, Ion was blessed with an easy night: he only had to call one penalty.

The *Colonist* delivered surpassing praise of Fredrickson's brilliant performance: "he was seen in some phenomenally spectacular play, and the fans were shrieking with delight at the way he outskated, outguessed and outmanoeuvred every Seattle opponent who got in his way." The performance brought Fredrickson level with Vancouver's Fred "Smokey" Harris for the lead in the individual scoring race, each with twenty-four points.

As the Aristocrats looked forward to their next game, the *Colonist* had good news for downtown merchants and shoppers. City council had decided to pave Government Street, with costs to be shared by the BC Electric Railway, operators of the city's streetcar system. Victorians could take pride that only two cities in Canada—neither of them Vancouver—had built streetcar systems before Victoria followed suit in 1890. Paving Government Street would make the city that much more up to date.

On March 2, the Aristocrats did it again: a 3-0 victory over the Mets, this time in Seattle. It was the Victorians' sixth straight victory over Foyston and company. That Fredrickson had impressed hockey fans throughout the PCHA was demonstrated when he was presented with a bouquet of flowers before the puck was dropped. Fredrickson scored the first goal for the visitors, with Oatman and Wilf Loughlin contributing the others.

The Aristocrats' next game, March 4, was one to remember. Ties were not tolerated in the PCHA. If a game was tied at the end of regulation time, teams played as long as necessary to break the tie, but on March 4, something extraordinary happened at the Epworth Street arena. Playing for the third time in a row, the Aristocrats and Metropolitans were tied at 4-4 after sixty minutes. A twenty-minute overtime period resolved nothing. As did a second. And a third. After 120 minutes of playing time, the teams were still knotted at 4-4. It was called off: the game went into the books as a tie.

It was a contest notable, not just for the length of time it took to play, but for another reason too. It was Moose Johnson Night in Victoria, and the big fellow must have been much moved by the praises and prizes awarded him. Moose was given a fine silver cup engraved with the league's assurance that we was the greatest defenceman in its ten-year history. On behalf of "his pals, the kids of Victoria," he was presented with a second silver cup by Lester Patrick. In case that was insufficient proof of the esteem in which he was held, there was more: diamond-encrusted gold cufflinks from the fans, and a handsome bouquet for Mrs. Johnson.

Sports writers are no strangers to hyperbole. If the *Colonist*'s reporter was fulsome in his account of the tributes and treasures bestowed upon Moose Johnson, his counterpart attached to the *Times* pulled out all the stops. "'Moose Johnson Night' will never be forgotten in the history of Victoria," he began. "In the dim and distant future when many of the young nippers who were the 'Moose's' guest last night are bouncing their grand-children upon their knees, this sensational event will be recalled."

With the game finally underway, it was the Mets who found their way in the early going, with goals from Riley and Foyston. Bobby Rowe did what he could to contain Fredrickson, but the big centre managed to set up goals by Oatman and Meeking. Oatman crashed into a goalpost and had to be carried off. With Dunderdale off for a boarding infraction, an unassisted goal by Foyston late in the third period cemented the tie that refused to be broken. Finally, with all the players and perhaps most of the paying clientele exhausted, it was police commissioner Joe North, supplier of Mrs. Johnson's floral bouquet, who decided enough was enough.

The Aristocrats' faint hope of a berth in the post-season playoff came to grief in Vancouver on March 7. Eight thousand people paid to see the final home game of the regular season; hundreds of them had travelled from Victoria. Perhaps buoyed by all the silverware and acclaim bestowed on him three nights earlier, Moose Johnson played a game the *Colonist*'s sports reporter saw as his best ever.

Fredrickson delivered spectacular skating rushes one after another. But it was all for naught. Hugh Lehman, the Hall of Fame goaltender stopped everything wristed his way. The Millionaires won, 5-0.

There was one more game to play, but it was of little consequence. The playoff slots were sorted out: Vancouver and Seattle were in, Victoria was out. With little at stake, the teams didn't bother to play defence in an 11-8 shootout at the Epworth Street rink, Victoria the winner. Cyclone Taylor scored twice for Vancouver, the final goals of his remarkable hockey career.

Perhaps the outcome mattered a little to Smokey Harris and Frank Fredrickson. Locked in a scoring race, each player's mates helped to push their man ahead. Fredrickson had a hat trick—three goals—to go along with two assists for a five-point night. Harris, understanding he'd fallen behind, put a move-on in the final period: he scored a hat trick of his own, and with the assist he'd earned earlier in the game, Smokey had four points for his evening's labours—which meant that the rivals finished the season in a dead heat, with thirty-two points each. Since Fredrickson had five more goals than Harris, his name appears first in the record of the league's leading scorers for 1920-21.

Only one other Aristocrat emerged with a place in the league's top ten scorers. Tommy Dunderdale had led the PCHA scoring parade the year before. This time he slipped from twenty-six goals to just nine. His points total was twenty, twelve in arrears of Fredrickson and Harris. At age thirty-two, were Tommy's best days behind him?

For the fourth year in a row, Seattle and Vancouver squared off for the league championship. The Millionaires had finished first in the regular season, and the two-game, total-goal playoff left no doubt as to which club was the PCHA's best in 1921. Vancouver prevailed, and it wasn't close. The Millionaires won, 13-2.

It was the west's turn to host the Stanley Cup final. The best-of-five series at the Denman Street arena made it clear for all to see that there was little to differentiate the best of NHL talent from the best in the west. The series attracted an audience of ten thousand for every game—a pro hockey record at the time—and went the full five games. Every game was decided by a single goal. On April 4, the Ottawa Senators won, 2-1, both goals scored by future Hall of Famer Jack Darragh. Darragh and mates relished the reward of raising the Cup in victory for the second year in a row.

Lester Patrick might have taken a measure of satisfaction that his prized new player had a share of the league's scoring title—and had boosted ticket sales everywhere he played—but the bottom line was that the Aristocrats had finished last again, just as they had done the year before. They were again mere bystanders while others competed for the Stanley Cup. If the addition of a gold-medallist scoring champion who had taken the PCHA by storm was not enough to lift Victoria out of the PCHA cellar, what would it take?

ELEVEN

1921-22

THE MOOSE DEPARTS

I N THE WINTER of 1921-22, the major professional hockey landscape of western Canada underwent a transformation. When
the nominally amateur Alberta Big-4 Hockey League collapsed
under the weight of accusations that it was amateur in name only,
a new professional league arose out of the Big-4 ashes. It was the
Western Canada Hockey League and comprised four clubs in its
inaugural season, two in Alberta—the Edmonton Eskimos and Calgary Tigers—and two in Saskatchewan—the Capitals of Regina and
Sheiks of Saskatoon. With this development, the number of elite
pro teams in the western reaches of the continent instantly bloomed
from three to seven. Over the next four years, the WCHL would neu-
tralize any doubts that the calibre of hockey it delivered was every
bit the equal of the PCHA and NHL. Given the quality of talent it
attracted from the get-go, it was clear to informed observers that
the new league demanded serious respect.

Among the people paying attention to developments in Alberta
and Saskatchewan was Lester Patrick. The previous winter, 1920-21,
was an aggravating one for the hockey impresario. He had managed
to bring to Victoria a man who would arguably become the greatest
player he ever signed to play for him, one who was an instant star

throughout the league, one who boosted ticket sales whenever and wherever he took to the ice. But the unhappy fact was that despite the presence of Frank Fredrickson in the Victoria lineup, the Aristocrats still finished last in the PCHA, albeit by the slimmest of margins. What could Patrick do to improve the Aristocrats' fortunes in the new season? Well, if one gold medal–winning member of the 1920 Canadian Olympic hockey team could be lured to the far west coast, what if he could persuade another to combine forces with his former teammate? And so it came to pass that a six-foot-three-inch, two hundred-pound collaborator in the gold-medal victory of 1920 joined Frank Fredrickson in Victoria.

He had been born with the name Halldor Halldorsson, but by late 1921, he was more widely known by an anglicized version of his Icelandic name. Harold Halderson—even better known by the nickname "Slim"—was three years younger than Fredrickson. Slim Halderson was twenty-two when he'd won Olympic gold and still just twenty-three when Patrick persuaded him to team up his with his fellow Winnipegger in Victoria. In 1920–21, while Fredrickson was making a big splash on the west coast, Halderson had been one of the leading lights with the Saskatoon Crescents of the Saskatchewan Senior Hockey League.

The amateur Saskatonians were no slouches. One of Slim's Saskatoon teammates was Rusty Crawford, a veteran former professional, who would one day earn a place in the Hockey Hall of Fame. Another was Bobby Benson, one more of the Icelandic–Canadians who had won gold in Antwerp. The Crescents included someone else familiar to long-time fans of the Victoria Aristocrats: Skinner Poulin had played for Lester Patrick from 1911 to 1915 before taking his act to Montreal to skate for the NHA Canadiens and Wanderers in the war years.

Other than the addition of Slim Halderson, Lester Patrick once again took a stand-pat approach to his team's roster. Just one departure offset the addition of Halderson: after seven seasons in Victoria, Bobby Genge finally decided to call it quits at age thirty-one.

As for the wide, wide world beyond Victoria, the *Daily Colonist* continued to keep readers abreast of major international events. Great Britain and the advocates for an Irish republic reached an agreement establishing an "Irish Free State" that conveyed a measure of self-determination equivalent to that enjoyed by the Empire's Canadian, Australian, and South African dominions. But it was not enough to pacify pure-of-heart Republicans, who desired complete independence from Mother Britain. Within a few months a civil war would be raging in Ireland.

The ongoing famine in China was compounded by another mass affliction: an outbreak of yellow fever. Famine raged in the Soviet Union, too, and the *Colonist* delivered regular dispatches on the cruelty and violence visited upon Russians viewed as enemies of the young Soviet regime.

Mohandas K. Gandhi led a campaign for independence in another part of the world. The leader of those aspiring to free India from colonial shackles was himself an advocate of non-violent measures for achieving that goal, but Gandhi was sometimes helpless to deflect some of his fellow nationalists from resorting to more violent means to realize their dream.

Political tides had turned in Canada, too, but they were typically not accompanied by the extremes of behaviour prevailing elsewhere. The day before the new PCHA hockey season got underway, Canadians delivered a resounding "No, thanks" to giving the Conservative government a renewed mandate to run the country. Sir Robert Borden, prime minister from 1911, had stepped down in 1920, replaced by Arthur Meighen. The Conservatives took only 49 of 235 seats in the December 6 election, reducing the Tories to third-party status behind a new affiliation, the Progressives. The distemper of the post-war times was mirrored in the election of small numbers of MPs from several other parties—Labour, Socialist, United Farmers, et al.—harbouring grievances related to conscription, underemployment, workers' rights, votes for women, and other issues many voters felt the Conservatives had failed to adequately address. After ten years in Opposition, a new Liberal leader, forty-seven-year-old Mackenzie King, was the country's new prime minister, the successor to former Liberal Party leader (and earlier prime minister), Wilfrid Laurier.

Important as these larger matters may have been, a segment of Victoria's population was happily distracted by the prospect that not one but two Olympic gold medallists might lead the Victoria Aristocrats to the promised land of a PCHA championship. The new season started on the road December 7, in the downtown Seattle Ice Arena. Slim Halderson wasted no time in establishing that Lester Patrick might have made an astute move in bringing a second Icelander to Victoria. The towering Manitoban scored his first goal as an Aristocrat in the opening period of his first game. Fredrickson followed suit shortly afterward.

Normally appreciated for the clean, non-violent style of hockey they usually played, the Metropolitans—or one of them—deviated from the script in the third period. Often dubbed "the Long Irishman" by the *Colonist* hockey writer, was Jim Riley perhaps out of sorts over events in the old country? Whatever, after the heroics of his rookie season, Frank Fredrickson was now a marked man. Riley cut him down "with a terrific crack across the ankle," and the man the *Colonist* frequently now dubbed "Freddie" had to be carried off the ice. "Men were men" back then, though, and Fredrickson returned in time to watch fellow future Hall of Fame teammate Tommy Dunderdale score the final goal in a 4-1 Aristocrats' victory. It was a fine start to the new season.

Two evenings later the same two teams faced off in a return engagement at Victoria. A new rule came into play. The Patricks had decided that if a full period of extra time failed to resolve a tie, the tie would stand. That is what happened December 9 when both goaltenders—Hec Fowler of Victoria and Hap Holmes of Seattle—distinguished themselves in a 1-1 standoff. But the man singled out by the *Colonist* as the finest performer on the Victoria side was Ernie "Moose" Johnson, the ageless star defenceman.

Two more victories followed, 2-0 in Vancouver on December 12 and 4-3 at home against the Millionaires on December 16. After four games the Aristocrats were undefeated and standing on top of the PCHA leaderboard with a record of three wins, one tie. Optimism must have soared in the heart of Lester Patrick.

A reversal of fortune ensued. At the winter solstice, December 21, Victoria lost narrowly in Seattle, 2-1. The Long Irishman—Riley— scored both Seattle goals, with Fredrickson replying for Victoria. Normal pleasantries set aside, Moose Johnson planted his stick in the ribs of former Aristocrat Bobby Rowe; Rowe reciprocated with stick slashes over Johnson's head. His attention focused elsewhere, referee Mickey Ion missed both violations of peace and fair play.

Lester's lads lost another close one to Seattle, 3-2 in overtime, at home on December 23. Victoria suffered from the absence of team captain Eddie Oatman, out with a wounded foot. That void was perhaps offset by another: league president Frank Patrick had sentenced Rowe to a one-game suspension for the damages inflicted on Moose Johnson's cranium in the previous game. The Icelanders— Fredrickson and Halderson—combined for the tying goal in the third period, but the ever-reliable Flash Foyston won it for Seattle in overtime, 3-2.

The Aristocrats lost twice more to Vancouver over the festive season, 3-2 in Vancouver on Boxing Day, and 5-3 at home, December 30. The *Colonist* called the December 26 game the best of the season, and no one could fault Fredrickson for the result: he scored both Victoria goals. After eight games he led the league's individual scoring parade, but the Aristocrats had tumbled from their lofty first-place perch to a 3-4-1 losing record as the new year beckoned.

As the second year of the 1920s made way for the third, the Victoria *Daily Colonist* endeavoured to balance its coverage of starvation, pestilence, and insurrection in the world's trouble spots with items of a lighter nature. On January 1, 1922, a large-type wish for A PROSPEROUS NEW YEAR TO ALL spread across the top of the *Colonist*'s front page. Yes, there were stories about turmoil in Ireland, famine in Russia, yellow fever in China, and agitation for independence in India, but the paper also reprinted advice from the famed and cherished Canadian humorist, Stephen Leacock, that had originally appeared in London's *Daily Mail*. The piece, entitled "Great Humorist on Humour," offered advice for turning life's vicissitudes into matters for merriment. "I have found," Leacock wrote at the end of his tutorial, "that the only kind of statement worthwhile is over-statement. A half truth, like half a brick, is always more forcible as an argument than a whole brick."

Elsewhere in the January 1 edition, under the section heading "A Page for Children," readers of any age could find the latest offering in the column "Wild Life on Vancouver Island" by Clement L. Kaufman. Mr. Kaufman's subject in this case was the sparrowhawk, a species we now know as sharp-shinned hawk. The bird's beautiful colouring, Mr. Kaufman wrote, would make it a favourite "were it not for its villainous habit of devouring small birds." After a detailed account of its life and habits, the writer comforted his readers with the assurance that the sparrowhawk's taste for small birds is offset by the public service it performs in reducing numbers of harmful insects and mice.

On January 1, there was news that motorists needed to heed closely. Most people still got around by streetcar or horse and buggy, but the privately owned motor car was becoming a more familiar sight in downtown Victoria, one posing hazards for both operators and pedestrians. On January 1, a full-page notice in the *Colonist* instructed streetcar passengers, pedestrians, and drivers on their roles in ensuring that Victoria's downtown streets remained safe and secure for everyone. But that was not all. Two other notices drew attention to motoring matters. The first reminded drivers that as of this date, cars had to be operated on the right side of the road, not the left, or the middle, or wherever else automobile drivers had grown accustomed to going about their business. Finally, yet another item informed motor car operators that Victoria police chief, John Fry, warned that his constables would be strictly enforcing new speed limits effective from 6:00 AM that New Year's morning: fifteen miles an hour on city streets but only ten in intersections.

A speed limit of fifteen miles per hour or the notion of operating a vehicle anywhere but on the right may sound absurd in our time, but some issues canvassed in 1921 and 1922 seem perfectly familiar even a hundred years down the road. No Canadian is surprised anymore when a US administration decides to slap a tariff on Canadian lumber. Such tariffs are repeatedly levied in our time even after international tribunals determine they are unjustified. They appear to have been as commonplace a century ago as they are now. An item in the *Colonist* of December 31 reported that American westcoast lumber interests were demanding the imposition of duties on Canadian lumber and shingles.

On January 28, under the headline DRUG EVIL GROWS IN TERMINAL CITY, the *Colonist* reported on an initiative aimed at driving "dope peddlers" out of Vancouver and initiating measures to deal with drug addicts now living there. A consortium of organizations—the Board of Trade, Rotary, and Kiwanis clubs among them—found the illicit drug situation in Vancouver more alarming than anyone had previously imagined. Particularly distressing was the discovery of the ravages of the drug habit among young women in the city.

If contemplating tariffs and drug ravages grew too burdensome, Victorians still had plenty of distractions for revelling in the arrival of the new year. Famed Hollywood star Harold Lloyd was onscreen at the Capitol in his new comedy, *Never Weaken*. Mary Pickford was the star of *Little Lord Fauntleroy* over at the Dominion. If westerns with plenty of combative "cowboys and Indians" were to a viewer's taste, he could look forward to seeing Hoot Gibson in *Sure Fire* at the Columbia. Theatre-goers of finer sensibility could opt for *Hamlet* at the Pantages.

A frequently used route took streetcar riders to the Epworth Street home of the Victoria Aristocrats, but Victoria's hockey pros went on the road for their first game of 1922. In Seattle, on January 4, the Aristocrats returned to winning ways with a 4-3 overtime

Mary Pickford in *Little Lord Fauntleroy*. VICTORIA *DAILY COLONIST*, DECEMBER 28, 1921

victory over the Metropolitans. The Mets had a 3-0 lead at the start of the third period, but two goals from Wilf Loughlin and a third from Oatman sent the game into overtime.

It was another game uncharacteristic of typical Victoria–Seattle encounters. Referee Mickey Ion ordinarily had an easy time of it in Mets–Aristocrats games, but not on this night. Ion called a dozen penalties, a PCHA record. Moose Johnson had to be carried off the ice after being whacked across the forehead by Gord Fraser. Clem

Loughlin and Bernie Morris engaged in the first bout of the night's fight card. Then the Icelander Halderson got into the action with the Long Irishman Riley. That led to "a little illegal checking" by Wilf Loughlin on Foyston. For a while it appeared that an insufficient number of players remained to play the rest of the game. But play they did, and it was Halderson who ended it on a pass from Dunderdale in the fifteenth minute of overtime.

Another item in the January 5 sports section might have caught the sports fan's eye after he'd read the account of the hockey game in Seattle. Under the headline FOOTBALL IS NO GAME FOR WOMEN, the *Colonist* reported that the British Football Association had put itself on record as opposed to "women's invasion of the football domain," and had issued directives to its member clubs that they deny women the use of their pitches. The FA's spokesman was quoted as saying "women's football is a travesty of the game . . . football is not, never was and never will be a woman's game." What must the Christine Sinclairs of 1922 have felt about *that*?

In the year that women finally won the right to vote as full citizens in most of Canada, it was clear from other stories reported in the *Colonist* that women's equality still had a long way to go. In December, the Victoria daily reported that the Streets Committee of Victoria city council was looking into plugging a loophole in the city's bylaws by disqualifying girls from working as downtown newspaper vendors. On January 21, a story datelined Cleveland, Ohio, reported that mayor Frederick Kohler had issued a ruling prohibiting women from watching prizefights with men. Clubs violating the ruling could expect to have their licences revoked.

On January 6, back home on Epworth Street, the Aristocrats enjoyed a game to savour against the unpopular Millionaires of Vancouver. Playing what the *Colonist* described as their best hockey of the season, Victoria took over first place again in the PCHA's standings. Playing "the game of his career," Wilf Loughlin scored three goals. Fredrickson delivered "his usual sterling game," setting up Loughlin's first goal and scoring two of his own. After performing poorly in his previous game, Halderson seemed to have got rid of the "stage fright, or whatever it was" that had hobbled his previous performance. Final score: Victoria 5, Vancouver 2.

Sixty-five hundred paying customers came to Denman Street to watch the visiting Victorians January 9. What they got for the price of admission was a game the *Colonist* reporter called the most exciting battle he'd seen in a long while. In the third period, with fifteen minutes left to play, referee Mickey Ion sentenced Aristocrats' goaltender Hec Fowler to a major penalty. In the modern game, someone else serves penalty time assessed to a goalie. Not in 1922. With no spare netminder to turn to, Lester Patrick "jumped into the nets without pads, played almost all the time on his knees," and stopped all but the last Vancouver shot directed his way. Now aged thirty-eight, Patrick was awarded a great ovation by the Vancouver clientele for his emergency service. But it was the Millionaires' goaltender, Hugh Lehman, who was the game star. Fredrickson, Dunderdale, and Wilf Loughlin all took turns at challenging the future Hall of Famer, and Halderson's stickhandling "was a revelation," but Lehman barred them all. Jack Adams, having himself a banner season, managed a hat trick, and Vancouver won, 4-0.

In what was turning into another topsy-turvy season, the loss levelled Victoria's season record at 5-5-1.

Four nights later, at home in Victoria, the Aristocrats vented their aggravation against Seattle. Harry Meeking was "brilliant," while Fredrickson and Halderson treated the home crowd to eye-catching combinations, one after another. Fredrickson played "wonderful hockey, and showed up as the most finished player on the ice." Victoria won, 5-2, with Fredrickson scoring twice, Halderson and Meeking once each. Moose Johnson also scored, a goal that would turn out to be not just the only one he would tally this season but the last of his major pro career.

Victoria won again, in Seattle, January 18. Fredrickson opened the scoring in the fifth minute, and then Riley scored twice to give Seattle the lead. Old age and treachery loomed large in the game. Masquerading as a teammate, Dunderdale fooled Riley into directing a no-look pass his way—and scored. Then Riley turned the table on Dunderdale and got away with the same trick. Fredrickson, "always good," led the way for the Aristocrats, but it was Halderson, on a pass from Dunderdale, who scored the winner in a 4-3 victory that restored the Aristocrats to the top rung of the PCHA ladder.

But not for long. On January 20, as Pope Benedict XV lay dying at the Vatican, Vancouver came to Victoria for another episode in the continuing saga of Frank Patrick's Millionaires versus his brother's Aristocrats. The *Colonist* celebrated the combined skill of Fredrickson, Halderson, and Dunderdale, but it was the Millionaires who prevailed, 4-3. The day's big story belonged to Ernie "Moose" Johnson: the Moose had not played, nor would he ever play again as a Victoria Aristocrat.

The *Colonist* published a statement in which Lester Patrick regretted to announce that Johnson had "broken his contract" and quit. He had grievances—"trivial and imaginary" ones in Patrick's view—that could have been remedied, but Johnson could not be persuaded to set them aside. The grievances were not disclosed in Patrick's public statement but it came to light that Johnson felt the boss had been parsimonious in allotting him playing time following an injury. The Moose may also have felt poorly supported by the Victoria fans. Whatever, Johnson, a proud man who would become an early inductee in the Hockey Hall of Fame, had decided that playing in Victoria was no longer tolerable. Less than a year after he had been showered with love, affection—and engraved silverware—by legions of fans at the Epworth Street arena, the Moose had had his fill of Victoria. But he was not done with hockey. As late as the winter of 1930-31—nine years later—Johnson was still playing, and playing very well, as the second-leading scorer of the San Francisco Tigers of the California Professional Hockey League. By then Moose Johnson was forty-five years old.

The Aristocrats recovered from their abandonment by Moose Johnson. On January 23, they steamed across the Strait of Georgia and delivered retribution to Vancouver on the Millionaires' own ice.

Harry Meeking took over for Johnson and quickly established to the satisfaction of the *Colonist* observer that he would be "a most formidable defender." Another big crowd of 6,500 watched the game. Trailing by 4-3 after two periods, the Aristocrats fought back to score two unanswered goals in the third period and won, 5-4. Fredrickson was again the principal rescuer: he netted the tying goal and enabled the winner, scored by Dunderdale. Halderson also scored, and had managed to remedy whatever worries Victoria followers might have had about his abilities. IIis performance marked Halderson "as one of the greatest stickhandlers in the league," his speed every bit the equal of Fredrickson's and Dunderdale's.

First place theirs again, the Aristocrats proceeded to lose two in a row. They fell at home to Seattle, by 4-0 on January 27, and again, in Seattle, by 3-1, on the first of February. Playing ever less frequently, Lester Patrick took to the ice in the January 27 game but made little difference. The loss levelled the Victoria record at eight wins, eight losses, and a tie.

In another see-saw season, they won a game at home, 2-1 over Vancouver, before embarking on their latest losing streak—three this time—between February 6 and February 15. Halderson starred in the narrow loss to Vancouver, but the February 15 game at Seattle was an embarrassment: the Metropolitans won by 7-0, with former Aristocrat Bernie Morris inflicting the lion's share of the damage. Morris scored a quartet of goals for Seattle, his confinement at Alcatraz a distant memory that clearly had done nothing to compromise his hockey abilities. The loss shrunk Victoria's season record to 9-11-1; they once again stood last in the PCHA standings.

As Victoria's hockey professionals stumbled, larger world events commanded the attention of *Daily Colonist* readers. An authentic hero to Victorians and to people the world over, Sir Ernest Shackleton had died unexpectedly at age forty-seven in January at Grytviken, South Georgia. Vancouver Islanders had been as mesmerized as everyone else by accounts of the courage and tenacity Shackleton displayed in saving the crew of his ship *Endurance* after it was lost in the Antarctic ice in 1915. By 1922, the explorer was back on South Georgia mobilizing another Antarctic endeavour.

In February, the *Colonist* kept readers informed about Shackleton's last voyage. The plan had been to take his body home. Grieving crowds and a grand ceremony greeted the arrival of the steamer *Woodville* at Montevideo, but when the *Woodville* departed Uruguay, it was not toward Britain that it steamed but back to South Georgia. Lady Shackleton had decided that her husband should be buried in the place he died and from which his Antarctic exploits had been launched. Nearly a century after his demise, Shackleton still has legions of admirers. Any who wish to pay homage at his gravesite must travel to latitude 54° south, where the great man's mortal remains lie in the English church cemetery at Grytviken.

Eighty-seven hundred miles northwest of Grytviken, the Victoria Aristocrats won a hockey game on February 17. Led by the Manitoban Icelanders, Victoria edged Seattle, 3-2, on their home ice. A pair of goals from Frank Foyston gave the Mets a 2-0 lead, but a Fredrickson-enabled marker by Oatman and Wilf Loughlin's goal on a penalty shot evened the score. The Olympic medallists won the game for Victoria in the third period, Halderson scoring with a helping hand from Fredrickson.

Victoria still had a shot at the playoffs, but the Aristocrats lost their penultimate game of the season, 5-1, in Vancouver. The final game, a 7-4 win over the Millionaires at home on Epworth Street mattered only to the players vying for individual scoring honours. Fredrickson added a goal and assist to his numbers, bringing his total to fifteen goals and twenty-five points for the season. That was good enough to lead the Aristocrats, but five points in arrears of Jack Adams, who had enjoyed the finest year of his Hall of Fame career.

The PCHA clubs finished the 1921–22 season with the closest result ever: Seattle and Vancouver ended with twelve wins, Victoria eleven. For the fifth straight year, Lester Patrick's Aristocrats had failed to reach the championship playoff. Vancouver won both games of the two-game, total-goal series by the same score, 1-0, and thereby put themselves in a position to battle the WCHL champion, the Regina Capitals, for the right to represent the western leagues for the Stanley Cup. Vancouver prevailed over Regina in the western showdown. Each team won a game, but the Millionaires outscored the Capitals by 5-2 in the goal count and thereby qualified themselves to take on the Toronto St. Patricks for all the marbles at the Mutual Street Arena.

Once again, it required all five games of the best-of-five series to decide the issue. Once again, the games alternated between western and eastern rules. Vancouver could boast two players who would one day have a tablet in the Hockey Hall of Fame—Mickey MacKay and Jack Adams—but the St. Patricks included *three* future Hall of Famers: Babe Dye, Harry Cameron, and Reg Noble. Once again—for the fourth time in a row—it was the NHA representative that won the bragging rights that came with a Stanley Cup victory.

TWELVE

1922-23

IN ROAR
THE COUGARS

OR THE TWELFTH season of the Pacific Coast Hockey Association, the Patrick brothers decided it was time for a few changes—some material, some cosmetic. After five straight last-place finishes, Lester Patrick perhaps decided his Victoria club needed a new identity, something a little less refined, a little more intimidating. He decided on a name change, one that might evoke more respect in the hearts of his PCHA adversaries. Perhaps a moniker denoting a large, dangerous, wild animal might command more attention in enemy hearts than one suggestive of bluebloods living in crumbled English castles. He decided to turn his Aristocrats into Cougars.

Across the Strait of Georgia, brother Frank had a similar change of heart. His Millionaires had enjoyed more than a little success in the first eleven PCHA seasons, but does the name Millionaires conjure notions of a scarily aggressive team of hockey warriors? Maybe not. Reflecting the primary, manly colour of his players' sweaters, Frank Patrick renamed his club the Maroons. Perhaps that was a telling choice: in 1924, when a new Montreal team was admitted to the National Hockey League, its owners decided to flatter by imitation: *they* called their new team the Maroons.

The Seattle skaters had also enjoyed more than a little success in their PCHA time, including a Stanley Cup victory in 1917. The team's moniker, the Metropolitans, perhaps implies cultivation, urbanity, and sophistication, but is it any more fearsome a handle than Aristocrats or Millionaires? Wouldn't any of "Sasquatches," "Seahawks," or "Steelheads" be a better name for an attack-oriented band of hockey players? Well, perhaps, but in the end, the Seattle management decided to stick with the familiar: the Metropolitans would keep their name.

Other new developments arose in the winter of 1922–23. After sticking to seven-man hockey throughout the PCHA years to date, the Patricks decided at last to follow the NHL example by eliminating the rover position. The brothers also expanded the regular season, from twenty-four games to thirty. Given the presence of another major professional league in western Canada, one that commanded a say in who would represent the west in the annual Stanley Cup showdown, the two leagues agreed on a measure of integration for the new season. PCHA teams would play WCHL squads, and the results would count in each league's regular standings. This was a good thing, given the possibilities of raising fan interest in teams and players they knew about, thanks to newspapers and word-of-mouth, but never had the opportunity to see.

In Victoria, whose fans had got ever so close to seeing playoff hockey the previous winter, Lester Patrick brought in new blood he hoped might deliver the extra push Frank Fredrickson and company would need to deliver playoff action to the Epworth Street arena. He secured the services of a man who had contributed to the success of the Calgary Tigers—surely a team name to reckon with—the previous two seasons.

John Wilberforce Anderson, better known as "Jocko," had been a member of the Sixty-first Battalion hockey team that won the Allan Cup as Canadian national amateur champions in 1916. That squad also included "Bullet" Joe Simpson who would go on to hockey glory and one day earn a place in the Hockey Hall of Fame. Jocko was a native Manitoban, albeit a more diminutive one—five feet, seven inches and 170 pounds—than his new teammates Fredrickson and Halderson. He would remain a Victoria Cougar for the remainder of his professional career.

Given his happy experience with players of Icelandic ethnicity, Patrick might have reasoned that if two Icelanders were good, wouldn't three be even better? Yet another Manitoban, Albert Christian Vigfusson Deildal, had grown up among fellow Icelanders at Glenboro, just over a hundred miles west of Winnipeg. Like Fredrickson, he had volunteered as a soldier in the war, enlisting in the 197th Battalion (Canadian Vikings). Lester Patrick had not had to look far for Deildal: he had been a leading light for two seasons with the Victoria Senators of the City Senior Hockey League, his exploits regularly reported in the sports pages of the *Daily Colonist*.

Given its expanded schedule, the new season began early—November 15—but not serendipitously. The Cougars went to Seattle and lost decisively to the Metropolitans, 4-0.

Two days later, November 17, the Cougars played their home opener against the archrival Vancouver Maroons. Fans agreed that the six-man game reduced congestion on the ice and facilitated greater speed. Clem Loughlin scored twice, with Meeking, Fredrickson, and Oatman adding singletons in the Cougars' 5-3 victory.

The same teams faced off again, in Vancouver, November 20, but this time one player dominated the scoring for Victoria: Frank Fredrickson scored all four goals in a 4-3 Cougars win at Denman Street. It was a telling start for a player who, at age twenty-seven, was just entering the prime of his hockey life. For the time being, the Cougars shared first place in the PCHA standings with Seattle.

On November 24, the Metropolitans came to town and rained on the Victoria parade. The *Daily Colonist* called it a "torrid" game that would linger long in fan memory. "When the puckchasers weren't playing hockey they were using their hickory over their opponent's skulls." The second period "will go down in history as probably the greatest ever played here." The greatest, and perhaps one of the nastiest, too. Wilf Loughlin and Bernie Morris initiated the first bout of the evening's fight card, then Eddie Oatman and Archie Briden another. Briden needed stitches for the damage done to his head by Oatman's stick. The paper commended Slim Halderson's rushing and stickhandling, but the man of the hour was once again the Long Irishman, Riley: he scored three goals in Seattle's 6-4 victory, and the Mets had sole possession of first place.

In the pages of the *Daily Colonist*, matters other than hockey competed for readers' attention. Antagonism continued between Irish nationalists and those defending the view that Ireland must remain part of the Empire, even by force of arms if necessary. Unrest grew in mainland Europe over conflicting views on the issue of the war reparations Germany had to pay the side that had won the war. Without the blessing of its allies, France sent troops to occupy the Ruhr region of Germany, the leverage it needed to extract the German coal it wanted for French industry. Greece and Turkey were at odds, too—and resorting to armed conflict to sort out their territorial disputes.

There were trouble spots on the other side of the Atlantic. In Chile a big earthquake killed more than a thousand people in November. In a story datelined New York, November 23, the *Colonist* reported that the Dyer bill, prohibiting lynching of black people, had passed by a vote of 230 to 119 in the US House of Representatives. But passage of the bill was condemned as unconstitutional—an infringement of state rights. One of the bill's attackers was the Ku Klux Klan, an organization, the *Colonist* reported, whose opponents claim has "served to arouse racial and religious hatreds and constitute a menace to the peace of the country."

Racial tensions were on display here at home too. Members of the British Columbia legislature considered a resolution calling on the federal government to "completely prohibit Asiatic immigration into Canada." On November 21, the resolution passed without a single dissenting vote. Liberals and Conservatives might disagree on many other matters, but on this issue they were all of one mind. Meanwhile, Victoria police continued to conduct frequent raids in

Open Till 7

Never a price so low
as now

$445

F.O.B. Ford, Ont.

Government Taxes
and Freight Extra

National Motor Co., Limited

831 Yates St.   Home of Ford in Victoria   Phone 4900

"Never a Price So Low." VICTORIA *DAILY COLONIST*, NOVEMBER 17, 1922

Chinatown to bust gambling clubs, opium dens, or laundries open past the 7:00 PM closing time stipulated under city bylaws.

The legislature was in the news for other reasons. Veterans' organizations objected that the assembly's newly appointed sergeant-at-arms was unworthy of the job because he had not been a soldier in the war. Veterans had reason to feel cranky: unemployment was a continuing social problem, particularly among soldiers who had come home to circumstances not at all like the ones they had expected and felt they deserved.

For people having a job and a decent wage, life had its rewards. The city provided diversions for those who could afford the admission price to one or another of the half dozen downtown theatres and cinemas. Though they weren't allowed to drive faster than fifteen miles an hour, individuals aspiring to become motor car owner–operators were given an assist by Henry Ford. The advantages of mass production enabled the automaker tycoon to provide his Model T to Victorians for $445—less than five thousand dollars in today's terms. You could have "any colour—so long as it's black," Ford famously offered.

Technology just in its infancy was in the news. On December 23, the *Colonist* reported that the growing number of Victorians owning radio receivers could listen to American broadcasts relayed by a Victoria station, CHCA. As Christmas approached, listeners could look forward to hearing a special seasonal concert from KFCB in San Francisco at 10:15 PM that night. A *Colonist* ad depicted headphone-wearing children gathered around a Northern Electric radio receiving set. "Lack of time perhaps prevents you from reading aloud to your children? Why not let RADIO do it?" The ad disclosed no price, but those tempted to investigate could go to Western Canada Radio Supply at 919 Fort Street to make inquiries.

One day in years to come, fans of the Victoria Cougars would be able to listen to radio accounts of their team's games, but in the meantime their sole live-action option was to watch in person and rely on the local newspaper to recap the details of their favourite players' exploits.

Riding high to start the season, the November 24 loss to Seattle was the start of a four-game losing skid, all of them by a single goal. On November 29, Bernie Morris won it for the Mets in the seventeenth minute of overtime. Seattle's Frank Foyston scored three times, including one blundered into his own net. Fredrickson and Halderson each scored a goal, and so did thirty-five-year-old Tommy Dunderdale. Tommy was a PCHA original, one of the 1911–12 Victoria Capitals. He had scored more than twenty goals in five different seasons, but in 1922–23, his last PCHA campaign, Dunderdale would be reduced to just two.

On December 1, the Cougars did win a hockey game, but it didn't count. The defending Stanley Cup champion team, the Toronto St. Patricks, came to Victoria for an exhibition game. Before a crowd of 3,500, Victoria won convincingly, 7-3. It was a "wonderful" game according to the *Colonist*'s observer, "an excellent exhibition of the great sport," and Toronto's first loss in its western tour. Five Cougars shared in the scoring, while Harry Cameron, the future Hall of Famer and hero of the St. Pats' Cup triumph the previous March, scored all three for Toronto.

A week later, December 8, the Cougars played another home game. It counted. They lost, 4-3, to Vancouver. According to the next day's *Colonist* report, the game lacked pep and aggressiveness "as though the ice dogs were unable to stand the six-man hockey pace." The most intriguing storyline of the game was the return of the great Cyclone Taylor. After two years in retirement, Taylor had decided at age thirty-eight to give it another go. He made a long rush or two that evoked memories of who he had been, but the Cyclone played only briefly. It would turn out to be the shortest of revivals: Taylor took a turn in that one game and never played another. In 1947, a quarter century after Victoria hockey fans witnessed his final game, Taylor would be inducted in the second draft of players enshrined in the Hockey Hall of Fame.

On December 11, the Cougars had a rematch with Vancouver and lost again. In "one of the fiercest battles" the antagonists had ever played, the Maroons won at home, 2-1. Frank Fredrickson scored the lone Victoria goal, but in the eyes of the *Colonist*'s hockey reporter, the star of the occasion was the first-year Maroon, twenty-one-year-old Frank Boucher. Boucher would play four years in Vancouver before making a big splash in the National Hockey League: between 1928 and 1935, he would win the Lady Byng Trophy seven times. The Byng silverware honoured the player judged to have exhibited the best combination of skill and sportsmanship. Boucher won it so often that Lady Byng, the spouse of Canada's Governor General, gave it to him permanently and replaced it with another. Boucher, too, would one day be awarded a plaque in the Hockey Hall of Fame.

As the Victoria Cougars were losing four in a row, the world continued to revolve as if it mattered little. A new item appeared routinely in Victoria's morning daily, "The *Colonist*'s Pictorial Page," featuring pictures and captions. On November 24, the photographs included one of Albert Einstein, noting the award of a Nobel Prize to the "father of relativity."

In the November British general election, voters had voted out of office a well-known Member of Parliament. The *Colonist* reported that while he awaited an opportunity for re-election to

Westminster, Winston Churchill kept himself busy with writing. Soon the newspaper began serializing Churchill's *Naval History of the Great War.*

Another war-related matter made the front page of the December 12 edition. The *Colonist* reported that the French government had decreed that the land surrounding a new Canadian war memorial at the summit of Vimy Ridge would be awarded to and forever become part of Canada. The story speculated that the Canadian memorial would be completed in five years but Walter Allward's design for the towering monument to the Canadians who had fallen in France and had no known grave would not be completed for another fourteen years, in 1936.

One of the Canadian soldiers who had fought—and was seriously wounded—at Vimy was one Mervyn Dutton of Russell, Manitoba. Just nineteen when he went over the top with the Canada Corps on Easter Monday, 1917, Dutton came close to losing a leg for his troubles. By 1922, his war wounds repaired, "Red" Dutton was a stalwart defenceman with the Calgary Tigers, someone who in days to come would tangle with the Victoria Cougars at the Epworth Street arena.

But that was for later. On December 15, the Seattle Metropolitans took the ferry steamer to Victoria to play the Cougars on their Oak Bay home ice. The Victoria hero this time was "Old Reliable," the Cougars' thirty-year-old goaltender, Hec Fowler. Fowler stopped all but one shot directed his way; Clem Loughlin and Fredrickson scored a goal apiece and Victoria prevailed, 2-1. The result left the two Franks—Foyston and Fredrickson—tied for the lead in the individual scoring race, with thirteen points each.

On December 22, the Cougars faced off in a milestone game: the season's first matchup with one of the WCHL sides, the Regina Capitals. It was a game that mattered: the result counted in each team's league official standings. The Capitals were a team to reckon with. Three of them—George Hay, Dick Irvin, and Barney Stanley—were destined for the Hall of Fame. Despite the advantage of playing at home in front of their loyal fans, the Cougars lost to the visitors in another one-goal decision, 2-1, their fourth such loss in five games.

Once upon a time, Skinner Poulin had been a valued member of the Victoria Aristocrats, but that was long ago; by this time Poulin was the WCHL's chief on-ice arbiter, and it was he who officiated in this first Victoria WCHL–PCHA encounter. The Victoria fans did not like his work: at times he "received harsh treatment from his former boosters." The Cougars played a fine game, but the *Colonist* awarded its top marks to George Hay, who scored the first Regina goal, with Barney Stanley scoring the other two. "Eddie and Freddie" continued to shine for the Cougars. Fredrickson enabled a goal by Oatman and then scored a second all of his own. Still, Regina prevailed, 3-2. The game left Fredrickson one point behind Frank Foyston in the individual scoring race, but the Cougars were back in their familiar last-place position, three games in arrears of Seattle.

The loss to Regina perhaps inspired the Cougars to try that much harder. Having recently endured a four-game losing run, they embarked on a roll more to Lester Patrick's and their fans' liking: they welcomed the new year by winning four in a row, the first three by the same narrow margin that applied in much of the losing slide—a single goal.

On December 29, they won at home against Frank Patrick's Maroons. Victoria fans reserved greater antipathy for the Maroons than other opponents and they were "tickled to death" to see their team beat Vancouver. One advantage the Cougars enjoyed was that Jack Adams, the man who had beaten Fredrickson for the PCHA scoring title the year before, was no longer in Vancouver. He had been parcelled up and shipped to Toronto in exchange for Corb Denneny. Skinner Poulin was again the referee, but this time he managed not to alienate the Victoria crowd. Harry Meeking won it for the Cougars, 4-3, on a pass from Fredrickson.

The Victoria fans got more for their admission money than the hockey game. During the intermissions, they were treated to a fine exhibition of "fancy skating" by Miss Mae Fielding and Mr. E.E.

Daniels, accompanied by the arena band. It had been a few years since the hockey followers had the privilege of seeing this sort of display, and they "greatly enjoyed... the spiral, waltz, jump, fourteen steps [and] Mohawk dance."

New Year's Day delivered more gratification for Cougars' fans. Seven thousand Vancouver customers went home disappointed at seeing the Maroons lose, 2-1. Another Halderson–Fredrickson combination produced the first Victoria goal, and Clem Loughlin won it for the Cougars in the ninth minute of overtime. The victory left the PCHA standings crowded, the Cougars only a game behind first-place Seattle, and Fredrickson just a point behind Vancouver's Lloyd Cook for the individual scoring race lead.

On January 3, "the snarling Cougars" returned to Seattle and delivered a performance to make a hockey purist's heart sing. It was a defensive gem; both goaltenders shone, and only one man scored: Fredrickson in the twelfth minute of the first period. "The lone goal was a darb," the *Colonist* reported. "Darb"? We learn on investigation that a darb is "an excellent thing." With his January 3 darb in Seattle, Fredrickson took a share of the scoring lead with Vancouver's Lloyd Cook, and all three PCHA teams were tied at twelve points each.

Two days later the Cougars further aggravated the Metropolitans with a 5-1 victory back in Victoria. Fredrickson, "the big Icelander," scored three of the Victoria goals and enabled a fourth by Harry Meeking. Fredrickson's first goal came just forty-two seconds into the game. "Freddie... demonstrated that he is one of the cleanest and most effective puckchasers that ever stepped into a hockey contest." The *Colonist* commended Meeking, too, and Halderson again impressed Cougar fans "by his remarkable stickhandling and his wonderful work on the defence." The win improved Victoria's season record to the league's best and Fredrickson's big night put him three points ahead of Lloyd Cook and Mickey MacKay in the individual scoring race.

Foul fortune followed fair: the Metropolitans paid the Cougars a visit, shutting them out in their own rink, 2-0, on January 8. Neither

Frank Fredrickson, Victoria Cougars. Many observers concur that Frank Fredrickson was the greatest player Lester Patrick ever recruited to play for his Victoria hockey club. Fredrickson played six seasons in the BC capital and was the team's leading scorer in all six. A five-time PCHA all-star with Victoria, he was inducted in the Hockey Hall of Fame in 1958.
COURTESY HOCKEYGODS

team scored in the first two periods. "Fredrickson worked heroically to score," and the "big blonde was skating and shooting in amazing form tonight, but the luck was not with him." Fraser and Riley scored for the Mets in the third, leaving all three PCHA clubs tied with fourteen points each.

January 12 delivered a diverting novelty to Victoria hockey fans: a catfight at the Epworth Street arena. The WCHL Calgary Tigers came to town to square off against the Victoria Cougars. Red Dutton, the young Vimy victim and future member of the Hockey Hall of Fame, was in action for Calgary that night, and so were two other future Hall of Famers: Herb Gardiner and Harry Oliver. But it was

Victoria's own eventual Hall of Fame luminary who shone brightest for the three thousand paying customers. Fredrickson set up goals by Meeking and Halderson and then scored one of his own in a 4-0 Victoria shutout.

The Meeking goal was a particular gem. Outwitting Dutton and Gardiner, Meeking "skated around them and slipped the gutta percha into the net." The *Colonist*'s hockey writer—who regrettably was never given a byline—liked his metaphors: "gutta percha" is a Malay term for the latex derived from a tree native to that part of the world and was one of the terms for "puck" the beat reporter occasionally pulled from his bag of synonyms. He capped his account of the game with a florid tribute to Fredrickson's compatriot: "Slim Halderson again demonstrated that he is a great defence star, when he sent to the islands beyond the seas the fondest hopes of the visiting tribe."

A story from beyond the seas and from ages past captivated not just readers of the *Daily Colonist* but people the world over. In January, excavators bankrolled by George Herbert, the Fifth Earl of Carnarvon, had unearthed the tomb of Tutankhamen, the boy pharaoh of Egypt who had been confined to his glorious final resting place some thirty-two centuries earlier. Throughout January and February, the Victoria daily enabled readers to share in the excitement of the tomb's discovery and marvel at the treasures Lord Carnarvon's crew were unearthing at Luxor.

City residents could read all they wanted about King Tut, but there were compelling diversions closer to home. The child film star, Jackie Coogan, enjoyed rave reviews for his performance in *Oliver Twist*, onscreen at the Royal. Not just Coogan's greatest picture, the *Colonist* ad proclaimed, but the first true screen presentation of the classic. "There could be no more perfect portrayal had Dickens written 'Oliver Twist' just for Jackie."

On January 19, the Cougars won again, this time a 3-2 extra-time victory over Vancouver. The game was played at home in the facility the *Colonist* now typically called the Patrick Arena. Lester Patrick, laid up with a bad cold, was at home in bed, briefed on the game's events by telephone. Team captain Oatman took over Patrick's role. The first star this time was Clem Loughlin, who played "a wonderful game . . . and engineered many of his characteristic speedy rushes." In what was becoming routine, the *Colonist* celebrated Fredrickson, too, for his speed, passing, checking, and scoring. The new man, Jocko Anderson, "performs more brilliantly every time he makes his appearance." In the second period, Meeking opened the scoring on an assist from Jocko, and then Fredrickson bagged his eighteenth of the season. Clem Loughlin, who had enabled Fredrickson's goal, won it for Victoria in overtime.

During the between-period intermissions, the not-hockey skaters—Miss Fielding and Mr. Daniels—were back by popular demand. Accompanied by the arena band, the couple "executed a number of dance numbers, in addition to some of the difficult arts of fancy skating." Their reward was "an even greater hand from the railbirds" than they had received the last time.

Meanwhile, on the far side of the Rocky Mountains, Seattle won narrowly over the Calgary Tigers, 4-3. Seattle's "old foxes" did all the damage: Bernie Morris and Frank Foyston scored one each, while Jack Walker had two. All three of them well into their thirties by this time; Walker, thirty-four, was the eldest, well advanced on his inexorable path to the Hockey Hall of Fame.

The evening's events left Victoria with the PCHA's best record—nine victories against seven losses—and Fredrickson three points in front of Lloyd Cook in the scoring parade.

Which ushered in another retreat. Unaccustomed to the view from top of the ladder, Fredrickson and company proceeded to lose two straight. Neither was close: they fell, 4-1, in Vancouver on January 22 and were blown out by the Maroons at their home arena, 8-4, on January 24.

In modern hockey, when a penalty shot is called by the referee, it is the player transgressed against who takes the shot. Not in 1923. In the Vancouver game, when Halderson was tripped en route to confronting Maroons' goaltender Hugh Lehman, referee Mickey Ion whistled a penalty shot. Lester Patrick called on Jocko Anderson to take the shot, "which caught Lehman amidships with a resounding thud." The Icelanders combined for the lone Victoria goal, Fredrickson scoring on a pass from Halderson.

In the January 24 return engagement, the Cougars started very well, Fredrickson scoring the first period's only goal. Then the Cougars collapsed. "Hec Fowler left his glasses in the dressing-room when he came out for the second canto," and surrendered six Vancouver goals in twenty minutes. Reliably brilliant Mickey MacKay had a hand in three of the Vancouver goals and thus found himself sharing the scoring lead with Fredrickson. Standing first just a few days earlier, the Cougars were back in the PCHA cellar, six points behind Vancouver. Lester Patrick must have wondered whether unhappy history intended to repeat itself.

Patrick managed to right the ship February 9. It was Saskatoon's turn to provide the hometown lads with a challenge from the rival western league. A nearly full house paid to see the team—now nicknamed "Crescents" rather than Sheiks—confront the Cougars. Led by the great Edward Cyrille "Newsy" Lalonde and two other players destined for the Hockey Hall of Fame—Bill Cook and Rusty Crawford—the Crescents did not rise to the occasion. Fredrickson, the Cougars' "shining star," scored twice and assisted on a third to lead Victoria to a 5-2 victory. The Iceland connection loomed large: in addition to Fredrickson's heroics, reliable Halderson "dazzled the fans with his speed and good stickhandling," and third-fiddle Albert Deildal came close to scoring twice.

Intermissions must have been something to behold in the PCHA of the early 1920s. On February 9, it was not the fancy skating of Miss Fielding and Mr. Daniels that charmed spectators but ice comedian Ralph Alcock, who was given a warm hand for "his comical stunts on the steel blades." If only a filmmaker of the time had taken the trouble to record an entire hockey game, including the entertaining events that went on between periods; such a film would be something to prize.

The Cougars lost twice more in early February, by 4-3 to Vancouver on February 2, and 5-2 in Seattle on February 7. They made amends February 9 with a 6-1 thrashing of Seattle at the Patrick Arena. The game stars were Meeking and Fredrickson, with "Freddie" combining three goals with an assist while Meeking contributed two goals and an assist. Fredrickson extended his scoring lead over MacKay to five points, and the Cougars closed to within five points of Vancouver. It is hoped, the *Colonist* observer ventured with his customary flair, that the win "will land the hockey gonfalon" in the BC capital this winter. Consulting the *Concise Oxford,* one finds that "gonfalon," derived from the Italian, is another word for "banner."

Gonfalon aspirations had to be put on hold after a 5-3 defeat in Vancouver, February 12, but then the Cougars embarked on a winning run. On February 16, as the inner chamber of Tut's tomb at Luxor was being opened for the first time in more than three millennia, the Cougars gave a warm welcome to the fourth WCHL club they would play this season at the Epworth Street facility, the Edmonton Eskimos. Yet another future Hall of Fame duo led the way for the Eskimos—Duke Keats and Joe Simpson.

Somewhat spent by their exertions in Seattle the previous evening, the Eskimos were not in their best form. By contrast, the Victoria club "was flying about on the pond like a well controlled aeroplane does among the clouds." Once again the WCHL crew attracted almost a full house to Epworth Street. The *Colonist* paid particular kudos to Clem Loughlin and Hec Fowler.

Two of the Eskimos also impressed. Joe Simpson "dazzled the railbirds with his great 'corkscrew rushes.'" The Iron Duke—Keats— "known and regarded as one of the best players in the hockey sport," was the worse for last night's wear in Seattle but showed flashes of his outstanding ability. Though he was an enemy skater, Keats "won the fans' praise when he almost made the figure eight in mid-ice when several of the local boys tried in vain to wrest the rubber biscuit from him." But then Keats "ferociously attacked" Anderson, and when he returned to the ice after serving penalty time, the fans' bouquets turned into boos and derision. Such is the human experience. When the final horn sounded, the Cougars were 4-0 winners, Clem Loughlin having scored twice, and the Icelanders— Fredrickson and Halderson—the others.

What followed the victory over Keats and company was the first long road trip in Victoria's PCHA history. Travelling by ferry and train, the Cougars crossed the Rockies and beyond. On February 19, they faced off against the Capitals in Regina. The *Colonist* again lauded the play of Fredrickson and Halderson, but it was Harry Meeking who scored both Victoria goals in a 2-1 victory over the Capitals.

In the years major pro hockey was played in the west, the nicknaming of players was a fine art. "Cyclone," "the Long Irishman," "Old Eagle Eyes," et al. flourished under monikers their mothers had never chosen. The man responsible for the sole Capitals goal was a fellow whose birth certificate established that he was Charles Henry McVeigh, but the Regina fans knew and cherished him by another name: "Rabbit."

The next stage of the Cougars' road trip took them 160 miles northwest to Saskatoon. According to the subheading of the next-day issue of the *Daily Colonist*, the February 21 game by the meandering South Saskatchewan River was the GREATEST PRO HOCKEY SASKATOON EVER SAW. All but a minute of a "dazzling, whirlwind" game had elapsed without a goal when Fredrickson ruined goaltender Tom Murray's day with his twenty-eighth goal of the season. Murray was, of course, the same Tom Murray who had guarded Victoria's goal in 1918-19.

Murray's opposite number in the Victoria goal was Hec Fowler, who had played close to a decade in Saskatoon and was still a fan favourite. Before the game started, Fowler was presented with a case of silverware by Saskatoon mayor Howard McConnell. The silverware obviously motivated Hec to put on a display of the skills that had so endeared him to Saskatoon. Perhaps on this occasion, Fowler's talents were a little less cherished than they had been in the past. The game's final score: Victoria 1, Saskatoon 0.

After two straight victories by a one-goal margin, the Cougars went to northern Alberta and made it three in a row. In a season already remarkable for his production, Fredrickson scored four goals in the Cougars' 5-4 victory over the WCHL-leading Edmonton Eskimos. Duke Keats was almost as productive for Edmonton: he had a hand in three of the four Eskimos goals. The win brought Victoria to within a single point of the PCHA lead. As for Fredrickson, his four-goal night pushed him to thirty-two for the season and his points total, forty-nine, was an even dozen better than Mickey MacKay's aggregate to date.

The Victorians had one more date on their WCHL tour, in Calgary, February 26. Alas for the Cougars, the Tigers delivered reprisal for their loss in Victoria the month before. This time the catfight result was Tigers 4, Cougars 2, in a match the *Colonist* called "sensational. "Fredrickson opened the scoring seven minutes into the first period, on a pass from Jocko Anderson. Fredrickson scored another in the second period. But *two* Andersons were on stage this night in Calgary, and it was Jocko's younger brother, Ernie, who dominated the sibling rivalry: Ernie scored twice; his first, in the second period, put Calgary up, 2-1, his second was the clincher in the Tiger's 4-2 victory. Fredrickson's two goals bumped his season total to thirty-four in the twenty-eight games he had played.

There was one more road game to endure before the Cougars returned home. On the last day of February, Victoria played in Seattle. In the past, Victoria–Seattle matches had been commended for their civility and composure, but with Vancouver having a lock on first place, the second playoff spot was still at issue, and neither team felt disposed to go easy on the other. Peace and tranquility forgotten, near the end of the first period the two captains—Oatman for Victoria, Foyston for Seattle—initiated a battle employing both fists and sticks. Referee Mickey Ion sent off both skippers and fined each man fifteen dollars. Then Rowe and Clem Loughlin squared off. The roughhouse events stretched the *Colonist* reporter's vocabulary. Knocked repeatedly to the ice, Riley and Halderson were "kissing the ice so often they must have learned all about astronomy in one evening."

In the third period, Meeking wrapped his stick around Foyston's midsection. Mistaking Oatman as his assailant, Foyston attacked the Victoria captain. The battle joined, Oatman "took one on the cheek and went down for the count." Ion banished Foyston, but Oatman had lifted himself from the ice in time to renew his reciprocal attack on Foyston, whereupon "it was only the cool-headedness of some of the old timers that prevented a free-for-all." When the combatants got around to finishing the hockey game it was the Metropolitans who prevailed, 5-3—which set up a do-or-die final confrontation for March 2, in Victoria: the Cougars had to win in a rematch with the Metropolitans or be knocked out of the PCHA playoff yet again.

The Cougars did not blink. With every seat at the Patrick Arena sold and occupied, the Cougars decided scoring was more important than fighting. Fredrickson surpassed himself, netting four goals and assisting on two more. Mickey Ion had an easy night, compelled to call only three minor penalties. Victoria overwhelmed Seattle, 9-2, and were at last in the post-season.

Fredrickson's final-game splurge lifted him to fifty-five points for the campaign—thirty-nine goals, sixteen assists—tying him with Bernie Morris for the PCHA's best-ever season total. Two other Cougars, Harry Meeking and Clem Loughlin, finished among the top ten scorers. By contrast, in his twenty-nine games, the formerly great Tommy Dunderdale had scored just twice, a far cry from his usual form. At age thirty-five, Dunderdale was clearly not the elite player he had been for so many years. He had reached the end of the line with Lester Patrick: he would not play for him again.

The first game of the playoff to determine who would advance to the next round against the NHL representative went ahead March 7 at home. Before a full house of four thousand-plus, the Cougars were greeted with prolonged cheers when they skated onto the ice. The arena band struck up "the Cougars' marching hymn," "Abe,

Frank Fredrickson, Victoria Cougars. From his arrival in Victoria in late 1920, Fredrickson was a star in his own Patrick Arena domain and a major draw wherever he played in western hockey rinks. AUTHOR'S COLLECTION

Abe, Abe, My Boy." The Maroons' defenders focused on Fredrickson, and the tactic worked: he was stymied and so was everybody else. Art Duncan, the former ace pilot, opened the scoring for

Vancouver, and Ernie Parkes scored twice to give the Maroons a 3-0 lead in the two-game, total-goal playoff.

It was too big a deficit to overcome. On March 12, the Cougars travelled to Vancouver for the second game at Denman Street. Nine thousand fans—the biggest PCHA crowd of the season—paid to watch. As the *Colonist* saw it, the "Islanders played a beautiful game." Fredrickson scored twice, and Oatman added a third. But the great Mickey MacKay, future Hall of Famer, scored twice for Vancouver. Victoria won, 3-2, but 3-2 was not enough. For the third year in a row, it would be Vancouver that moved on.

In 1923, the rival leagues had settled on a revised format for the Stanley Cup showdown: the PCHA and NHL champions would battle to determine who would meet the WCHL winners in the Cup final. Ottawa had beaten Vancouver in 1922 and they did it again this time, prevailing in the best-of-five series by three games to one. Ottawa thus qualified to meet Duke Keats and the Edmonton Eskimos for the right to raise Lord Stanley's silverware in triumph.

The league bosses agreed to play the final at a neutral site, Vancouver. In another two-game, total-goal series, the games were closely contested. On March 29, Ottawa won, 2-1. Two days later, the last day of March, another man destined for the Hockey Hall of Fame, Punch Broadbent, scored the game's only goal. For the third time in four years, the Ottawa Senators were kings of the hockey hill.

THIRTEEN

1923-24

THE TEAM IS REFURBISHED

A S THE THIRTEENTH season of the Pacific Coast Hockey Association got underway, shadows of a war recently ended and auguries of another yet to come commanded attention in the pages of the *Daily Colonist*.

On November 11, thousands of Victorians gathered on the grounds of the BC Legislature to mark the fifth anniversary of the day the day the guns fell silent along the Western Front. Accompanied by the pipes and drums of the Sixteenth Canadian Scottish band and led by Colonel Cy Peck, VC, five hundred war veterans marched from the city library to Parliament Square, past the throngs gathered along Yates and Government Streets.

Soldiers whose war wounds prevented them from marching gathered on the legislature driveway to await the arrival of their comrades. At 11:00 AM, the city came to a standstill. People stopped what they were doing, and streetcars and motor cars halted as two minutes of silence descended upon Victoria. It was, in the eyes of the *Colonist*'s reporter, "a worthy observation of a great anniversary... a striking commentary upon the way in which the simple ceremony has seized the imagination of the Allied peoples of the Great War."

Peace and tranquility had not settled over the continent where the war had principally been fought. CHAOS IN EUROPE IS VAST PROBLEM ran the front-page headline in early December. Viscount Grey of Fallodon delivered a speech in London in which he observed that the continent was drifting back into the old arms race and headed for another war.

A *Colonist* story datelined Munich, November 14, reported that a man who had led an unsuccessful nationalist revolt in Bavaria was being held in the Landsberg prison fortress. "We have to be careful about who are his jailers," an official said, "or he will make them a speech and have them cheering for the revolution." Everyone agreed, the story went on, that the man "radiates a personal influence that is almost hypnotic." The man's name was Adolf Hitler.

By the early to the mid-1920s, it seemed that Victoria moviegoers could see one or more different Mary Pickford films every month. In 1919 Pickford had co-founded United Artists with Charlie Chaplin, Douglas Fairbanks, and the celebrated director, D.W. Griffith. Throughout the rest of the silent-film era, until 1927, the movies kept coming. Pickford, Chaplin, and Fairbanks appeared in many.

Movie lovers who preferred Wild West action movies to the sort cherished by Pickford fans had options, too. The big cowboy stars of the era such as Hoot Gibson, Tom Mix, and William S. Hart appeared routinely on Victoria's big screens. Sometimes movie fans could see a double bill—perhaps Gibson in *The Ramblin' Kid*, or Chaplin in *Sunny Side*—for the price of a single admission.

A building across town offered a different kind of mass entertainment from the sort available onscreen at the movie houses. In the autumn of 1923, Lester Patrick engineered a big makeover of his Victoria Cougars hockey team. Among the players who had enabled the Victoria club to end a long losing streak and savour playoff hockey for the first time in years, four were gone.

Wilf Loughlin had been an important cog in Lester's machine in the 1920–21 and 1921–22 seasons, but his production had slipped in 1922–23; in October, Patrick dispatched Loughlin to the NHL's Toronto St. Patricks for cash. Albert Deildal, the third-fiddle Icelander on Patrick's roster, had produced only a little in 1922–23, so Patrick declined to invite him back for an encore in the new season.

Tommy Dunderdale had contributed a good deal to Victoria's hockey successes right from the beginning, in 1912, but now aged thirty-six, his best days behind him, Dunderdale was expendable, too. In November, Patrick sold his services to the rival western club in Saskatoon. Old Tommy could expect to be warmly greeted by Victoria fans when he returned to play with his new team, and he would be.

Eddie Oatman, the Cougars' team captain, had played six seasons for Lester Patrick and had combined strong leadership skills with a well-established ability to put the puck in the enemy net. But by late 1923, Oatman was thirty-four years old. Patrick perhaps concluded that he, too, was past his prime; the Victoria boss decided to trade his veteran to the Calgary Tigers for a player seven years younger, Jimmy Gibson.

A native of the beguilingly named northwestern Ontario community of Rat Portage (later renamed Kenora), Gibson had enlisted as an infantryman in the Canada Corps while still a teenager, in 1916. He had distinguished himself as a soldier, twice being awarded the Military Medal for gallantry. It is easy to understand why Lester Patrick might have wanted to see Gibson in a Cougars sweater: in 1922–23, Gibson was Calgary's second-leading scorer, with eighteen goals in twenty-nine games. But as a new member of the Calgary Tigers, Oatman would have the motivation—and the opportunity—to demonstrate that it might have been dangerous to trade away the Cougars' reliable captain.

Patrick may have been persuaded to sign Clem Trihey to a Cougars contract not just because Trihey had established himself as an accomplished amateur in Montreal, but also because of his bloodlines. Clem's uncle, Harry Trihey, had twice been a Stanley Cup winner while playing with the Montreal Shamrocks at the turn of the century, and in time to come would be an early inductee in the Hockey Hall of Fame.

Wilfred Harold Hart, born at Brandon, Manitoba, early in Wilfrid Laurier's second term as Canada's prime minister, had enjoyed a superlative season with the Weyburn Wanderers of the South Saskatchewan Senior Hockey league in 1922–23. Hart led the Wanderers to the SSSHL title, scoring twenty goals in just ten games. If it was young blood Lester Patrick was keen to add to the Cougars roster, Hart fit the bill: he was just twenty-two when the Cougars boss persuaded him to sign his first professional contract.

The money yielded by the sale of Loughlin and Dunderdale perhaps helped in the acquisition of the fourth new Cougar. Edward Archibald Briden, better known by any of his alternate names—Archie, "Bones," or "Red"—had played for the NHA Toronto Blueshirts in 1916–17 before enlisting as a nineteen-year-old in the 228th Battalion Northern Fusiliers in the spring of 1916. On returning from the war, Briden played two years with Duke Keats in Edmonton before signing with the Seattle Metropolitans for the 1921–22 season. Red Briden was in his third season in Seattle when Lester Patrick acquired him for cash in January, 1924.

On November 14, as Herr Hitler languished in his Bavarian lockup, the Victoria Cougars' new season got off on the wrong foot. The new man, Gibson, scored twice for the Cougars in Seattle, as did Slim Halderson, and the Cougars and Mets were tied at 6-6 at the end of three periods. But it took less than two minutes of overtime for Lester Patrick's former chattel, Bobby Rowe, to settle the game in Seattle's favour.

The Cougars' November 16 home opener against Vancouver delivered a happier outcome. Gibson and Hart make Great Hit shouted a subhead in the next day's issue of the *Daily Colonist*. "Lester Patrick trotted out a pretty nifty bunch of hockey players onto the Willows rink [the Patrick Arena] last night, and they delivered in whirlwind fashion." The *Colonist* credited Frank Fredrickson with producing the highlight play of the game, and "Freddie" scored a goal of his own while setting up Hart for another to deliver "Frank Patrick's hirelings a bitter lacing," 5-1.

It did not take long for the uncherished Maroons to take retribution. On November 19, the Cougars travelled to Vancouver to receive a 7-1 thrashing at the hands of Frank Patrick's hirelings. In the battle between the former Great War fliers, it was Vancouver's Art Duncan who prevailed over the Cougars' Fredrickson. Duncan accomplished a genuine hat trick—three straight goals—straddling the first and second periods, while Fredrickson would have been little comforted that his goal was the only one Victoria could muster against Old Eagle Eyes Lehman, the Maroons' goaltender.

Following the Vancouver debacle, Lester Patrick had given his skaters what the *Colonist* called a heart-to-heart talk. The chat appeared to have done some good: Fredrickson and company redeemed themselves on November 23 in a home game against Frank Foyston's Seattle Metropolitans. Fredrickson matched Art Duncan's performance four days earlier, scoring the Cougars' first three goals. Jimmy Gibson continued to supply evidence that the trade for Oatman had been inspired: he scored the final goal in the Cougars' 4-2 win.

The *Colonist*'s game account ended with a paragraph demonstrating in one way how very different late 1923 was from our own time. A new rule took effect for the November 23 game: smoking was no longer permitted in the arena. Those wishing or desperately needing to smoke were confined to smoking rooms on the main floor.

Competing cigarette ads were everyday features of the *Colonist*, and they would have been an important revenue source for the Victoria daily, but until this new innovation—no smoking in the arena—the air at Epworth Street was typically so thick with tobacco smoke that fans were prevented from seeing the hockey action from all parts of the rink. And what was the reaction of those in attendance? In the *Colonist*'s account, the new rule was well observed and "working out with satisfaction to the players and the fans alike"—especially, no doubt, to those who preferred breathable air.

The last day of November brought the season's first inter-league encounter with one of the teams of the WCHL. Inspired by the title of a smash-hit Rudolph Valentino movie, the Saskatoon club had been the Sheiks in their inaugural WCHL season. But the team performed poorly—a record of 5-19 in twenty-four games—and low attendance had driven them to Moose Jaw by the end of the campaign. In their second season, back in Saskatoon, the unlucky Sheiks had a new name, the Crescents, but the name change failed to deliver better results: in 1922–23, Saskatoon won only eight times in thirty games. They reverted to their original moniker. The Sheiks came to Victoria hoping that the reversion would deliver better fortune. It didn't.

Despite the presence of the formidable, fearsome Newsy Lalonde in the Sheiks lineup, the "local knights of the blades [the Cougars] romped to victory" by 7-1. The *Colonist* lauded Fredrickson, Harry Meeking, and the Weyburn wonder, Hart, for their contributions to the victory. Hart, who in time would be better known as "Gizzy" than Harold to his fans, scored three goals—Fredrickson had two, with Gibson and Harry Trihey's nephew Clem adding the others. With this big win, the Cougars now lagged just a game behind first-place Seattle, and Fredrickson had surged to the lead the pack in the individual scoring race, two points ahead of Art Duncan.

In their December 7 visit to the Cougars' lair, the Calgary Tigers were less accommodating than Saskatoon had been. More than three thousand fans paid to see the popular castoff, Eddie Oatman, lead the Tigers onto the ice. Oatman did step onto the ice early—and was accorded a warm, enduring ovation—but his initial role, shared with Lester Patrick, was to officiate, not play. Referee Mickey Ion had missed the morning ferry out of Vancouver and arrived too late to do his duty from the start of the game. Oatman and Patrick filled in until Ion arrived, ten minutes late.

Though the game was said by the *Colonist*'s man to be the fastest, most thrilling of the season, Oatman's Tigers outplayed the other big cats in the rink and won, 3-1, behind Harry Oliver's two goals and another by Herb Gardiner, both men future Hall of Famers. The

Calgary defence, led by Gardiner and Red Dutton, effectively bottled up Fredrickson and kept him off the score sheet.

The *Colonist* continued to keep readers informed of world news, not all of it bad. Lord Carnarvon, excavator of King Tutankhamen's tomb at Luxor, had died unexpectedly in April from a mosquito bite infected by a razor cut. Tut's excavation continued despite Lord Carnarvon's demise. One story after another on the project took up column inches in the *Colonist*. X-rays disclosed the skeletons of shrouded mummies. Investigators reported relics of matchless beauty. The men working at Luxor retrieved a life-sized statue of Tut, made of gold. Tut's sarcophagus was to be opened. One thrill followed another.

Following the Calgary loss, the Cougars departed on this season's tour of WCHL cities. Their last experience had gone well for Lester Patrick's men: they had won three of the four games played the preceding February. Their December junket would turn out to be a different story.

The Cougars' first stop was Edmonton, December 10. Before the opening faceoff the Edmonton audience paid homage to Foley Martin, a native Albertan and member of the previous year's edition of the Calgary Tigers. Martin had died in circumstances about as quirky as those that ended the life of Lord Carnarvon. Home remedies for everything from piles to pimples, grippe to lumbago, and catarrh to corns were as lucrative a source of advertising in the nation's newspapers as were cigarettes and tobacco products. Corns, the thick, hardened calluses growing on toes unhappy with the shoes they are jammed into were a particular focus of 1920s advertising. Instead of investing in any of the advertised treatments on offer, Foley Martin had sliced off his corn with a razor blade. The blood poisoning resulting from this self-surgery killed young Martin at the age of twenty-two. The Calgary Tigers did something special in memory of Foley Martin: they retired his sweater number—number five—the first time in North American professional sports that a player was so honoured.

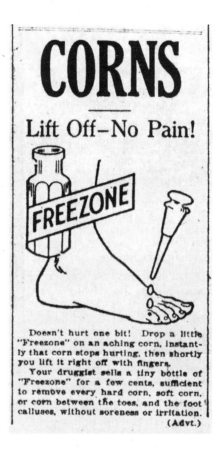

CORNS

Lift Off–No Pain!

Doesn't hurt one bit! Drop a little "Freezone" on an aching corn, instantly that corn stops hurting, then shortly you lift it right off with fingers.

Your druggist sells a tiny bottle of "Freezone" for a few cents, sufficient to remove every hard corn, soft corn, or corn between the toes, and the foot calluses, without soreness or irritation.

(Advt.)

VICTORIA *DAILY COLONIST*, DECEMBER 14, 1924

Without the advantage of artificial ice, the Edmonton Eskimos had to deal with the vexations that go along with hockey played on natural ice. Edmonton had not yet experienced a hard freeze this December, with the result that only a half inch of ice separated the players' skates from the sawdust floor of the Eskimos' rink when the Eskimos skated out for their game against Victoria. Soon enough the ice gave way and watery sawdust began emerging on the playing surface. Players had to slalom a course around holes in the ice. Clem Loughlin scored first, on a shot that bounced fortuitously out of a hole in the ice, over goaltender Hal Winkler's shoulder.

The players were fortunate: no one was injured on the corrupted ice. Fredrickson scored a goal, Hart added another. The Cougars won, 3-1, and were now tied with Seattle for the PCHA lead at four wins, three losses each. With nine goals and ten points in his seven games, Fredrickson now had a two-point lead over his fellow former flier, Art Duncan.

One column over from its account of the game in Edmonton, the *Colonist* reported that a highlight of the carnival of ice sports scheduled the following evening for the home arena was basketball on ice. The contest, pitting a Willows team against Oak Bay, was expected to "produce some of the finest comedy that has ever been staged at the Arena." The game would be played under established basketball rules with the hoopsters wearing rubbers over their shoes. Ralph Alcock, "the Charlie Chaplin of the ice," would serve as referee. If only a videographer had been equipped and available to record what happened.

As basketball on ice tipped off at the home rink, the Cougars carried on with their Prairie adventure, which would prove less serendipitous than the opener in Edmonton. On December 12, the Saskatoon Sheiks looked anything but the cellar-dwelling losers they had been the season before. Despite the lightning-fast pace described in the *Colonist* game dispatch, the result was a blowout, Saskatoon winning by 9-3. Future Hall of Famer Bill Cook led the way for Saskatoon with three goals. Once again opposition defenders focused on bottling up "the great Frank Fredrickson." He was again shut out of the scoring: no goals, no assists, no glory.

One of the Sheiks joining in the scoring fusillade was Tommy Dunderdale. Keen to show Lester Patrick that he was still a player, Tommy scored Saskatoon's eighth goal late in the third period. Might Dunderdale have felt it was one of the sweetest of his entire Hall of Fame career?

On December 14, a three-part challenge between the PCHA and WCHL clubs delivered evidence as to which league's brand was currently superior. Vancouver lost, 1-0, in Calgary, Seattle fell to the Sheiks by 2-1, and the Cougars lost, 4-2, in Regina. These results left all three Coast clubs with losing records. At Regina the Capitals won their fourth straight in a game played on "sticky" ice. The Cougars were hurt by penalties—Meeking and Fredrickson the prime offenders—when the Capitals capitalized on having the manpower advantage. The winning goal, by Barney Stanley, came with two Cougars sitting on the penalty bench. Fredrickson scored one of the Victoria goals and took a three-point lead in the scoring race.

Three days later, December 17, the WCHL clubs did it again: three wins in three games against PCHA opponents. The Victoria-Regina match, played at Winnipeg, was the most one-sided. The Capitals won, 4-1, as the *Colonist* saw it, "because they had more finish and staying power." Barney Stanley and Rabbit McVeigh divided the Regina scoring equally—two goals each—while Fredrickson's eleventh of the season was the only goal the Cougars could manage against Regina goaltender Red McCusker.

On December 19, two more defeats left the PCHA teams winless in eight tries on their mid-December road tour. Finally, at the winter solstice, December 21, Vancouver and Victoria both managed Prairie victories: Vancouver by 4-3 in Regina, Victoria by 3-2 in overtime over Saskatoon. That game, like the December 17 encounter against Regina, was played at Winnipeg.

After a first-period goal by Fredrickson—his twelfth of the season—Harry Meeking tied the game at 2-2 in the third. It took Clem Loughlin only a minute of overtime to win it, on a pass from Jimmy Gibson. The Cougars' win–loss record stood at 5-6. That mix would have left them in the WCHL basement, but in a season marked by one-sided results in inter-league games, 5-6 was the PCHA's best. At least for a while, the Cougars stood first among the coast teams. Meanwhile, the former fliers were locked in a duel for the individual scoring title: with thirteen points each, Fredrickson and Art Duncan had a four-point lead over the rest of the field.

The Cougars' prosperity did not endure. Before a Christmas Day crowd of five thousand, the Vancouver Maroons celebrated a 3-1 victory over the Cougars at the Denman Arena. But three days later the Cougars returned the favour with a narrow 3-2 win at home in

Victoria. The new guy, young Harold Hart, was the Cougars' hero, breaking a 2-2 tie with the winning goal in the fourth minute of overtime. Fredrickson assisted on Jocko Anderson's first-period goal, but he also missed a penalty shot. With a hand in both Vancouver goals, Art Duncan pushed three points ahead of Fredrickson in the battle for individual scoring honours.

As 1923 passed into 1924, the *Daily Colonist* saw to it that fans of the Victoria Cougars understood there was more to life than hockey. Early in the new year, two world figures breathed their last: Vladimir Lenin and Woodrow Wilson. In death, the Soviet leader and wartime US president would have something in common: out-of-the-ordinary interment arrangements. Lenin's body was put on display in Moscow's Red Square mausoleum, and Wilson's was placed in a sarcophagus in Washington's National Cathedral—the only US president to be awarded that honour.

Shortly after Wilson's death, former British prime minister David Lloyd George caused a sensation with the claim that Wilson and French president Georges Clemenceau had reached an agreement—behind their allies' backs—in which Wilson had given American blessing to the French occupation of the coal-rich Ruhr region. That occupation—which would not end until the summer of 1925—and the punishing war reparations forced on Germany by the victorious side in the war were just two of the issues inspiring the inmate of the Landsberg prison and his devotees to rise up against their vengeful oppressors.

European nations—not just Germany—still struggled with the social and economic upheavals generated by the Great War. On the other side of the Atlantic, Mexican president Álvaro Obregón continued to battle insurgencies that had divided his country for a decade and a half. In September, an earthquake had killed an estimated 140,000 people in Japan. In December, it was Mexico's turn: a quake in Sonora compounded Obregón's troubles.

Closer to home, a string of events demonstrated how perilous travel by sea was for west-coast people dependent on ships to get them where they wanted to go. On December 17, ten crew members were lost in the wreck of the steam schooner *C.A. Smith* near Coos Bay, Oregon. Four days later, December 21, the steamer *Astorian*—in just its second run on the Bellingham–Seattle route—rammed a barge in dense fog and sank in fifteen minutes. All twelve passengers and the crew were saved. Not so fortunate were the captain and two crew members of the tugboat *Tyee*, sunk at Pedder Bay in the fury of an early winter storm on Christmas Eve. The Christmas Day issue of the *Daily Colonist* reported that the same storm imperilled ships all along the coast, including the crew of the British steamer *Author*, "drawing ever closer towards the relentless rocks of the Washington coastline."

On dry land there was more welcome news for people wishing to journey from one place to another. On January 11, after years marked by cost overruns and controversy, the new Johnson Street Bridge finally opened. Victoria Mayor Reginald Hayward presided in a ceremony attracting several thousand citizens. The lead story in the following day's edition of the *Daily Colonist* exulted that "a huge procession of motorcars passed over the structure to Victoria West, while at the same time the afternoon train pulled slowly out of the depot and across the railway span."

The new bridge would serve Victorians for close to a century until it was replaced in 2018 by another span, one that, like its predecessor, was beset by controversy and cost overruns, a bridge that skeptics doubt will do its duty as the old "Blue Bridge" did for ninety-four years.

In 1924, the new bridge would perhaps enable residents of Victoria West and Esquimalt to join the crowds gathered at the crosstown hockey rink to watch their local hockey heroes in action.

The Cougars travelled to Seattle to take on the Metropolitans in their first game of the new year, January 2. Jack Walker, the future Hall of Famer, was the man of the hour in Seattle. Though he was thirty-five by this time and "thin-thatched," Walker liked to call himself "Young Jack." Despite his age, it was Walker who broke a scoreless tie in the second period. Jack Arbour made it 2-0 for Seattle before Harold Hart scored the Cougars' lone goal of the night. The result left the three clubs of the PCHA closely bunched, a single point separating first from last. None of them had a winning record. Fredrickson, who the year before was steamrolling his way to the scoring title, was blanked again and now trailed Duncan by four points.

The same teams played again two days later, in Victoria, and this time the Cougars prevailed. Again the game was tied after three periods and it might have remained that way until, with only four minutes left in the extra period, Fredrickson charted a course through the entire Seattle team and beat Hap Holmes for the winning goal. The *Colonist* raved about Fredrickson's performance and another Cougar, the stalwart thirty-one-year-old guarding the Victoria goal, Hec Fowler.

Fredrickson and company waited a week for their next engagement. Perhaps that was too long. On January 11, Duke Keats and the Edmonton Eskimos came to Victoria to play the latest round of "Which is the Better Brand, WCHL or PCHA?" Perhaps the joy of playing on ice they needn't worry might melt and rupture under their skates, the Eskimos answered the question conclusively. Edmonton won, 4-2. The great Keats scored the first and final goals for his team and choreographed the middle two, by Joe Simpson and Ty Arbour, Jack Arbour's kid brother. In this latest showdown between two future members of the Hockey Hall of Fame—Keats and Fredrickson—the Iron Duke left no doubt as to who was the alpha dog on this day. With just a single assist for his efforts, Fredrickson fell further behind Art Duncan.

The Cougars travelled to Vancouver and beat the Maroons on January 14, to close within a game of levelling their season record; they then proceeded to drop two in a row, to Calgary on January 18, and to Vancouver on January 23. The January 18 encounter, at home against the Tigers, must have been especially aggravating for Lester Patrick. The Tigers won convincingly, 7-3, and the castoff Eddie Oatman was a key player in the unhappy drama. Oatman led the way in several Tiger charges and scored Calgary's second goal.

Harold Hart, fast becoming a fan favourite in Victoria, scored all three Victoria goals. Fredrickson assisted on Hart's final goal but was otherwise successfully hobbled by the opposite side's defenders.

On January 25, the Cougars managed a narrow 2-1 home victory over Vancouver. Then the rudder fell off the good ship *Cougar*. Lester's skaters lost three in a row, the first to Regina, the latter two to Seattle. The February 6 through February 8 home-and-home series would have been especially galling for Patrick, as the Cougars lost by an aggregate 12-2 margin: 8-1 in Seattle on February 6, then by 4-1 on their own ice two days later.

Amid all the misery, Victoria's hockey fans might have taken comfort from events in far-off Chamonix in the French Alps. Frank Fredrickson and Slim Halderson had played leading roles in Canada's 1920 Olympic victory at Antwerp, and they must have revelled in what their successors accomplished at Chamonix in the 1924 Games. The Canadians won gold again, and did so even more convincingly than the Icelandic Canadians had managed four years earlier. They swatted aside the Czechs, Swedes, and Swiss by an aggregate 85-0 margin in the opening round. The semi-final against Britain was a little closer, 19-2; then, on February 3, the Canadians won gold by 6-1 over the United States.

In Victoria, the Cougars, season standing at 9-14 on February 8, their season appeared irredeemably lost, but the team resuscitated themselves well enough to beat Seattle, 4-1, on February 11; they then did it again in a February 15 rematch at home against Duke Keats's Edmonton Eskimos.

LESTER PATRICK'S HOPEFULS DECISIVELY TROUNCE IGLOO DWELLERS, ran the subhead in the following day's game account in the *Colonist*. In fairness, the paper conceded, the "Igloo Dwellers" were handicapped by injury, one missing in action, two skating wounded, including Joe Simpson. Harold Hart and Fredrickson were the Cougars' bright lights, with Hart scoring twice and Fredrickson once. Tables were turned. Though he had netted five goals against Seattle two nights earlier, the "Iron Duke" was held scoreless by the Cougars.

A sidebar event charmed the Eskimos audience. Saskatoon had sold Tommy Dunderdale's contract to Edmonton, and Tommy was now ranked among the Eskimos playing with Keats and Simpson. He played only five minutes in relief of Keats in the second, but Tommy was warmly welcomed by the fans for whom he had played so brilliantly all those years in Victoria. It was the last time Dunderdale played a game in Victoria.

Remarkably, though they still had a losing record—11-14 after twenty-five games—the Cougars were not yet out of it. The Prairie teams having been so dominant in inter-league play, *none* of the PCHA clubs had a winning record. The Cougars were just two points behind Seattle with two games in hand and five still to play.

In mid-month, Lester Patrick's crew left home for their second tour of WCHL cities. Between February 18 and February 27, they played five times. But for a 1-1 tie in Edmonton, they lost them all. The disaster started with a 4-3 loss in Calgary and ended with another in the same town, a 7-1 shellacking at the hands of the Tigers. For Lester Patrick, it was an ignominious end to a sad season. For Eddie Oatman, now the Calgary "skipper," it must have been delicious.

Was there a silver lining? Not much of one. The Cougars ended the campaign at 11-18-1—just eleven wins in thirty games. Fredrickson had enjoyed a season for the ages the year before. His 1923-24 numbers—excellent by ordinary-mortal standards—were only half as radiant as they had been the year before. A year ago he had left everyone far behind in the individual scoring race. This time he came second—to Art Duncan—his nineteen goals and twenty-seven points far behind the thirty-nine-goal, fifty-five-point pinnacle he had savoured the previous season.

Two other Cougars, Harold Hart and Clem Loughlin, managed to slip into the top-ten scorers list. As for the bigger picture, the league's final standings could not hide the fact that the PCHA clubs had been humbled by their WCHL opponents. Seattle finished first, with a losing record—fourteen wins, sixteen losses—just three victories better than last-place Victoria.

Relegated to the sidelines yet again, Lester Patrick and the 1923-24 Cougars could only daydream about what might have been. In the ensuing PCHA playoff—the usual two-game, total-goal arrangement—Seattle narrowly prevailed over Vancouver, 4-3. This qualified the Maroons to take on the WCHL-champion Calgary Tigers for the right to meet the NHL winners. After losing the first game in a best-of-three round, the Tigers asserted their authority, beating the Maroons by 5-3 and 3-1 in the subsequent games.

In the Stanley Cup final, played at Montreal's Mount Royal Arena and the Auditorium in Ottawa, the Tigers discovered that the Montreal Canadiens bore little resemblance to any of the PCHA opponents they had faced in the west. Montreal won, 6-1, on March 22 and by 3-0 on March 25. The Seattle Metropolitans had won the Cup in 1917 but, excepting 1919, when the Spanish Influenza wiped out the final, the NHL representative had prevailed in the Cup final eight straight times.

From Lester Patrick's point of view, the picture looked even gloomier. His Victoria pros had won the PCHA title in 1913 and 1914 but had claimed not a single one since. Over the past eight seasons, he had been a mere spectator as Seattle won three league titles and his younger brother Frank five in Vancouver.

FOURTEEN

1924-25

SPOILS OF AN ILL WIND

N 1924, A HOCKEY ill wind blew through the city of Seattle and the whole Pacific Coast Hockey Association. The owners of the land on which the Seattle Ice Arena stood decided they had a better purpose for their property than the playing of professional hockey: a parking lot. There was a need to provide ample parking for the well-heeled clientele that would be staying at the new, state-of-the-art Olympic Hotel on University Street between Fourth and Fifth Avenues. The Seattle Metropolitans, Stanley Cup winners in 1917 and four-time PCHA champions, were suddenly without a home.

For a time the Patrick brothers, Lester and Frank, together with their Seattle collaborators, sought alternate arrangements so that Seattle hockey fans could continue to watch and root for their hockey heroes. The efforts came to naught; the Seattle Mets were obliged to fold operations. A hockey league with just three teams is lean enough, but a two-team configuration is beyond the pale: after thirteen seasons the PCHA itself was obliged to call it a day. Fortunately for the Patricks and hockey fans in the surviving PCHA cities—Vancouver and Victoria—the previous two seasons had featured inter-league play between the PCHA clubs and those of the Western Canadian Hockey League. It thus came to pass that the

Vancouver Maroons and Victoria Cougars joined the WCHL, expanding that circuit's members to six teams for the 1924–25 season.

With nowhere to play anywhere near Puget Sound, the men who had toiled as Seattle Mets were obliged to look elsewhere if they wished to continue their careers in pro hockey. Jim Riley decided to take a break from one sport to focus on another: baseball. Bobby Rowe and Alvin Fisher joined NHL clubs. Jack Arbour signed with the Calgary Tigers. Two players, Fred Harris and Gordon MacFarlane, agreed to play with Frank Patrick's Maroons in Vancouver.

But it was Frank's elder brother who salvaged the greatest haul from Seattle's sinking: *four* Metropolitans agreed to Lester Patrick's terms for playing hockey in Victoria in the winter of 1924–25. At age thirty-three, Frank Foyston mulled the possibility of retiring. He let Patrick know that if he was to play in Victoria he wanted to be joined by his long-time teammates, Jack Walker and Hap Holmes. The Victoria boss made it happen: he persuaded all three to become Victoria Cougars. Neither Walker nor Holmes could imagine their best years were ahead of them; at age thirty-six, the sidekicks were even older than Foyston. It was nonetheless a windfall for the Victoria owner: every one of the trio would one day join Patrick and Frank Fredrickson in the Hockey Hall of Fame. Each of the former Mets would demonstrate in the new season that even in their mid-thirties, they were still valuable players.

The fourth Metropolitan, Gordon Fraser, was no slouch either. By late 1924, Fraser was a veteran of eleven hockey seasons. In 1923–24, he had been Seattle's third-best goal-scorer, behind Foyston and Walker, with fourteen goals in thirty games. Fraser was effective, and combative, too. In one category he had led not just the Mets but the entire PCHA—in penalty minutes. Already thirty when he agreed to play in Victoria, Fraser had plenty left in the tank: he would still be playing pro hockey in 1936 at the advanced age of forty-one.

But what were the consequences of Lester's new signings for the men who had worked for him in 1923–24? To make room for the new quartet, four of the 1923–24 Cougars were shown the door.

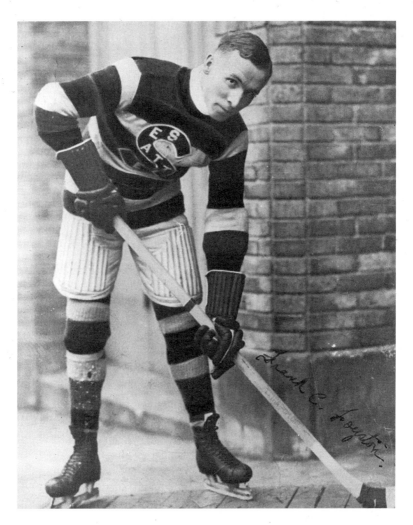

Frank Foyston, Seattle Metropolitans, 1917. Foyston's Stanley Cup triumph with the Victoria Cougars in 1925 was his third. He won his first with the Toronto Blueshirts of the National Hockey Association in 1914. His second came with the 1917 Seattle Metropolitans of the Pacific Coast Hockey Association. Foyston was awarded his place in the Hockey Hall of Fame in 1958. COURTESY HOCKEYGODS

The war hero, Jimmy Gibson, had won kudos for his play a year ago, but he was out, and would never take another shift in professional hockey. Clem Trihey had not been productive in Victoria—just a single goal in twenty-four games—and would not be missed. Archie Briden had enjoyed a solid fifteen-goal season with the Mets and Cougars the year before, but he was dispatched to the Edmonton Eskimos, where he would be an occasional stone in Lester's shoe during the new season.

Perhaps the Cougar given the shortest shrift was the veteran goaltender, Hec Fowler. Fowler had guarded the Victoria goal for six seasons and was an occasional PCHA all-star. But with the arrival of the great Hap Holmes in Victoria, old Hec was suddenly dispensable. He was shipped to the NHL Boston Bruins for cash. In Boston, Fowler played a few games with the Bruins before he was let go. He then signed with Edmonton, where he played effectively and would enjoy a measure of payback in 1925, when the Eskimos faced off against his former teammates.

As Lester Patrick's refurbished hockey club prepared for its first post-PCHA hockey season, the world beyond the Patrick Arena continued its worrisome ways. Unemployment remained a problem in post-war Canada. The price of wheat fell through the grain-elevator floor, causing hardship for Prairie farmers. Debate persisted in the British Columbia legislature about how to confront the "yellow peril"—immigration from China and Japan.

In the world beyond the nation's borders, Germany wore the albatross of enormous war reparations around its collective neck. Afflicted with myriad other economic problems, Germany continued to roil in political turmoil. Demands for German rearmament grew within the Fatherland. Informed outside observers worried that unless Germany's reparations burden was materially eased, another war was inevitable.

As auguries of a future war raised alarm, commemoration of the one ended just six years earlier grew in importance. In Ottawa, proposals for a national war memorial got underway. It would take a dozen years, but the proposal was grandly realized in 1936, when King George VI and Queen Elizabeth dedicated the monument around which the country's principal Remembrance Day ceremony has been conducted ever since.

The Victoria *Daily Colonist* provided distractions for folks looking for relief from war and rumours of war. A new feature—the daily crossword puzzle—appeared in the pages of the Victoria daily. Spoilsports fretted that crossword puzzles were a frivolous waste of time and would diminish people's intelligence. The *Colonist* printed them anyway.

An entire new section appeared, one devoted entirely to the wonder of radio. The section became a regular item in the paper's Sunday edition. Its content included detailed instructions and diagrams for building a receiving kit of one's own. The *Colonist* also delivered guides—what to listen to—to assist a clever kit assembler after the receiver was built and operational. Not everyone thought radio a good thing. Those whose livelihood was rooted in other entertainment forms feared that radio would be their undoing. RADIO IS THEATRE'S GREATEST MENACE, one *Colonist* headline fretted. COMPOSERS DECLARE NEW WAR ON RADIO, ran another.

Perhaps the worrywarts needn't have stewed. In Victoria people still paid to see the latest Hollywood offerings. They still paid big bucks to see Anna Pavlova or Sergei Rachmaninoff when such international stars performed in Victoria.

Soon there would be another city amenity to which Victorians could go to spend their quarters and dollars. A year earlier, voters had approved by a margin of eight to one a proposal to spend public money for the construction of a public amusement centre. By the new year of 1925, the foundation for the Crystal Garden had been laid and the city was well on its way to having its first indoor swimming pool, a handsome steel-and-glass structure unique in Canada.

Designed by prominent architects Francis Mawson Rattenbury—designer of the BC Legislature and Empress Hotel—and Percy Leonard James, the Crystal Garden played an important part in the city's social development. Even a century after its construction, the building retains its architectural allure, a registered Canadian Historic Site and enduring tourist attraction.

Apart from the city's theatres, cinema houses, and soon-to-be-completed Crystal Garden pool, citizens seeking diversion and entertainment also had hockey. Fans could go to the Patrick Arena to pay as little as twenty-five cents or as much as a buck and a half to watch the Victoria Cougars in their latest grail quest for the Stanley Cup.

The reconstituted Cougars skated off on the right foot to start the new season. They travelled to Winnipeg, a city without a WCHL franchise, to play the first two games of the season. On December 8, the Cougars paid homage to their former captain Eddie Oatman by handing the Calgary Tigers a 4-1 beating. As seen by the *Colonist*, the result was "a victory for science over brute strength. "One of the new guys, Jack Walker, did most of the damage for the Cougars, with two goals and an assist.

Three days later, still in Winnipeg, the Cougars made it two in a row with a 4-3 victory over Frank Patrick's Vancouver Maroons. The Manitoba Icelanders—Fredrickson and Halderson—led the way for Victoria, each recording a goal and assist.

Then, for a while, the Cougars reverted to old ways: they took the train across the Rockies and proceeded to lose three in a row to Prairie adversaries. After losing by 4-1 in Saskatoon on December 13, they dropped another in Edmonton by 2-0 on December 16. It was a game the *Colonist* described as one of the fastest ever played in Edmonton. Perhaps it was no wonder the players moved swiftly: outside the building, Edmonton's air temperature had fallen to minus forty degrees Fahrenheit, an outlandish state of affairs for players accustomed to the version of winter enjoyed along the margins of Juan de Fuca Strait and Puget Sound.

In Calgary, on December 17, "[the] snarling Victoria Cougars we've heard so much about, turned out to be as gentle and harmless as a house kitten playing with grandma's ball of yarn." Twenty-five hundred Calgary fans braved minus-thirty-five-degree-Fahrenheit weather to see another super-fast game. Two future Hall of Famers dominated the Calgary scoring: Harry Oliver with two goals, Red Dutton with another. Calgary won, 4-2.

The new Cougar blood saw to it that the losing streak did not continue. On the way back home, Victoria stopped at Denman Street three days before Christmas and vanquished the Maroons, 1-0. It was Fredrickson who scored the game's lone goal midway through the second period.

The win over Vancouver was the first of four in a row. On Christmas Day, a Thursday, the Maroons came for a return engagement in Victoria. They lost again. The Cougars sent "three thousand local railbirds home happy on Christmas afternoon, and in the right humour and with an appetite for a nice turkey dinner." Fredrickson shone again, scoring three goals in a 4-2 Victoria win.

On December 27, the Victoria lineup provided fresh evidence that the Cougars were a team to fear in 1924–25. The Regina Capitals came to town for a 5-0 thrashing at the hands of Lester Patrick's reinforced team. After two goals from Harry Meeking, it was the new arrivals who looked after the Victoria scoring: Fraser with two goals, Foyston with a goal and assist.

If a 5-0 score had failed to impress anyone paying attention, the Cougars' next game, on New Year's Day, erased any residual doubt. Victoria welcomed the new year in Vancouver, where they proceeded to hammer the Maroons by 11-2. One of the Cougars joining in the January 1 feeding frenzy was another new member of the team. Wally Elmer scored twice and handled himself well enough to have the *Colonist*'s hockey reporter pay him particular notice.

It was a special day for Wallace Druce Elmer: January 1 just happened to be his twenty-seventh birthday. He had played the previous two seasons in Saskatoon, where it was hard to stand out in the proximity of Newsy Lalonde, Bill Cook, and Rusty Crawford, but those future Hall of Famers had an advantage over Elmer: they had two eyes with which to see; Wally had to make do with one. Elmer would play just the one season for Lester Patrick, but it would prove to be a momentous one.

On January 3, motivated perhaps by the ill treatment inflicted upon them three days earlier, the Maroons revived and managed a 3-0 victory in the Cougars' own Victoria lair. But that turned out to be just a bump in the Cougars' road. Victoria won two more, 5-1 against visiting Calgary on January 7, and 3-2 over Saskatoon, January 10. This raised their season record to 8-4, eight wins in twelve games.

The Calgary game gave the *Colonist* reporter plenty to gloat about. In his view the Cougars outplayed and outclassed the Tigers throughout the game, and he seemed to take particular relish that Eddie Oatman, the former Cougar captain, had showed he'd "slowed up a lot" since his previous appearance in Victoria. Perhaps Oatman was soured by his own and his mates' performance. He resorted to a sideshow of fisticuffs—with Slim Halderson—and both were rewarded by referee Mickey Ion with ten-minute penalties for their troubles.

After their narrow January 10 win over Saskatoon, Victoria managed just two victories in their next six games, and thus diminished their season record to 10-8 by January 28. Then they beat George Hay, Dick Irvin, and the other Regina Capitals in back-to-back games at home in Victoria at the end of January.

In the ten-day period starting February 4, they lost four times in five games, which left Lester Patrick's crew in positive territory by just a single game—thirteen wins, twelve losses—with three games left to play in the regular season. Some of the Victoria "railbirds" perhaps wondered if, despite the infusion of excellent new talent, the Cougars were reverting to old habits. With three WCHL teams ahead of the Cougars in terms of games lost, Cougars fans must have worried: was gold going to turn to dross yet again?

They needn't have allowed their precious sleep to be disrupted. Lester Patrick had successfully reconfigured his Victoria personnel. Determined to keep their fate in their own hands, the revitalized

Cougars won all three of their remaining games. On February 18, Victoria shut out the visiting Maroons, 4-0. Five days later, February 23, they did it again, this time by 3-2 at the big Denman Street arena. The final game of the regular season, March 1 at home in Victoria, turned out to be a 5-1 waltz against Saskatoon.

When the smoke cleared, the Victoria Cougars had made it to the post-season. They finished two points in arrears of first-place Calgary and one behind second-place Saskatoon. In the new six-team WCHL landscape, that was good enough. The second and third finishers were obliged to face each other for the right to play Calgary for the WCHL championship. The semi-final would once again be a two-game, total-goal affair, commencing March 6 in Victoria.

In the meantime, where had Frank Fredrickson finished in the contest for bragging rights in the individual scoring competition? The season before, he had finished second to Vancouver's Art Duncan. "Freddie" was a runner-up this time too. Four future members of the Hockey Hall of Fame—Mickey MacKay, Harry Oliver, Duke Keats, and Bill Cook—were bunched within a point of one another on top of the scoring ladder, with MacKay and Oliver at thirty-three points, and Keats and Cook at 32. Fredrickson finished two points behind them—thirty for the season—to finish fifth overall, the only Victoria Cougar to make the top-ten list.

"All roads lead to the Willows tonight," the *Colonist* reported on the opening day off the Saskatoon-Victoria playoff. The rush for tickets was said to have broken all records. Fans could "hardly wait [for] the time when Mickey Ion will let the elusive disc slide out of his hand—and start the rival clans of puckchasers off to the merriest fracas of the season."

The fans crowded into the Patrick Arena got what they wanted. Fredrickson eased anxiety early, scoring the game's opening goal just four and a half minutes into the action. His fellow Olympian, Halderson, made it 2-0 midway through the second period. Corb Denneny's goal with less than six minutes left to play in the third made it 2-1 and "put heart in the visitors and those in the audience who were anxious for the Saskatchewan outfit to win." Two minutes later pandemonium broke loose and the "rafters echoed with the lusty cheers" that erupted when Jack Walker scored the clincher in a 3-1 Victoria win.

Now the fans had to wait four fretful days as the Cougars travelled to Saskatoon for the deciding game. There was just cause for worry: in the regular schedule the Cougars had won all three times they had faced the Sheiks in Victoria—and Saskatoon had won all three played on their home ice.

In a game the *Colonist* called one of the "most sensational played here this winter," both teams rose to the occasion for the March 10 finale. The former Metropolitans opened the scoring, Foyston making it 1-0 on an assist from Jack Walker. Victoria watched the most dangerous of the Sheiks, Bill Cook, "like a hawk," which delivered opportunity to the former war hero's teammates. Fred Gordon scored for Saskatoon in the second period to tie the game at 1-1. Fredrickson answered, giving the Cougars a 2-1 lead going into the third. The Sheiks scored twice in the final period but the other Frank—Foyston—did, too, and the game ended 3-3, delivering victory to the Victoria Cougars by a 6-4 margin for the series.

This qualified the Cougars to square off against Eddie Oatman's Calgary Tigers for the WCHL championship in another two-game, total-goal series. Having finished first in the regular schedule, the Tigers won the right to be the host team for Game 1.

By March 15, the morning after the first game on the far side of the Rockies, the Cougars' story was not just the lead item in the *Colonist* sports section, but the headline news item of the newspaper's front page. The latest developments in the progress of the League of Nations could not compete with the hockey story. Nor could the discoveries reported from the opening of another ancient pharaoh's tomb in Egypt. Victoria Holds Calgary to Draw on Prairie Ice, ran the banner headline in the March 15 edition.

The Calgary arena was "packed to the roof, the crowd being the largest and most enthusiastic that ever witnessed a hockey contest

Jack Walker, Victoria Cougars. Together with teammates Frank Foyston and Hap Holmes, Jack Walker had won the Stanley Cup in 1914, with Toronto, and three years later with the PCHA Seattle Metropolitans in 1917. By 1925 the trio were all in their mid-thirties, but they won again in 1925 with Lester Patrick's Victoria Cougars. Walker was recognized by the Hockey Hall of Fame as one of the all-time greats in 1960. COURTESY HOCKEYGODS

in Calgary." For the first two periods, goaltenders and defencemen controlled the game. Neither team scored in the first period, nor in the second. Finally, in the sixth minute of the third, Jack Walker made it 1-0 for Victoria. Cully Wilson tied it for Calgary on a goal enabled by ex-Cougar-captain Eddie Oatman, but that was it:

neither team managed to break the tie. The Tigers and Cougars would return to Victoria to settle the championship on March 18.

The front page of the March 19 edition of the *Victoria Colonist* reported on memorial services for the recently deceased Chinese president, Sun Yat-sen. Marquess Curzon, former Viceroy of India, was near death in London. Agnes McPhail, sole female member of the Canadian House of Commons, was in the news for the penitentiary reforms she was pursuing in Ottawa. But none of these front-page items, except for a lethal tornado in the US, could compete with the day's biggest story: VICTORIA'S HOCKEY TEAM BRINGS CHAMPIONSHIP TO CITY.

Accompanied by a photo of Lester Patrick, formally attired in suit and tie, the lead began with this: "Hail to the Victoria Cougars, champions of the Western Canada Hockey League, and contenders for the coveted Stanley Cup." Victoria had won the deciding game the night before by 2-0. The scoring heroes were the ever-reliable Jack Walker and Frank Fredrickson. The big Icelander, "one of the most brilliant players that the hockey sport has ever produced... elicited for him the cheers of the vast assemblage, which jammed every corner of the Willows rink, and saw the game of games."

Praise for Walker was almost as golden: "There is a crafty man on the Cougars' roster upon whom too much praise cannot be lavished... [Walker] is in the game from start to finish, always employing his cunning to superb advantage." And with that, the Victoria Cougars were in the Stanley Cup final.

Having successfully confronted one ambush of Tigers, Victoria might have proceeded directly to another. Rather like the Cougars of Victoria, the Hamilton Tigers had been chronic losers, finishing last in every one of their first four years in the National Hockey League. But in 1924-25 the Tigers went from worst to first, finishing with the NHL's best record. Sudden success perhaps turned the Tigers a little giddy. Led by the brother act of Red and Shorty Green and reinforced by a former Victoria chattel of Lester Patrick's, Goldie Prodgers, the Hamilton lads decided their first-place finish gave them some unaccustomed leverage.

The Tigers demanded that the Hamilton owner pay each player an extra two hundred dollars to supply their services in the NHL playoff, or else they wouldn't play. It turned out to be a decision of surpassing hubris. Distinctly unamused, the hard-as-nails league president, Frank Calder, not only refused to let Hamilton general manager Percy Thompson accede to the players' demands, he suspended them all and disqualified the team from the playoffs. The Tigers' March 9 regular-season game against Montreal would be the last they ever played. In the subsequent off-season, the Hamilton assets were sold off and the former Tigers morphed into the New York Americans. The first strike in major pro history had turned out very badly for the players.

With the first-place Tigers dismissed from the stage, the league championship was sorted out by a playoff between the second- and third-place finishers, the Montreal Canadiens and Toronto St. Patricks. In the usual two-game, total-goal format, it was the Canadiens who prevailed. After winning the first game at home in Montreal, 3-2, on March 11, they put Toronto out of its misery with a 2-0 victory at Toronto's Mutual Street Arena on March 13.

Winners of the Stanley Cup in 1924, the Canadiens were a formidable troupe. The roster was shot through with players destined for a place in the Hockey Hall of Fame—*five* of them. One, Sprague Cleghorn, a brutal, bruising defenceman not celebrated for his on-ice ethics, was in the fourteenth year of his long NHA–NHL career. He had led the NHL in penalty minutes in 1921-22, and more significantly, had been a Stanley Cup winner in 1920, 1921, and 1924.

Georges Vézina, the Canadiens goaltender and the player honoured in the naming of the NHL's best-goaltender award, was another fourteen-year veteran. The three remaining future Hall of Famers were just entering their hockey prime. Twenty-three year old Aurèle Joliat had led the Canadiens' goal scorers with thirty during the regular season. Silvio Mantha, still just twenty-one, was a robust defenceman who would win the Stanley Cup three times while playing in Montreal. The last of the future Montreal Hall of Famers was a twenty-two-year-old in his second season. Howie

Morenz lagged just two goals behind Joliat in the season just ended and would become a player widely regarded as one of the best of all time.

The Cougars had their work cut out for them, but thanks to the decision to convert the Seattle Ice Arena into a parking garage, Victoria could also boast a roster crowded with future Hall of Famers—Fredrickson, Foyston, Walker, and Hap Holmes.

Rather than the familiar two-game, total-goal format, the Stanley Cup final in 1925 would be a best-of-five arrangement—the first team to win three games would be kings of the professional hockey mountain. The Cougars enjoyed a significant advantage before the first faceoff. It was the west's turn to host the Cup final: every game would be played on the west coast. The Cougars would be buoyed by the support of a loud and loyal legion of fans.

The opener went ahead on home ice on the first day of spring, March 21. A major front-page story in the following day's edition of the Victoria *Daily Colonist* reported that the newly established League of Nations had been delivered a serious blow by Great Britain's refusal to go along with an important League protocol.

But not even a significant threat to European peace and security could displace the headline story in the city of Victoria. Cougars Jump into Lead in World's Ice Series, ran the banner headline. More than four thousand people had sardined themselves into the Patrick Arena to see the game. The *Colonist* called it "a very spectacular affair"; it was a fiercely contested one, too. The Canadiens "laid the hickory on the local boys in plentiful fashion," delivering nasty cuts to the faces of Slim Halderson and Clem Loughlin. When Joliat and Jocko Anderson came to blows, the maestro referee, Mickey Ion, was hard-pressed to keep the match from tumbling out of control. But he did.

The players who rose to the occasion for Victoria were the ones Cougar fans might have predicted would do it. Jack Walker scored the game's first goal in the fourth minute of the first period. Then Slim Halderson made it 2-0 in a fine combination with Fredrickson. In the second, Jack Walker scored another. Ahead 3-0 going into the third, Gord Fraser, playing his best match of the year, made it 4-0. The Canadiens' Billy Coutu broke the drought to make the score 4-1, but Fraser replied with his second of the game a half-minute later. Morenz scored Montreal's second goal later in the third, but it was too little, too late. Victoria had prevailed in Game One by 5-2.

The privilege of hosting the series' second game went to the Patrick Arena on Denman Street in Vancouver. With its ten-thousand-seat capacity, the Denman rink promised a much bigger payday for the principals, Lester Patrick and the Canadiens owner, Léo Dandurand.

The gambit worked. Before "one of the largest crowds of fans that ever jammed into the big hockey arena," the Cougars won again. The following morning the Cougar' victory was only the second-biggest story on the *Colonist* front page. The lead headline reported that European leaders had agreed to hold a conference to fix borders and sort out the continent's security issues. Despite that weighty matter, it was clear that the *real* story of the day in Victoria was the result of the hockey game the previous night in Vancouver. In its lead paragraph, the *Colonist* exulted that the Victoria Cougars now needed "only another match and the hockey championship of the universe is theirs."

The "Old Fox," Walker, worked his magic again. He scored the game's first goal at 8:15 of the opening period. Halderson, playing what the *Colonist* called his best game of the season, facilitated another, by Fredrickson, before the end of the period. "The two Franks, Fredrickson and Foyston, had a great night, and they were prominent factors in the Cougars' signal win," wrote the *Colonist* reporter.

Early in the second period, a Joliat–Cleghorn collaboration narrowed the Montreal deficit to 2-1, but in the third period, Walker ingratiated himself with Cougars' fans, scoring his second of the game to make the final score Victoria 3, Montreal 1.

All the Cougars needed to send Victoria hockey fans into a frenzy was to deliver a third straight victory back in their own rink on March 27. But *les Canadiens* were not done yet, or perhaps the

VICTORIA *DAILY COLONIST*, MARCH 31, 1925

Cougars relaxed a little. In the result, Montreal won by 4-2 and thus threw a spanner into Lester Patrick's best-laid plans. Showing phenomenal speed, the "Flying Frenchmen" raced out of the gate. The superstars, Joliat and Morenz, divided the Montreal scoring equally between them—two goals each. It was left to two Cougar lesser lights, Gizzy Hart and Jocko Anderson, to answer for Victoria.

Even after years of inter-league play, there were still variations between the NHL and WCHL rulebooks. Game Four would be played under NHL rules, a fact that must have worried the Cougars and their fans as the clubs anticipated the next game, in Victoria, March 30.

Had the Montrealers overextended themselves in the effort to avoid elimination in the third game? Whatever the case, the anxiety that might have troubled Victoria players and fans in advance of Game Four was quickly remedied by what happened on the second-last evening of March. Nothing else that might have taken place in the world during the preceding twenty-four hours could possibly displace the story of the day in the Garden City. The headline, in inch-and-a-half type, that ran across the front page of the *Daily Colonist* said it all: COUGARS WIN STANLEY CUP. The Cougars won, and it had not been close: the final score was 6-1 for Victoria. With perhaps a soupçon of overstatement, a subheading offered this sober reflection: PRIDE OF VICTORIA UPHOLD HONOUR OF CITY IN CRUCIAL CONFLICT.

To the editor of the *Daily Colonist*, the clinching Stanley Cup game and all the playoff games that led to the final 6-1 triumph over

Harry "Hap" Holmes was a member of more Stanley-Cup-winning teams than any other player Lester Patrick brought to Victoria. The goaltender won his first Cup with the Toronto Blueshirts in 1914, his second with Seattle of the PCHA in 1917, his third with the NHL Toronto Arenas in 1918, and his last with the Victoria Cougars in 1925. Holmes' recognition as a Hockey Hall of Fame player came about in 1972. COURTESY HOCKEYGODS

Montreal was *news*. And not just any news, but the lead front-page story of the day. Another editor saw things differently. For the man in charge of deciding what warranted front-page treatment in the *Daily Times*, the Cougars' victory was strictly a *sports* story—and, of course, to many sensible people, that is all it was. On March 15, the same day the *Colonist*'s headline story described the game as an event in which the Cougars had upheld the honour of the city in a "crucial conflict," the game rated barely a mention on the front page of the *Times*. There was a small box indicating that the hockey team would be favoured by a civic reception. Nothing else. *Times* subscribers looking for details of the great victory had to turn to the sports page for what they wanted.

Who in particular had saved the city's honour? In a series marked throughout by his prowess in the Victoria goal, Hap Holmes had had another outstanding game. Holmes had allowed the Canadiens an average of only two goals a game, half as many as Vézina had surrendered. As he had done throughout his five seasons in Victoria, Frank Fredrickson had delivered all that great occasion demanded: he scored the game's first goal and then added another to put the Cougars up by 5-1 in the final period. Hart, Halderson, Foyston, and team captain Clem Loughlin contributed goals of their own. On this night, Jack Walker wasn't indispensable: the Old Fox went without a goal. Aptly, however, Fredrickson and Walker finished the series tied for individual scoring honours, each with three goals and five points.

For the first time since 1917, a western team were Stanley Cup champions. Merchants sought to capitalize on the Cup victory: to honour the city's hockey heroes, the auto dealer, Plimley's, ran an ad in the *Colonist* offering discounts on their stock of used cars.

The city organized a congratulatory banquet for the Chamber of Commerce auditorium, with Mayor Pendray presiding. The Rotary Club orchestra provided musical accompaniment. Gold medals happily paid for by the citizens of the city were struck and awarded to the players. Members of the Chamber of Commerce exulted that the Stanley Cup victory would provide Victoria with "publicity of the highest order in all the newspapers of America."

For Lester Patrick, Cougars owner, manager, and sometime player, the Cup victory of 1925 must have felt something like a providential gift. It had been eleven years since his club had won a league championship, eleven years since his previous shot at the

The 1924–25 Stanley Cup-winning Victoria Cougars. Clockwise from upper left: Gord Fraser, Wally Elmer, Lester Patrick, Clem Loughlin, Jack Walker, Harold Hart, Harry Meeking, Jocko Anderson, Hap Holmes, Frank Fredrickson, Harold Halderson, Frank Foyston. Patrick, Foyston, Fredrickson, Walker, and Holmes would eventually be inducted in the Hockey Hall of Fame. COURTESY DAVID MACDONALD

Stanley Cup. A world war enduring more than four years had come and gone. His Pacific Coast Hockey Association had also come and gone. After a long stretch in the hockey wilderness, he was once again on top of the hockey world. With the team of luminaries he had put together in the wake of the Seattle collapse, he must have looked forward to 1925–26 with unrestrained optimism.

FIFTEEN

1925-26

LAST TIME AROUND

THROUGHOUT THEIR FIFTEEN-YEAR regime as western hockey tycoons, *change* had been a constant companion to Lester and Frank Patrick. Much of the change was of their own choosing. The brothers, with Frank in the lead role, had been the greatest innovators in the history of the game. By 1925, hockey was a very different affair from what it had been a decade and a half earlier. The blueline, forward pass, penalty shot, changing on the fly, and the moving goaltender are among the most prominent Patrick innovations, but the list is longer than those five.

Other changes—ones forced upon the brothers—occurred routinely as one season of major professional hockey in the west led to another. Only one team stayed the entire fifteen-year course: Frank Patrick's Vancouver club, variously named the Terminals, Millionaires, and Maroons. The original team based in New Westminster came and went, as did clubs in Spokane, Portland, and Seattle. Lester Patrick's own Victoria club lost two seasons when the Epworth Street arena was commandeered for war purposes by the Canadian military in 1916.

In Saskatoon, owning and operating a top-level pro hockey club had never been an especially profitable venture. In 1921–22, the inaugural season of the Western Canada Hockey League, attendance at games of the Saskatoon Sheiks had been so ungratifying for those bankrolling the team that they packed up and temporarily transferred operations to Moose Jaw.

In the late fall of 1925, one more unwelcome change disrupted proceedings in the west. The other Saskatchewan club, the Regina Capitals, were adept at losing money too. The number of people in Regina willing to pay for the joy of watching the Capitals was insufficient to cover the team's operating costs. The bosses decided to move the team south of the Forty-ninth Parallel: the Regina Capitals morphed into the Portland Rosebuds. It had happened before.

The first incarnation of the Portland Rosebuds, 1914–17, had been brought about by the demise of the New Westminster Royals. That, too, had been a move prompted by notions of the grass being greener elsewhere, but the Rosebuds lasted only three years before most of the players were packaged up and used to stock Lester Patrick's Victoria club when the war finally ended and his Aristocrats were allowed to take back their arena.

That forced another change. It wouldn't do to adhere to the name Western *Canada* Hockey League if one of the league members was based in the United States of America. The WCHL became the WHL, a shorter, more apt acronym.

As the 1925–26 hockey season unfolded in the northwestern reaches of the continent, the world beyond the happy confines of Victoria remained as dangerous and discouraging as ever. Ships continued to sink, with the loss of the passengers and crewmen who relied on them to get where they were going. The year 1926 was a bad time to be a miner, too. A mid-January disaster cost the lives of ninety-three miners in Wilburton, Oklahoma. Two days later nineteen coal miners perished in a mine explosion at Fairmont, West Virginia. A fortnight after that, a blast trapped another twenty-one miners underground at Horning, Pennsylvania. In Australia, two hundred firefighters battled a huge bushfire near Wagga Wagga, New South Wales.

Troubles continued to torment war-ravaged Europe, but by the winter of 1925–26 conflict also roiled in other regions. The death of Sun Yat-sen led to a war of succession in China. A *Daily Colonist* front-page story in late December described a battlefield covered with dead on the Yangtsun Front. The Italian dictator Benito Mussolini seized Somaliland. Terms of the Treaty of Versailles peace delivered unintended consequences in the Near East: in an augury of troubles to come, violence erupted in Syria and Iraq.

But distant places also delivered positive, even exciting news. Archaeologists continued to make stirring finds in the tombs of the ancient pharaohs of Egypt. In early January, the *Colonist* reported on a new expedition aimed at discovering the continent long believed to be hidden in the Arctic. Partly sponsored by the National Geographical Society, the expedition would rely not on ships to realize their objectives, but flying machines. It was hard to keep up: in no time at all, five different parties were planning to make Arctic inroads using airplanes. One party announced that once it had found land near the North Pole, it planned to claim it for the US. Yet another far-removed expedition planned on using aircraft to "conquer" Mount Everest.

Scientists made headlines too. Geologists determined a new calculation of the planet's age: 1.5 billion years, appreciably closer to the 4.5 billion-year antiquity calculated by modern geoscientists.

Hollywood continued to produce of the sort of movies Victorians loved to see. Mary Pickford remained a celebrity, but early in the new year she had a new rival: Man o' War, the great racehorse, starred in *Kentucky Pride*, available for viewing at the downtown Columbia cinema for a mere twenty cents.

Celebrated performers continued to make Victoria a stop on their tours. Though almost entirely forgotten now, Anna Case was an acclaimed soprano who had been recorded by Thomas Edison. In early December, Ms. Case came to town, her performance on the Royal Victoria stage rapturously received by an adoring Victoria audience.

In only a short time, the new Crystal Garden was already appreciated as a major city amenity. On December 4, the *Colonist* reported that one of the most elaborate cabarets ever arranged in the city had captivated those on hand to play bridge or mah-jong in the afternoon, or to watch the splendid display of swimming and diving that followed. But that was not all. Later, a remarkable evening of music and dance ensued, featuring Ivo Henderson's orchestra. A particular highlight was the Egyptian fantasy, "Long Ago in Egypt," featuring a troupe of female performers singing and dancing in costume in an exotic "Oriental" setting. What a grand affair it must have been.

But, of course, Victorians had more: they continued to enjoy the benefit of major-league professional hockey. Now that their Victoria Cougars were champions of the entire universe, the Epworth Street rink continued to be a magnet for those preferring exciting live entertainment to what was available on downtown movie screens.

Over the years, Lester Patrick had tended to take a see-saw approach to personnel matters: in some seasons he left well enough alone, keeping the team roster largely unchanged from the preceding season. In other years, he saw to it that his club underwent a substantial overhaul. Given that the 1924–25 team had won the Stanley Cup the preceding March, Patrick gave essentially the same cast the opportunity to do it again. In the new season he made just one personnel switch: Russell Oatman took over for Wally Elmer.

If the name Oatman rings a bell, there is good reason. Russell Warren Oatman was the fifteen-year-younger brother of Eddie Oatman, the loyal Cougar captain Lester Patrick had traded away once the Cougar boss decided he might no longer be the reliable goal producer he had been in his six seasons at Victoria. Russell was familiar to Patrick: he had played three seasons with teams in the Victoria City Senior League. In 1924–25, the younger Oatman had played a season with the Minneapolis Rockets of the United States Amateur Hockey Association. In Minneapolis his teammates included two men—Ching Johnson and Cooney Weiland—who would go on to successful careers in the NHL and eventually be welcomed into the Hockey Hall of Fame.

The defending-champion Cougars started the season with several players slowed or absent due to injury. They lost their opening game by 4-1 in Vancouver and then proceeded to go winless in four more. On December 18, heading into a game that evening against the revived Portland Rosebuds, the Victoria season record had fallen to 0-3-2—just two ties to show for their efforts in the season's first five games. The Cougars managed to beat Portland narrowly at home by 2-1 and then proceeded to lose two more. By December 23, their record had shrivelled to 1-5-2: a single victory in eight games, hardly the sort of record that champions of the entire universe had much of a case to brag about.

Christmas Day delivered the gift of a 4-1 win over the Calgary Tigers, and then a week later, on New Year's Day, the Cougars won a second-straight by 4-0 over Duke Keats and the Edmonton Eskimos. The pair of victories might have set up the Victorians to imagine they had turned their season around, but in home-and-home games with Frank Patrick's Vancouver crew, the Maroons defeated the Cougars by the same 1-0 score on January 4 and again on January 8. Another win-one-lose-one combination left the Cougars at 4-8-2—just four wins in fourteen games—as they approached the midpoint of the season.

So desperate had Lester Patrick become that he inserted someone who had played no hockey in four years into the Victoria lineup: himself. Patrick had played just twice in 1921–22 and not at all in the three subsequent seasons, but at age forty-two, the Silver Fox amazed everyone in sight—perhaps none more than himself—by playing effectively almost a quarter-century after the launch of his adult hockey career.

On January 18, Lester began to right the ship. A victory in Portland, January 18, led to a string of five wins, two ties, and two losses in nine games, bringing the Cougars record to 9-10-4 by February 10—just a single game short of levelling their season standing.

Perhaps they had a shot after all of earning their way to a playoff for the second straight year.

Earn it they did: between February 12 and March 5, Lester's crew won six in a row, all but one of the victories convincing ones. By March 5, the Cougars had improved their standing to 15-10-4 and assured themselves of a playoff berth. Perhaps the winning run had made them a little complacent. Without needing a victory in their last game, in Calgary March 9, they perhaps relaxed; they lost to the Tigers by 2-0. It didn't matter: for a second year in a row, Victoria was in the playoffs, with another shot at the Stanley Cup.

The 1925–26 season was Frank Fredrickson's sixth in Victoria. In all six he had led his team in scoring. This time he had managed sixteen goals and twenty-four points in his team's thirty games. Those numbers, his lowest in Victoria, came nowhere close to matching the thirty-five-goal, forty-five-point total achieved by Edmonton's Art Gagné, but "Freddie" had still made the league's top-ten scorers list, the only Cougar to do so.

The first step in deciding the WHL championship in 1926 was the same as it had been the year before: a two-game, total-goal series between the second- and third-place finishers in the regular season. The principals were also the same: second-place Saskatoon would face off against third-place Victoria. By finishing ahead of Victoria, the Sheiks won the advantage of having the first game played on their home ice.

That first game did not turn out the way Sheiks' fans desired. Saskatoon didn't lose the match, but they didn't win either. It took less than four minutes of the first period for the Cougars to put themselves ahead by 2-0. No surprise, the man who engineered the early lead was Fredrickson. He scored in the third minute and then enabled Russell Oatman's goal just seventy seconds later.

But the Sheiks were led by the great Bill Cook, and it was he who saw to it that the deficit did not endure. Cook narrowed the Victoria lead to 2-1, then teammate Laurie Scott tied it at 2-2 before the end of the first. In the second period, Gord Fraser restored the Victoria lead but as he took his shot, Fraser was accosted by Sheiks' defender Leo Bourgeault, who managed to break the Cougar's stick in two and leave nasty cuts on his opponent's forehead and cheek. Then Cook took the spotlight: six minutes after Fraser's goal, the WHL's leading goal scorer in the regular season answered for Saskatoon. The score was tied, 3-3, and that is how it remained. The teams headed back to Victoria for the second game.

In Victoria, history repeated itself: not only were the Cougars the talk of the town in the sports section, but the lead news story on the *Colonist*'s front page, too. A full house on Epworth Street watched the Cougars and Sheiks play three periods with no one at all managing to score. It was a game in which much was demanded of both sides—and much delivered. The Hall of Fame referee, Mickey Ion, handed out seventeen penalties, including ten-minute majors for fighting to Russell Oatman and Bill Cook's twenty-two-year-old kid brother Fred, who would eventually be better known as "Bun" and would join his brother in the Hockey Hall of Fame. Finally, in the ninth minute of overtime, it was Gord Fraser, facial lacerations notwithstanding, who ushered the fans into euphoria. Fraser's goal won the game for the Cougars by 1-0 and the series by 4-3. With the victory, Lester Patrick's crew qualified themselves to take on first-place Edmonton for the league title in another two-game, total-goal series.

On the day of the spring equinox, March 21, the front page of the *Daily Colonist* relayed news about the latest events out of Egypt: eight hundred "urchins" were nearly done with the task of digging the Sphinx out of the desert sands of Giza.

Frank Fredrickson knew a little about the Sphinx and Giza. During the war he had trained as a flier at a British air base nearby and had had himself photographed riding a camel, with the Sphinx as backdrop. But the big story in the *Colonist* of March 21 was not the Sphinx but the Cougars' victory over Edmonton the evening before.

A front-page sidebar story informed readers that something remarkable had happened. Fans unable to get to the sold-out game in Victoria had gathered in front of the *Colonist* building to listen to a play-by-play radio broadcast of the game by way of a Premier radio installed in Mr. A.W. Carter's automobile. The *Colonist* paid particular tribute to Mr. Jack Potts, "the best announcer radio fans of the city had ever heard." Not only was every word as clear as could be, but Mr. Potts "managed to convey the excitement of the game in a most realistic manner."

As for the game, there was no room for anyone extra to sit or stand in the home arena; fans occupied every seat and every foot of standing room to see the hometown lads win by 3-1 and leave the Edmonton "Igloo Dwellers" facing a two-goal deficit in the second game of the series. After a scoreless opening period, Foyston and Halderson scored for the Cougars in the second. "The packed stands went wild with joy... and the rafters resounded with prolonged applause and deafening cheers" after Halderson's goal.

Euphoria turned to something else when Mickey Ion disallowed a goal that would have been Halderson's second. The fans booed their heads off and hurled paper, oranges, and other markers of their displeasure onto the ice. Miffed at being overruled, the goal judge left the premises and Ion had to reach into the crowd for a replacement.

The emotional tide turned again when Harold Hart made it 3-0 early in the third period. Barney Stanley narrowed the gap by one, scoring Edmonton's lone goal of the game midway through the third, but that is as far as the Eskimos got.

The ice in the Eskimos' rink had been problematical in the past and it was again as spring bloomed in northern Alberta. Edmonton's "home game" was moved to better ice on Vancouver's neutral ground for the second game.

Entrepreneurs rose to the opportunities availed by Game Two. Eager fans wouldn't have to gather in front of the *Colonist* building to share communally in hearing a radio broadcast of the game: the Hudson's Bay people announced that they would sponsor a play-by-play broadcast by Victoria radio station CFCT. Those lucky enough to own a radio receiver could look forward to listening to the broadcast from the comfort of their favourite chair at home. On game day, the 2:15 PM ferry provided a group discount for as many as 150 people expected to journey through Active Pass to watch the big showdown.

Though their own Maroons were far removed from the action, nine thousand fans paid to see the March 22 game in Vancouver, the largest crowd of the season. The hero of the game was the Flash, Frank Foyston. Edmonton needed to beat the Cougars by at least three goals, but all they could manage was a 2-2 draw, Foyston scoring both Victoria goals. After the game, fans swarmed the Victoria dressing room and "Foyston was almost mobbed by his many scores of admirers."

Duke Keats, Edmonton's leading light, was not on the ice to observe the game's final moments. Assessed a penalty in the third period by Carl Battell, the judge of play—the second game official—Keats did not immediately head to the penalty bench. Battell issued a second directive, whereupon something unthinkable in today's game unfolded. Keats dropped his stick, removed his gloves, darted at Battell and "landed several blows on his countenance." Battell retaliated, landing "a couple of nice wallops" of his own. Players intervened and ushered Keats off the ice. "The fans were disgusted with Keats' behavior, and showed their resentment very plainly." No one need wonder why.

Edmonton had finished first in the regular season and had three men among the league's top ten scorers—Gagné, Keats, and Stanley—but the Eskimos would be bystanders as Victoria took the next step toward a return engagement for the Stanley Cup.

Immediately after the game, Victoria mayor John Carl Pendray directed his congratulations to Lester Patrick. Nowadays a mayor might choose to use Twitter as the vehicle of choice for such a message. But there was no Twitter in 1926, and no Facebook or email. Mayor Pendray *wired* his sentiments to the Cougars' boss: "Lester, we are proud of you and your wonderful team. Please convey my hearty congratulations to the boys who put up such a magnificent fight for the honour of Victoria."

In the fight for the honour of the city, history was about to repeat itself in an important way: once again Victoria would meet Montreal for the Stanley Cup. Montreal, yes, but not the same Montrealers the Cougars had faced the year before.

Stanley Cup finalists in 1925, the Montreal Canadiens came nowhere close to duplicating the achievement a year later. From 1910 to 1925, Georges Vézina, the man for whom the NHL's top goaltender award is named, was the only player to guard the Canadiens goal. In the first game of the 1925–26 season, Vézina played the first period of the game against Pittsburgh. He stopped every shot fired his way despite what was clear to everyone having eyes to see: Vézina was not a well man.

Over a span of a few weeks, Vézina had lost thirty-five pounds of body weight. In the intermission between periods, he vomited blood, had a high temperature, yet returned to the game. Not for long. At the start of the second period, Vézina collapsed to the ice and had to be taken away. A day later the veteran goaltender was diagnosed with tuberculosis. He never played another game for *les Canadiens* or anybody else. Vézina died March 27, 1926—just three days before the start of the 1926 Stanley Cup final. Without Vézina in goal and deprived of several other players instrumental in the Canadiens' success the year before, the Canadiens were a pale shadow of what the team had been. In the 1925–26 regular season, they finished last in the seven-team NHL, four points behind the second-worst Toronto St. Patricks.

Having defeated the Canadiens a year earlier, the Victoria Cougars now faced off against the Montreal Maroons in the 1926 edition of the Stanley Cup final. In just their second year in the NHL, the Montreal club had gone in the opposite direction to the Canadiens. Second-last in 1924–25, they had improved to second-best a year later, then narrowly defeated the Ottawa Senators for the right to face Victoria.

The Maroons were led by a twenty-three-year-old rookie, Nels Stewart, who had done pretty well as a first-year player: he scored thirty-four goals in his thirty-six games, six better than anyone else, and thereby won the NHL's individual scoring title by six points. The remaining Maroons' cast was just about as distinguished as Stewart himself. Another rookie, Babe Siebert, would one day join Stewart in the Hockey Hall of Fame, as would two other Montreal skaters, Reg Noble and Harry Broadbent. Clint Benedict, the man in charge of guarding the Maroons goal, would eventually make it a Hall of Fame quintet. The Maroons were a formidable opponent.

The Cougars were a year older and faced the disadvantage of having to make a long train journey to defend their 1925 championship. It was the easterners' turn to host the Cup final: all games in the best-of-five series would be played at the year-old Montreal Forum, a state-of-the-art hockey facility with a seating capacity of 9,300 in 1926, and standing room for another 1,600.

The teams played the first game March 30, under NHL rules. Back in Victoria, a big crowd gathered in front of the *Colonist* building on Broad Street to listen to a radio broadcast of the game. Those owning a new-fangled receiver could hear the same broadcast at home.

According to the next day's headline story in the *Daily Colonist*, "[the] tilt was witnessed by 10,500 fans who were treated to as fine an exhibition of Canada's national game as they could wish to see." For Victoria fans, the end result was not nearly as fine. Nels Stewart opened the scoring early, just past the three-minute mark of the first period. Three minutes later, Broadbent made it 2-0 for the Maroons. After a scoreless middle period, Stewart dispatched the Cougars with his second goal of the game late in the third period. For all their Hall of Fame firepower, the Cougars could not beat Benedict and the Maroons' defence. Montreal won, 3-0.

Another serious loss compounded Victoria's misery: already wounded with a broken bone in one hand, Jocko Anderson was left with a broken leg and dislocated hip by a mid-ice collision with Siebert. Jocko was lost not just for the series, but permanently. He would never play another game.

With two days' rest and the comfort of knowing that Game Two would be played under western rules, the Cougars no doubt approached the second encounter, on April Fool's Day, in a mood of enhanced optimism. But the fates care not a whit about optimism: the Cougars lost again, by the same 3-0 score. Destiny disregards human ambition. Humans are fickle. Given a second straight 3-0 loss, the *Colonist*'s attention waned. Yes, the game result was still front-page news on April 2, but not the sort commanding a headline in one-inch type.

Nels Stewart was again the man of the hour: he scored a goal of his own and assisted in another by Merlyn Phillips in the second period. As Stewart had done in the opener, Dunc Munro made it 3-0 late in the third period.

The result of game three encouraged the *Colonist* editors to revert to inch-high type for the paper's front page of April 4: Victoria Trims Montreal 3-2 in Third Game. Loughlin played brilliantly, the *Colonist* reporter exulted, and "Fredrickson was tireless and effective both in attack and in wrecking Maroon rushes." Yes, the *Colonist* conceded, Montreal had been disadvantaged because Stewart suffered from the grippe and played with a temperature, but the Cougars were full value for their victory.

Siebert put Montreal ahead early in the first period, but a Halderson goal late in the first and another by Clem Loughlin midway through the second gave Victoria a 2-1 advantage. Fredrickson made it 3-1 well past the midpoint of the third. Grippe or not, Nels Stewart was still effective: he brought the Maroons to within a goal late in the third, but Montreal needed more than one. The Cougars won, 3-2, and with that there was a resurgence of joy and hope back in Victoria.

In a sidebar item beside the front-page account of the hockey game, the *Colonist* enjoyed a bit of deserved self-indulgence, reporting that "scores of telegrams and telephone calls" had poured into radio station CFCT and the newspaper building to voice fans' gratification at the broadcast and the *Colonist*'s sponsorship of it.

A piece in the April 6 edition told readers that a Montreal win in the series was no longer a sure thing. Montrealers conceded that Victoria stood a fair chance of winning that night's game at the Forum and forcing a fifth, deciding contest.

Another item in the April 6 sports section, HOCKEY CONJECTURE IS RIFE JUST NOW, conveyed worrisome news for western hockey fans. The story indicated that Frank Patrick would meet with NHL president Frank Calder to discussed unspecified subjects. Frank's brother, Lester, took pains to deny rumours that Frank Fredrickson and Slim Halderson would be playing in the east a year hence. But the story stated that the Edmonton and Saskatoon owners were looking to put their teams on the market, and suggested that "Western players are likely to be seen in the East next year." Fans of the Cougars must have fretted at the last sentence in the piece, which indicated that both Fredrickson and Halderson would like to play in the NHL.

That evening, April 6, another full house crowded the Forum to watch the fourth game of the series. The Maroons had won the first two games without surrendering a goal to Victoria. They did it again in Game Four.

An opportunistic souvenir hunter had managed to appropriate Stewart's stick after Montreal's deciding victory over Ottawa in the NHL playoff. The rookie put out "an SOS" asking to have his stick back. The emergency call worked: the stick was returned, and Stewart, no longer disabled by the grippe and no longer without his lucky stick, scored both goals in the Maroons' 2-0 final victory. Clint Benedict claimed his third shutout of the series, the first goaltender to do so in a Stanley Cup series.

The *Daily Colonist* had never given its hockey reporter a byline, but someone else working the city's hockey beat was better recognized by his employer. In the April 7 edition of the *Victoria Daily Times*, Archie Wills' byline appeared twice. Like some of the players he covered as a *Times* sportswriter, Archie Wills had been a soldier in the Great War. He would go on to a long career with the *Times*, ultimately serving as the paper's managing editor from 1936 to his retirement in 1951.

Wills' first *Times* story on April 7 described particulars of the Cougars' last game of the Stanley Cup final; the other was a human-interest piece focused on the game's ending and the players' plans for the summer of 1926.

The Cougars had made a great impression on Montreal fans for their sportsmanship, Wills reported. "A minute before time, when Lester Patrick realized that his club had been eliminated he had all his substitutes ready on the fence to rush over the second the bell rang." The Cougars shook the winners' hands. "This is the first time this form of offering congratulations has been sprung, and the fans stopped in their homeward way to watch." As the Cougars made their exit, the Montreal fans gave them "thunderous rounds of applause."

It would be the last applause the Victoria Cougars ever heard.

Though few people realized it then, it was the final time that a team not part of the NHL would compete for the Stanley Cup. Lord Stanley had provided his silver bowl to honour Canada's best amateur hockey teams, but as of this date, the Cup would effectively become the private property of the National Hockey League. After April 6, 1926, only NHL teams would compete for the Stanley Cup and only NHL teams would win it. The Victoria Cougars would become the answer to trivia questions. What was the last non-NHL club to win the Stanley Cup? What was the last one to compete for it?

The April 6 Victoria–Montreal game was the last the Cougars ever played, the last game of the Western Hockey League, and the day the Patricks' western dream took its final exhausted breath. The denials and assurances Lester Patrick had delivered to Victoria fans in April turned out to be empty. Barely a month after the Montreal Maroons' Stanley Cup victory, an assets disposal sale was in full flight.

Over the preceding year and a half, the western owner-operators had struggled to keep their finances in the black. One of the ways in which the Patricks and other owners had sought to keep revenues in balance with expenditures was to exchange players for cash. In late 1924, Frank Patrick had sold two players, Alf Skinner and Lloyd Cook, to the Boston Bruins. Fred Harris, formerly a Vancouver Maroon and Seattle Metropolitan, went to the same destination for the same consideration: money. In September, two months before the start of the 1925–26 season, the Edmonton Eskimos' bosses sold not just one but *three* of their players to the New York Americans. One of the trio was the great Bullet Joe Simpson, a future Hall of Famer. It was not that the Eskimos no longer had use for John Morrison, Roy Rickey, and Bullet Joe—at age thirty-one, Simpson especially was still a top-drawer talent—but they needed the money to stay afloat.

It had come to this: by the time the Stanley Cup was sorted out for 1926, the Patricks and other WHL operators determined that they could no longer compete with the growing power of the National Hockey League. They could not command the audiences available to watch NHL games. They could not afford to match the players' salaries that big audiences enabled NHL owners to pay.

In 1911, at the time the Patricks conceived the Pacific Coast Hockey Association, the NHL was still eight years in the future. The Patricks built the PCHA largely by raiding the National Hockey Association. It was from the wreckage of the defunct NHA that the NHL had risen in 1917. The new league had not been born a mighty entity: it began the 1917–18 seasons with four clubs but one—the Montreal Wanderers—didn't survive that inaugural season. But in the years between 1917 and 1926, the NHL didn't just endure, it steadily flourished and expanded. By 1926, the tables were turned. By then there were seven NHL franchises, three of them in big American cities—Boston, New York, and Pittsburgh—whose populations included enough hockey enthusiasts to keep big arenas well filled with paying customers.

By the spring of 1926, the Stanley Cup was back in NHL hands and the western show was over. Frank Patrick led the effort to sell league assets—the players—to the NHL. By the end of May 1926, the deal was done. Victoria's players went principally to the city of Detroit, where Frank Fredrickson and eight other members of the 1925-26 Victoria club would become—what else?—the Detroit Cougars. Most of the Portland Rosebuds, seven players, went to Chicago to man another brand-new NHL team, the Blackhawks. A third new team, the New York Rangers, would be assembled in part from pieces of the Saskatoon Sheiks, including the great Bill Cook, and the Vancouver Maroons, including another future Hall of Famer, Frank Boucher.

By opening day of the 1926-27, season most of the men who had played WHL hockey the preceding year found themselves scattered throughout the NHL: former western-leaguers emerged on every NHL roster. There was a final marker for hockey fans in Victoria: the man chosen by the owner of the New York Rangers to run his team was a fellow by the name of Lester Patrick.

In the city of Victoria, hockey would still be played but, it would not be the calibre of the hockey delivered by the PCHA and the WHL. Thousands had paid to watch the Cougars at Lester Patrick's Epworth Street arena. They had followed the exploits of Lester's lads in the sports section of the *Daily Colonist*. They had become devoted fans of Frank Fredrickson and his mates. By the fall of 1926, those who had lost their team but still cared about its players would have to turn their attention 2,500 miles to the east—to the fortunes of the NHL's Detroit Cougars.

POSTSCRIPT

O N NOVEMBER 18, 1926, the brand-new Detroit Cougars faced off against the Boston Bruins in their opening game of the 1926–27 National Hockey League season. The players were ready to go, but because the new Olympia Stadium was not, the teams played a short distance south of Detroit—yes, south—in the Borders Cities Arena across the Detroit River in Windsor, Ontario. Indeed, Detroit would play *all* of its home games that inaugural season in another city, another country.

Of the ten skaters lined up to play for the Cougars in that first game, *eight* were members of the Victoria club that had played for the Stanley Cup in April: the Manitoba Icelanders Fredrickson and Halderson; two players Lester Patrick had brought from Seattle in late 1924, Walker and Foyston; and four other men who had so recently played for Victoria fans at the Patrick Arena—Clem Loughlin, Gizzy Hart, Harry Meeking, and Russell Oatman. Another former Victorian, Hap Holmes, would have brought the number of Victoria alumni to nine, but Hap was taken suddenly ill before the game and had to be replaced in the Detroit goal by Herb Stuart.

The Cougars lost that first game by the same score that had clinched the Stanley Cup for the Montreal Maroons in April, 2-0.

Like the Cougars, Boston was largely comprised of former WHL players, five of them. Two former western luminaries scored the Boston goals: Duke Keats, barely two minutes into the opening period, and Archie Briden, less than three minutes later.

That same evening, at Madison Square Garden in New York City, the Stanley Cup–champion Montreal Maroons took on another new NHL club, the New York Rangers, and won by the same score, 2-0, with Harry Broadbent scoring both Maroons goals. The man behind the New York bench was Lester Patrick.

Far away in Victoria, both games were newsworthy: the next day's issue of the *Daily Colonist* gave the NHL action two columns' worth of attention. No trace of resentment or rancour about the city's lost team appeared anywhere in the two columns. Thus began the first day of a new era, one in which a solitary major professional hockey league had endured, the NHL.

Fredrickson did not linger long in Windsor–Detroit. On January 6, 1927, he experienced a first-time event: a trade. He was packaged up with Harry Meeking and shipped to the Boston Bruins for none other than Duke Keats and Archie Briden, all four of them veterans of western hockey wars, all of them well known to one another. It turned out to be a good day for the former Victoria players: Boston was going places this season, whereas the Detroit team was destined for a last-place finish in the NHL's new American Division.

In Victoria the *Colonist* had nothing to say about the trade of the former local hockey hero, but the *Times* did. The city's afternoon daily published a three-paragraph story in boldface type: FRED-RICKSON PLAYS LAST GAME WITH HIS SIX-YEAR ICE PALS. The *Times* ventured that a change in surroundings "may help Fredrickson get back into his scoring mood." After the trade was announced, Clem Loughlin sent a wire to the *Times* in which he reported that Fredrickson would report to Boston immediately, with Keats and Briden joining Detroit on Sunday. The next encounter between Boston and Detroit "will be an interesting one," the *Times* speculated.

Observers waited only a week to find out. Boston and Detroit faced off at the Windsor arena January 13. Fredrickson, Meeking, and Harry Oliver led the way for Boston, but it was Keats who won post-trade bragging rights: he scored a goal for his new team, and the Cougars won, 3-2.

But five days later, January 18, Fredrickson provided evidence that Bruins management knew what they were doing: he scored four goals in a 7-3 victory over the New York Rangers. A Boston crowd of better than nine thousand watched the action. As the *Boston Globe* saw it, the crowd "yelled with delight as the greatest attack of the season was unloosed with Eddie Shore and Fredrickson going wild."

It must have been particularly sweet for Fredrickson to accomplish the feat over the team managed by his former Victoria boss, Lester Patrick.

The blonde Manitoban had been twenty-five when he came to Victoria in 1920; now he was thirty-one. Rare is the player whose best years come about beyond the age of thirty. But Fredrickson was still an accomplished producer. He finished the 1926–27 season with eighteen goals and thirty-one points in his forty-four games for Detroit and Boston. That was good enough to place him third among American Division scorers, behind two other refugees from western hockey, Bill Cook and Dick Irvin.

Another success followed. After finishing second in the American Division, the Bruins faced the third-place Chicago Blackhawks in the first round of the playoffs. Fredrickson's two goals led the Bruins to a 6-1 victory in the first game. Boston won the two-game series by 10-5 and proceeded to the second round against Lester Patrick's first-place New York Rangers. After playing to a scoreless draw in the first of another two-game series, the Bruins won the second game, 3-1, with Fredrickson choreographing two of the Bruins goals.

For the third year in a row, Fredrickson was in the Stanley Cup final. But that was a contest against Ottawa, the team with the best record that year, and it was the Senators who prevailed—for the fourth time in the 1920s.

A year later, Frank Fredrickson passed into hockey shadowland. In 1927–28, Boston finished first in the American Division, but at age thirty-two, Fredrickson was no longer the powerhouse he had been in Victoria. He finished the season with ten goals, third-best among that year's Boston lineup. But in the second round of the playoffs, the Rangers turned the tables on Boston and won the two-game series by 5-2. In just their second NHL season, the Rangers then went on to defeat the Montreal Maroons to win the Stanley Cup.

Fredrickson liked Boston. He was happy there and would have been content to play out the rest of his hockey career as a Bruin, but on December 20, 1928, he was traded to the Pittsburgh Pirates for another former star of western-league hockey, Mickey MacKay, and a bundle of cash. Fredrickson finished the season with a combined six goals for the two franchises, a far cry from his Victoria heyday when he might score six in a week.

The former Olympian played two more seasons of NHL hockey. In 1929–30, he filled a dual role in Pittsburgh as both player and coach. The player suffered a season-ending knee injury in his ninth game, and the coach led the Pirates to the NHL's second-worst record: just nine wins in forty-four games. As a player, Fredrickson had been productive enough in his nine games—four goals and eleven points—that he decided, at age thirty-five, to give it one more go in 1930–31. Perhaps he shouldn't have. Fredrickson went back to Detroit as a free agent. In twenty-four games with the Falcons (formerly the Cougars), he was a faint shadow of his former self, scoring but a single goal in twenty-four games.

Though finished as an elite player, there would be more to the Fredrickson story. In 1933, he took on a new role as coach of the Ivy League Princeton Tigers. At Princeton, he made a friend of a man who had decided that Adolf Hitler's Germany was no longer a place he wanted to call home. The man's name was Albert Einstein.

Fredrickson is one of just two members of the Hockey Hall of Fame—the other being Conn Smythe—who answered the call of duty in both world wars. He commanded a Royal Canadian Air Force flying school at Sea Island, where the present-day Vancouver

International Airport is situated, and coached the air force hockey team in the Vancouver City Senior Hockey League. One of the men who skated for Fredrickson's RCAF team was James Norman ("Dutch") Gainor, someone who had been Fredrickson's teammate with the Boston Bruins twelve years earlier. After the war, Fredrickson coached the University of British Thunderbirds—and was cherished by the Thunderbirds who played for him.

Leader of the first gold-medal winning Olympic hockey team, leader of the last team not part of the NHL to win the Stanley Cup, friend of Albert Einstein, veteran of two world wars, Fredrickson lived a remarkable life.

But what of the other Victoria Cougars who had won a Stanley Cup championship in 1925 and competed for another in 1926? What became of them?

Some players insisted on carrying on well after they had passed the peak of their playing prowess. Harry Meeking accompanied Fredrickson to Boston, but despite his accomplishments in Victoria, he lasted just the one season in the NHL, managing a single goal in twenty-nine games with Detroit and Boston. From 1927 to 1930, Harry played three years of minor-pro hockey with a motley array of teams: the New Haven Eagles and Philadelphia Arrows of the Canadian–American Hockey League, Toronto Millionaires, and London Panthers of the International Hockey League (IHL), and finally, the Kitchener Dutchmen of the Canadian Professional Hockey League.

Jack Walker played two seasons in Detroit, then another five in minor-pro hockey, first with the Seattle Eskimos of the PCHL, the minor league that western hockey fans had to make do with after the collapse of the WHL. By 1932, at age forty-three, Walker was in Tinseltown, player–coach of the Hollywood Stars of the California Professional Hockey League.

Russell Oatman played four years in the NHL with Detroit and Montreal and then, at the end, in 1928–29, for Lester Patrick's New York Rangers. Harold Hart, better known as Gizzy, played parts of three NHL seasons in Detroit and Montreal before settling for a long career in minor-pro and senior amateur hockey. He was still at it as late as 1938, when his teammates with the Weyburn Beavers of the South Saskatchewan Senior League included the Montreal Canadiens' future Hall of Famer Elmer Lach.

Clem Loughlin, the Cougars' captain in 1925 and 1926, was no longer a young man when he became a first-year NHLer in late 1926. At age thirty-four, he had been a hockey player since 1910, but Clem managed to hang on for three seasons in the NHL, with Detroit and Chicago; he then played three more in the minor-pro IHL, by which time he was forty. Once his playing days were done, Clem turned to coaching, first with the IHL's London Tecumsehs and then with the NHL Chicago Blackhawks from 1934 to 1937. Clem eventually owned and operated a hotel in Viking, Alberta, where his coaching would influence brothers by the name of Sutter—six of whom would play in the NHL.

Frank Foyston played parts of two seasons with the Detroit Cougars, then three more with the Detroit Olympics of the IHL. He, too, found it hard to get hockey out of his system. He spent a decade as a coach, first with the Olympics and eventually, from 1933 to 1937, with the Seattle Seahawks—not the football Seahawks, but the hockey variety that formed part of the short-lived North West Hockey League.

Jocko Anderson never played another game after his catastrophic injury in the Stanley Cup final against the Montreal Maroons, but in 1929–30, he took a turn as coach of the Victoria Cubs, the minor pro team burdened by having to fill the big skates of the Cougars after their departure for Detroit.

The younger of the 1920 Olympic gold medallists Lester Patrick cajoled into coming to Victoria, Slim Halderson, lasted just a single season in the NHL: after three games with Detroit, Halderson was traded to the Toronto St. Patricks. He played a full forty-four-game season but scored only three goals. Still in his twenties, Halderson remained in the game: he played ten seasons of minor league hockey—mostly with American Hockey Association clubs in Kansas City, Duluth, and Wichita—through the 1936-37 season.

Gord Fraser went on to play as long a stint in the NHL as any of the Cougars who had won the Stanley Cup in 1925. Together with all the others, Fraser's contract had been parcelled off to the Detroit owners in May of 1926, but before playing a single game for the Cougars, Detroit sent Fraser to Chicago with Art Gagné for the rights to Art Duncan, the former flier Frank Fredrickson had battled for the PCHA scoring title in 1923-24. After playing parts of two seasons in Chicago, Fraser was dealt back to Detroit. He played two seasons there before moving on again, to Pittsburgh in 1929-30 and Philadelphia in 1930-31. Cast off by the NHL clubs, Fraser played five more seasons in the IHL and NWHL, finally retiring as a player at age forty-two in 1936.

Hap Holmes was the Detroit goaltender for two NHL seasons before turning to coaching. After two years at the helm of the Toronto Millionaires, Hap went to Cleveland, where he took charge of the on-ice fortunes of the Indians and Falcons of the IHL and IAHL—International-American Hockey League—from 1929 to 1937. The great goaltender's legacy is reflected in this: since 1948, the trophy annually awarded to the man selected as best goaltender in the American Hockey League is the Harry "Hap" Holmes Memorial Trophy.

Then, of course, there is Lester Patrick himself. In the Victoria Cougars' final season Patrick somehow managed, after a three-year retirement, to be the Cougars' third-leading scorer, at the age of forty-two. A year later he was the coach of the New York Rangers, but for a single game he was a player, too.

Halfway through the second game of the 1928 Stanley Cup final against the Montreal Maroons, April 7, Rangers' goaltender Lorne Chabot was struck by the puck and suffered an eye injury that made it impossible for him to carry on. The man the Rangers' coach turned to as Chabot's replacement was himself. He stopped eighteen of nineteen Montreal shots, enabling the Rangers to win. The feat remains unprecedented: at age forty-four years and ninety-nine days, Patrick is the oldest man to have played in a Stanley Cup final.

Patrick led the Rangers to a Stanley Cup victory that year, 1928; he then carried on as the man behind the New York bench all the way through the 1938–39 season. In 1966 the NHL and USA Hockey inaugurated an annual award to honour individual contributions to hockey in the United States. The award is the Lester Patrick Trophy.

In the years 1912 through 1926, some forty-nine men played for one or another of the incarnations of Lester Patrick's pro hockey team in Victoria: the Capitals, Aristocrats, and Cougars. A good number of the forty-nine played only a season or two, some only a few games. But included among the forty-nine are seven who would eventually be awarded a tablet in the Hockey Hall of Fame. Just seven. Established in 1943, the Hall's first members were inducted in 1945. The class of 1947—the Hall's second—included Lester Patrick.

Ernie "Moose" Johnson had played only the final four of his major-pro hockey seasons in Victoria. By the time he arrived on South Vancouver Island late in 1918, Ernie was thirty-two, but he was as effective as he had ever been and quickly became a fan favourite in Victoria. After departing Victoria in 1922, Johnson carried on, playing minor-pro hockey as late as 1931, when he was forty-five. In 1952, Johnson became the second Victoria pro welcomed into the Hall of Fame.

The year 1958 ushered two more into the hockey pantheon: the two Franks—Fredrickson and Foyston. Then, in 1960, it was Jack Walker's turn. Unhappily, the honour came too late for Walker to enjoy it. He had died ten years earlier, in Seattle where Walker had enjoyed the finest hours of his long career in hockey.

Hap Holmes became a Hall of Famer in 1972; alas, that was also too late for the happy goaltender to know or care about the tribute. Holmes had departed his life more than three decades earlier, in 1941, at Fort Lauderdale, Florida.

The last of the old Victoria pros to be awarded a Hall of Fame plaque was Tommy Dunderdale, one of the seven originals who played every minute of every game with Lester Patrick in 1912. After he was finally jettisoned in 1923, Dunderdale dispensed his post-prime services in Saskatoon and Edmonton before staging a brief comeback at age thirty-nine with the Los Angeles Maroons of the California minor-pro league in 1926–27. For Tommy Dunderdale—like Jack Walker and Hap Holmes—the Hall of Fame honour came too late to be of much good: by 1972, the year of Dunderdale's induction, he had been at rest under a Winnipeg grave marker for more than a decade.

Hall of Fame selectors never made a place for Eddie Oatman in the Hall, but for six years Oatman was an important cog in the Cougar machine—a highly popular team captain and productive scorer. It is regrettable that Oatman is largely forgotten, because he had a remarkable career. Oatman began playing professional hockey in 1909–10 with the Waterloo Colts and Galt Pros of the Ontario Professional Hockey League. Arriving on the west coast in 1912, he played five seasons in New Westminster and Portland before joining the Victoria Aristocrats in 1918.

By the time the western league sank beneath the waves in 1926, Eddie was thirty-seven years old—too ossified to attract interest in the NHL; but Oatman carried on anyway. Between 1926 and 1934, he played minor-pro hockey in Minneapolis, Boston, Buffalo, and St. Paul. And he still wasn't done. In 1938–39, thirteen years after the demise of the Victoria Cougars and three decades after the start of his professional career, he was playing for the Duluth Zephyrs of the International-American Senior Hockey League. By that time his fiftieth birthday was on the near horizon, as was the Second World War. When someone took the time to count them all, Eddie Oatman had played thirty-two seasons. All that hockey did not wear Eddie out: he lived to the age of eighty-four. Oatman isn't in the Hall of Fame, but he should be.

Another western-league Hall of Famer merits attention here despite having been a Victoria *opponent* throughout the 1922–26 period. Bill Cook, just a year and a half younger than Fredrickson,

From left: Lester Patrick and sons Muzz and Lynn, New York Rangers, circa 1940. For a period of several years, from the late 1930s to the mid-1940s, the New York Rangers counted three Patricks among their ranks: the team coach, Lester, and his two sons, Lynn and Murray—the latter better known as "Muzz." Lester was inducted into the Hockey Hall of Fame in 1947. Lynn joined his father among Hall of Fame players in 1980. Lester and Lynn Patrick are one of only three father-and-son combinations to have been inducted as Hall of Fame players. COURTESY VICTORIA SPORTS HALL OF FAME

flourished in the NHL not just for a year or two but an entire decade. He was twice NHL scoring leader, in 1927 and 1933. By 1933 none of the former Victoria Cougars was still playing in the NHL, but twenty-goal seasons were still routine for Cook. In 1932–33, playing for

Lester Patrick's New York Rangers, he accomplished something extraordinary. He finished six points ahead of his nearest rival in the scoring race, and did so despite being thirty-six-and-a-half years old at the time. To this day, Bill Cook remains the oldest player to have won a full-season NHL scoring title.

Bill Cook was still in the NHL at age forty, in 1936–37. During his time in Saskatoon from 1922 to 1926, Cook had battled Lester Patrick's Cougars on several occasions. By 1936 he had shared three seasons in New York with someone who would be an all-star, win a Stanley Cup, and eventually earn himself a place in the Hockey Hall of Fame. That someone was Lynn Patrick, son of Lester.

One other man demands attention in the context of the Hockey Hall of Fame. It is widely agreed among hockey historians who have paid sufficient attention that in matters of innovation and invention, it was the younger Patrick brother, Frank, who took the lead role. After a long career as innovator and coach—all those years in Vancouver and two more in Boston from 1934 to 1936—Frank Patrick was inducted in the Hockey Hall of Fame, Builders Division, in 1958, the same year as Fredrickson and Foyston were admitted as players.

In Victoria, across the street from the site where crowds once gathered to watch the best of professional hockey, there is a monument to the Patrick brothers and to their achievements and innovations. What became of the Victoria and Vancouver buildings the Patricks built, the ones that pioneered artificial ice in Canada, the buildings in which hockey thrills and disappointments ebbed and flowed over a fifteen-year period?

In the early hours of Remembrance Day, November 11, 1929, the Patrick Arena in Victoria burned to the ground. The fire was thought to have been deliberately set, but no one was ever arrested or convicted of arson.

On August 19, 1936, a crowd of four thousand fight fans attended a boxing exhibition featuring former heavyweight champion Max Baer at the Denman Arena in Vancouver. Later that night, a fire broke out nearby and soon spread to the arena. Stan Patrick, the youngest Patrick brother and the man who managed the arena, was among those who watched helplessly as the fire burned out of control. The blaze destroyed the building, killed two people, and injured three firemen.

Buildings come and go, and so do people. Life sometimes resembles a drawn-out session of Russian roulette. Some of the Victoria pros lived long and well. Some did not.

Charles Tobin played a single season in Victoria, 1918–19, when only Tommy Dunderdale accumulated more scoring points in the Aristocrats' first post-war season. Tobin endured barely as long as the PCHA: he died of complications from stomach ulcers at age thirty-eight in the spring of 1924.

Stan Marples was Tobin's Victoria teammate in 1918–19. Like Tobin, it was Marples' only season in Victoria. In Marples' case the Victoria season was his last in professional hockey. From 1919 to 1922, the Winnipeg native played four seasons of amateur hockey with the Moose Jaw Maple Leafs of the Saskatchewan Senior Hockey League. Like Tobin, Stan Marples did not enjoy a long post-hockey life: he was only thirty-six when he expired in January 1928, at Moose Jaw. He had made good friends in hockey: several former teammates formed a guard of honour at his funeral and served as pallbearers.

Ken Mallen played only the 1915–16 season in Victoria. He accompanied Lester Patrick to Spokane to play the following year with the Canaries. That would turn out to be his last year as a player, but he remained in hockey as a skating coach and, in 1926–27, as referee in the Canadian-Pro league. Three years later, in the spring of 1930, he was gone. Felled by pneumonia, Mallen took his last breath in the same place he had drawn his first, Morrisburg, Ontario. He was forty-five.

Goldie Prodgers played only the 1912–13 season in Victoria before taking his hockey act back east to play ten seasons in the NHA/NHL through 1925. After a two-year stint as coach of the London Panthers of the Canadian-Pro league, 1926-28, Prodgers had

Lester Patrick, 1960-61 O-Pee-Chee hockey card series. In 1960 a bubble-gum company included a subset of "All-Time Greats" in its annual hockey card series. The Lester Patrick card was No. 1 in the series. O-Pee-Chee might have selected a picture of Patrick from his glory years in Victoria, but instead they chose an image of Patrick from his last appearance as a player, when, at age forty-four in 1928, he replaced his injured goaltender and helped the New York Rangers to a Stanley Cup victory. AUTHOR'S COLLECTION only a little time to savour middle age. He died of a heart attack at age forty-four in 1935.

Big Bobby Genge played eight seasons of professional hockey, every one of them with Lester Patrick. What counted as the highlight of his hockey career was doubtless the battle against his first cousin, Scotty Davidson, for the 1914 Stanley Cup. The Hall of Fame cousin was a casualty of war in 1915; Genge lasted somewhat longer. He died of sepsis in 1937 at age forty-seven.

And so it went.

Bobby Rowe was one of the players Lester Patrick had poached from the Renfrew Creamery Kings when he put together his Victoria hockey club in 1911-12. Rowe played hockey for a quarter century, much of it either as Patrick's collaborator or opponent in western-league hockey. After the demise of the WHL in 1926, Rowe was an NHL rookie with the Boston Bruins at age thirty-nine—five years older than any other Bruin. He would remain in the game long after his playing days were done. He coached the Portland Buckaroos of the minor-pro Pacific Coast league for seven seasons through 1938. He endured until 1948, by which time he had reached the age of sixty-three.

Too many among the cast of Victoria's hockey professionals were denied a generous life span. Others were luckier. Some of the boys of winter circa 1912 to 1926 were still in the land of the living late into the 1970s. Clem Loughlin endured until 1977, Wally Elmer until 1978. The great Fredrickson lasted until May of 1979; by then he had lived eighty-four fruitful years.

But Frank was only the second-last of the Victoria lads to depart his life. The very last of the Victoria pros persevered another nine years, to July 30, 1987. He had delivered five seasons of loyal service to Lester Patrick before the collapse of the Seattle Metropolitans delivered a mother lode of players to Victoria and enabled Lester to give Hap Holmes the job of Cougars goaltender. The man Hap replaced lived into his ninety-fifth year: he was Hec Fowler.

In 1960, Canadian boys who loved hockey and liked collecting bubblegum cards displaying the image of NHL players were treated

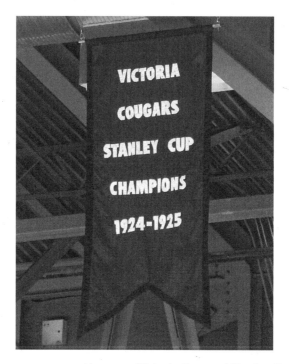

The banner commemorating 1925 Victoria Cougars' Stanley Cup victory, Victoria Save-on-Foods Memorial Centre, Victoria. The Cougars were the last non-NHL team to win the Cup and—a year later—they were the last team not part of the NHL to compete for it. AUTHOR'S PHOTO

to something special. The 1960–61 series of O-Pee-Chee hockey cards included a special subset of twenty-seven "All-Time Greats" interspersed among thirty-four current players. Three of the twenty-seven all-time greats were former Victoria professionals. Ernie Johnson, wearing the sweater of the Montreal Wanderers, was card number four in the series. Frank Fredrickson's card was number thirty-four.

The first card of the O-Pee-Chee series, number one, featured someone decked out in goaltender gear and wearing the colours of the New York Rangers. The back of card number one described the player as "One of the prime leaders of hockey's growth as player, coach and builder over 50-year span." The player of course was Lester Patrick.

Though he had made his fortune over a period of many years in the Big Apple, Patrick did not sever his ties with Victoria. In 1913, he had built a fine, architect-designed home in the Craftsman bungalow style in Victoria's Fairfield community. The bungalow remained his principal residence throughout the years, and it was in Victoria that Lester lived after his career in hockey was finally over.

The same year that O-Pee-Chee introduced its All-Time Greats hockey cards, 1960, brought a conclusion to the story of the man depicted on card number one: Lester Patrick died June 1 that year. His brother Frank followed just four weeks later, on June 29. Teammates, collaborators, innovators, and leaders throughout their lives, the brothers share post-mortem common ground, their graves just a few feet apart from one another at Royal Oak Burial Park in Victoria.

For a fifteen-year span the enterprise, initiative, and imagination of Frank and Lester Patrick delivered great delight and reward to the city of Victoria, reward not isolated to the city's hockey fans. The presence of a major professional hockey team in the city lured other attractions to town. Lester Patrick's hockey players put Victoria on the map, making the city a go-to place. The Cougars' Stanley Cup victory in 1925 generated a burst of civic pride—and left something permanent to prize.

From time to time a banner has hung from the rafters of the city's modern hockey arena—*Victoria Cougars Stanley Cup Champions 1924–1925*. The Victoria Cougars are and will always be the last team not part of the NHL to have accomplished that wondrous feat.

APPENDIX A

CHAMPIONSHIP WINNERS, 1912-26

PCHA Champions, 1912–1924
WCHL / WHL Champions, 1924–25, 1925–26

1912: New Westminster Royals
1912–13: Victoria Capitals[1]
1913–14: Victoria Aristocrats
1914–15: Vancouver Millionaires
1915–16: Portland Rosebuds
1916–17: Seattle Metropolitans
1917–18: Vancouver Millionaires
1919: Seattle Metropolitans
1919–20: Seattle Metropolitans
1920–21: Vancouver Millionaires
1921–22: Vancouver Millionaires
1922–23: Vancouver Maroons
1923–24: Vancouver Maroons
1924–25[2]: Victoria Cougars
1925–26[3]: Victoria Cougars

1   Also sometimes known as Victoria Senators
2   Western Canada Hockey League
3   Western Hockey League

APPENDIX B

VICTORIA PLAYER YEAR-BY-YEAR STATISTICS (REGULAR SEASON), 1911-16; 1918-26

[GP: Games Played; G: Goals; A: Assists; Pts: Total Points;
PIM: Penalties in Minutes; GAA: Goals-Against Average]

1911–12: 7 wins, 9 losses

PLAYER	GP	G	A	PTS	PIM
Dunderdale	16	24	0	24	25
Smith	16	19	0	19	22
Patrick	16	10	0	10	9
Rowe	16	10	0	10	62
Poulin	16	9	0	9	48
Smaill	16	9	0	9	34

Lindsay: GAA: 5.54

1912–13: 10 wins, 5 losses

PLAYER	GP	G	A	PTS	PIM
Dunderdale	15	24	5	29	36
Patrick	15	14	5	19	12
Rowe	15	8	7	15	34
Smaill	10	7	5	12	9
Poulin	15	5	4	9	64
Prodgers	15	6	0	6	21
Genge	8	2	4	6	17
Ulrich	5	2	1	3	0

Lindsay: GAA: 3.62

1913–14: 10 wins, 6 losses

PLAYER	GP	G	A	PTS	PIM
Kerr	16	20	11	31	45
Dunderdale	16	24	4	28	34
Poulin	15	9	9	18	47
Rowe	12	8	7	15	11
Smaill	16	9	5	14	8
Genge	16	9	4	13	15
Patrick	9	5	5	10	0
Ulrich	9	2	0	2	0

Lindsay: GAA: 4.74

1914–15: 4 wins, 13 losses

PLAYER	GP	G	A	PTS	PIM
Dunderdale	17	17	10	27	22
Kerr	17	14	4	18	15
Patrick	17	12	5	17	15
Morris	10	7	3	10	0
Poulin	16	4	4	8	47
Rowe	12	6	1	7	13
Smaill	13	3	1	4	6
Genge	17	1	1	2	36

Lindsay: GAA: 6.60

1915–16: 5 wins, 13 losses

PLAYER	GP	G	A	PTS	PIM
Kerr	18	16	12	28	46
Patrick	18	13	11	24	27
Nichols	11	12	10	22	3
Box	11	8	6	14	6
McDonald	16	10	3	13	32
Mallen	18	7	5	12	31
Genge	14	3	3	6	21
Riley	12	4	1	5	14
O'Leary	4	1	1	2	6

McCulloch: GAA: 5.55

1918–19: 7 wins, 13 losses

PLAYER	GP	G	A	PTS	PIM
Oatman	18	11	5	16	13
Marples	15	8	3	11	0
Tobin	20	10	1	11	3
Dunderdale	20	5	4	9	28
Patrick	10	2	5	7	0
Johnson	15	3	3	6	0
C. Loughlin	15	1	3	4	3
W. Loughlin	7	1	3	4	0
Barbour	10	2	1	3	0
Irvin	4	1	0	1	0
Genge	13	0	0	0	12
Kerr	1	0	0	0	0
Cook	1	0	0	0	0
Box	1	0	0	0	0
Poulin	1	0	0	0	0

Murray: GAA: 3.88

1919–20: 10 wins, 12 losses

PLAYER	GP	G	A	PTS	PIM
Dunderdale	22	26	7	33	35
Oatman	22	11	14	25	38
Kerr	19	8	1	9	12
H. Meeking	22	4	3	7	57
W. Loughlin	21	4	1	5	19
Johnson	21	0	5	5	22
Patrick	12	2	2	4	3
C. Loughlin	22	2	2	4	18
Genge	17	0	0	0	6
Murphy	1	0	0	0	6

Fowler: GAA: 3.21

1920–21: 10 wins, 13 losses, 1 tie

PLAYER	GP	G	A	PTS	PIM
Fredrickson	21	20	12	32	3
Dunderdale	24	9	11	20	18
Oatman	22	6	11	17	11
H. Meeking	24	13	2	15	15
W. Loughlin	24	8	5	13	15
C. Loughlin	24	7	3	10	21
Johnson	24	5	2	7	26
Patrick	5	2	3	5	13
G. Meeking	9	1	0	1	0
Adams	1	1	0	1	0
Genge	3	0	0	0	6

Fowler: GAA: 3.43

1921–22: 11 wins, 12 losses, 1 tie

PLAYER	GP	G	A	PTS	PIM
Fredrickson	24	15	10	25	23
Dunderdale	24	13	6	19	37
Oatman	21	9	6	15	28
W. Loughlin	24	8	3	11	27
Halderson	23	7	3	10	13
C. Loughlin	24	6	3	9	6
H. Meeking	24	2	4	6	33
Johnson	13	1	1	2	12
Patrick	2	0	0	0	0

Fowler: GAA: 2.86
Patrick: GAA: 4.62

1922–23: 16 wins, 14 losses

PLAYER	GP	G	A	PTS	PIM
Fredrickson	30	39	16	55	26
H. Meeking	28	17	9	26	43
C. Loughlin	30	12	10	22	24
Oatman	29	12	7	19	49
Halderson	29	10	5	15	26
Anderson	29	1	5	6	10
W. Loughlin	26	0	2	2	9
Dunderdale	27	2	0	2	16
Deildal	16	1	0	1	0

Fowler: GAA: 2.76

1923–24: 11 wins, 18 losses, 1 tie

PLAYER	GP	G	A	PTS	PIM
Fredrickson	30	19	9	28	22
Hart	29	15	1	16	4
C. Loughlin	30	10	6	16	18
H. Meeking	29	8	6	14	28
Gibson	30	6	4	10	2
Briden	12	8	1	9	6
Halderson	30	6	2	8	36
Anderson	29	5	2	7	4
Trihey	24	1	0	1	0

Fowler: GAA: 3.32

1924–25: 16 wins, 12 losses

PLAYER	GP	G	A	PTS	PIM
Fredrickson	28	22	8	30	43
H. Meeking	28	12	2	14	28
Walker	28	7	7	14	6
Hart	26	8	6	14	9
Fraser	28	9	3	12	64
Foyston	27	6	5	11	6
C. Loughlin	28	9	2	11	46
Halderson	28	3	6	9	71
Anderson	26	6	2	8	3
Elmer	4	2	1	3	0

Holmes: GAA: 2.25

1925–26: 15 wins, 11 losses, 4 ties

PLAYER	GP	G	A	PTS	PIM
Fredrickson	30	16	8	24	89
Walker	30	9	8	17	16
Patrick	23	5	8	13	20
R. Oatman	30	8	4	12	38
Hart	27	6	4	10	2
C. Loughlin	30	7	3	10	52
Foyston	12	6	3	9	8
Anderson	29	6	0	6	30
Halderson	23	3	1	4	51
H. Meeking	20	1	1	2	20
Fraser	7	1	0	1	12

Holmes: GAA—1.68

Note: In the 1916–17 and 1917–18 seasons, there was no Victoria team in the Pacific Coast Hockey Association.

APPENDIX C

CAREER STATISTICS, VICTORIA PLAYER, BY TOTAL POINTS SCORED

[First: First Season in Victoria; GP: Games Played; G: Goals; A: Assists; PTS: Total Points; PIM: Penalties in Minutes]

PLAYER	FIRST	GP	G	A	PTS	PIM
Fredrickson, F	1920	163	131	63	**194**	206
Dunderdale, T	1911	181	144	47	**191**	233
Patrick, L	1911	160	65	44	**109**	99
Oatman, E	1918	112	49	43	**92**	139
Loughlin, C	1918	203	56	32	**88**	188
Kerr, A	1913	69	58	28	**86**	106
Meeking, H	1919	175	57	27	**84**	224
Rowe, B	1911	55	32	15	**47**	120
Halderson, H	1921	133	29	17	**46**	197
Poulin, S	1911	63	27	17	**44**	206
Hart, H	1923	82	29	11	**40**	15
Smaill, W	1911	55	28	11	**39**	57
Loughlin, W	1918	102	21	14	**35**	70

PLAYER	FIRST	GP	G	A	PTS	PIM
Walker, J	1924	58	16	15	**31**	22
Anderson, J	1922	113	18	9	**27**	47
Genge, B	1912	88	15	12	**27**	113
Nichols, S	1915	11	12	10	**22**	3
Foyston, F	1924	39	12	8	**20**	14
Johnson, E	1918	73	9	11	**20**	60
Smith, D	1911	16	19	0	**19**	22
Box, T	1915	12	8	6	**14**	6
Fraser, G	1924	35	10	3	**13**	76
McDonald, R	1915	16	10	3	**13**	32
Mallen, K	1915	18	7	5	**12**	31
Oatman, R	1925	30	8	4	**12**	38
Marples, S	1918	15	8	3	**11**	0
Tobin, C	1918	20	10	1	**11**	3
Gibson, J	1923	30	6	4	**10**	2
Morris, B	1914	10	7	3	**10**	0
Briden, A	1923	12	8	1	**9**	6
Prodgers, G	1912	15	6	0	**6**	21
Riley, J	1915	12	4	1	**5**	14
Ulrich, J	1912	14	4	1	**5**	0
Barbour, A	1918	10	2	1	**3**	0
Elmer, W	1924	4	2	1	**3**	0
O'Leary, M	1915	4	1	1	**2**	6
Adams, E	1920	1	1	0	**1**	0
Deildal, A	1922	16	1	0	**1**	0
Irvin, A	1918	4	1	0	**1**	0
Meeking, G	1920	9	1	0	**1**	0
Trihey, C	1923	24	1	0	**1**	0
Cook, L	1918	1	0	0	**0**	0
Murphy, F	1919	1	0	0	**0**	6

APPENDIX D

GOALTENDER STATISTICS,
VICTORIA CAREER,
BY MINUTES PLAYED

[First: First Season in Victoria; GP: Games Played; GW: Games Won; GL: Games Lost; GT: Games Tied; SO: Shutouts; MP: Minutes Played; GA: Goals Allowed; GAA: Goals-Against Average]

GOALTENDER	FIRST	GP	GW	GL	GT	SO	MP	GA	GAA
Fowler, H	1919	130	58	69	3	9	8025	417	3.12
Lindsay, B	1911	64	31	38	0	0	3968	342	5.17
Holmes, H	1924	58	31	23	4	7	3577	116	1.95
Murray, T	1918	20	7	13	0	0	1251	81	3.88
McCulloch, F	1915	18	5	13	0	0	1103	102	5.55
Patrick, L	1921	2	0	0	0	0	13	1	4.62

GATEWAY ARCH
St. Louis, Missouri

STATUE OF LIBERTY
New York, New York

HOOVER DAM
Arizona/Nevada Border

OAK ALLEY

GOLDEN GATE BRIDGE
San Francisco, California

JEFFERSON MEMORIAL

Washington, D.C.

OLD FAITHFUL
Yellowstone National Park, Wyoming

MONTEZUMA CASTLE

Arizona

GRAND CANYON
Arizona

EMPIRE STATE BUILDING

New York, New York

WASHINGTON MONUMENT
Washington, D.C.

GRAND CENTRAL STATION
New York, New York

PORTLAND HEAD LIGHTHOUSE

Maine

MOUNT RUSHMORE
South Dakota

MONUMENT VALLEY
Navajo Nation Reservation, Utah

THE HOLLYWOOD SIGN
Los Angeles, California

IN THIS TEMPLE
AS IN THE HEARTS OF THE PEOPLE
FOR WHOM HE SAVED THE UNION
THE MEMORY OF ABRAHAM LINCOLN
IS ENSHRINED FOREVER

LINCOLN MEMORIAL
Washington, D.C.

TIMES SQUARE

New York, New York

HAVASU FALLS

Supai, Arizona

GREAT SMOKY MOUNTAINS
Tennessee and North Carolina

UNITED STATES CAPITOL
Washington, D.C.

THE ALAMO

San Antonio, Texas

RED ROCKS

Sedona, Arizona

ELLIS ISLAND

New York, New York

THE BROOKLYN BRIDGE
New York, New York

CLIFF PALACE

Mesa Verde National Park, Colorado

DEVIL'S TOWER

Wyoming

SPACE NEEDLE

Seattle, Washington

CRATER LAKE

Crater Lake National Park, Oregon

YANKEE STADIUM
The Bronx, New York

THE WHITE HOUSE

Washington, D.C.

MOUNT MCKINLEY
Alaska

MARTIN LUTHER KING, JR. MEMORIAL
Washington, D.C.

INDEPENDENCE HALL

Philadelphia, Pennsylvania

ARCHES NATIONAL PARK

Utah

REDWOOD FOREST

Redwood National Park, California